VOLUME 2

THE COLLECTED WORKS OF ARTHUR SELDON

The State Is Rolling Back

THE COLLECTED WORKS OF ARTHUR SELDON

VOLUME 1 The Virtues of Capitalism

VOLUME 2 The State Is Rolling Back

VOLUME 3 Everyman's Dictionary of Economics

VOLUME 4 Introducing Market Forces into "Public" Services

VOLUME 5 Government Failure and Over-Government

VOLUME 6 The Welfare State: Pensions, Health, and Education

VOLUME 7 The IEA, the LSE, and the Influence of Ideas (includes an index to the series)

Arthur Seldon

VOLUME 2

THE COLLECTED WORKS OF ARTHUR SELDON

The State Is Rolling Back

Essays in Persuasion

ARTHUR SELDON

Edited and with a New Introduction
by Colin Robinson

LIBERTY FUND, Indianapolis

This book is published by Liberty Fund, Inc., a foundation established to encourage study of the ideal of a society of free and responsible individuals.

The cuneiform inscription that serves as our logo and as the design motif for our endpapers is the earliest-known written appearance of the word "freedom" (*amagi*), or "liberty." It is taken from a clay document written about 2300 B.C. in the Sumerian city-state of Lagash.

Printed in the United States of America

08 07 06 05 04 C 5 4 3 2 1
08 07 06 05 04 P 5 4 3 2 1

Library of Congress Cataloging-in-Publication Data

Seldon, Arthur.
The state is rolling back: essays in persuasion/Arthur Seldon; edited and with a new introduction by Colin Robinson.
p. cm.—(The collected works of Arthur Seldon; v. 2)
Originally published: London: E. & L. Books in association with the Institute of Economic Affairs, 1994.
Includes bibliographical references and index.
ISBN 0-86597-543-4 (alk. paper)—ISBN 0-86597-551-5 (pbk.: alk. paper)
1. Welfare state. 2. Welfare state—Great Britain. 3. Public welfare. 4. Public welfare—Great Britain. 5. Privatization. 6. Privatization—Great Britain. 7. Capitalism. 8. Capitalism—Great Britain. I. Robinson, Colin, 1932– II. Title.

JC 479 .S45 2004
330.12'6—dc22 2004048483

LIBERTY FUND, INC.
8335 Allison Pointe Trail, Suite 300
Indianapolis, Indiana 46250-1684

CONTENTS

INTRODUCTION

Volume 2 of the Collected Works of Arthur Seldon comprises one book—*The State Is Rolling Back*, published in 1994 by Economic and Literary Books in association with the Institute of Economic Affairs. *The State Is Rolling Back* assembles fifty-four of Arthur Seldon's shorter articles, taken from 231 such articles that he wrote in newspapers and periodicals, including the *Times*, the *Daily Telegraph*, the *Sunday Telegraph*, the *Economist*, the *Spectator*, the *Financial Times*, the *Times Higher Education Supplement*, *Crossbow*, the *Building Societies Gazette*, and *New Universities Quarterly*.

The articles appear in six sections and, within each section, in the order in which they were published. Each article has a short explanatory note by the author that puts it in the context of the time when it was written and, in some cases, comments on subsequent developments. The first paper appeared in 1937, and the last in 1992. Cumulatively, the papers represent fifty-six years of publishing in this particular genre—namely, in which the author addresses himself, without any technical jargon, to audiences that are far more numerous and far broader in terms of interests and prejudices than any academic paper, or even any think tank paper, can ever hope to reach.

In his prologue to the book Seldon points to the changes in "mood and style" of the essays from

> the severely clinical in the early and middle years to the impatient and in a few cases, I confess, the mildly contemptuous as they survey the repeated excuses and subterfuges of intelligent and informed politicians to explain away, rather than explain, their failures (p. xxxiii).

It is true that some of the later pieces display a degree of understandable impatience, particularly with the very slow pace of reform of the welfare state under the Thatcher governments and with the failure of those governments to reduce significantly the size of the state.

Through its description of and comment on events, the book is an impressive catalogue of government failure over more than fifty years. Rather than merely examining the proximate causes of the economic and social problems it analyzes, the book addresses the underlying reasons for those problems and the likely long-term consequences of actions taken by governments with short-time horizons.

It is unusual to have so long a record of the development of a scholar's thought as in *The State Is Rolling Back*. In these short articles, virtually all the major elements of Seldon's ideas and his proposals for reform emerge. The book demonstrates, in particular, how long-standing and how fundamental have been Seldon's criticisms of the welfare state, and well over half the articles in *The State Is Rolling Back* are about the welfare state. Early in the postwar years, long before most people had woken up to the distortions and difficulties that would result from state provision of "welfare," Seldon foresaw these problems.

Seldon constantly emphasizes the tensions inherent in representative political systems such as those in the United States and Britain.[1] "Shopping in open markets" gives more influence to ordinary people than does voting. The search for the optimal size of government is vain: it will always be too big or too small. Over-government is the greater risk because big government will inevitably suppress the "natural recuperative powers of a free society." A democracy should therefore take a risk on under-government. But politicians find withdrawal difficult because it would be a confession of failure, and it would mean dissolution of the empires they have built.

But, despite the problem of persuading politicians to withdraw, Seldon's prologue (written in 1994) is optimistic. All the doctrines that "rested on the supposed power of government to right wrongs—communism, socialism, social democracy—have collapsed like packs of cards in a few years" (pp. xxxvi). Moreover, the power of politicians is in decline. They cannot control markets, which have become more important as free trade has spread and as technology has advanced. People have discovered they can escape from government to private suppliers, to suppliers overseas, and to the "underground" economy.[2] The state is rolling back and will continue to do so.

In part I, entitled "The Battle of Ideas for the Good Society," Seldon explains the dangers of collectivism and the virtues of competitive markets. The first paper, written when Seldon, then twenty, had only recently gradu-

1. As he did in later writings. See, for example, volume 5 of these Collected Works (forthcoming), especially *The Dilemma of Democracy* and *Government: Whose Obedient Servant?*

2. For a longer discussion of these "escapes," see *The Dilemma of Democracy*, in volume 5 of these Collected Works.

ated from the London School of Economics (LSE) and published in the LSE students' journal in March 1937, has already been referred to in the general introduction to these Collected Works.[3] It is a piece that sets the scene for the rest of the book because, like so many of Seldon's writings, it is in advance of its time. Given the intellectual climate of the late 1930s, Seldon would probably have found few sympathizers, among his fellow students, for the ideas he sets out. In the article, Seldon reviews a book, *Economists and the Public,* by W. H. Hutt, and takes the opportunity, in academic style, to compare and contrast communist and capitalist systems, at the same time stressing the virtues of competition. Seldon describes consumers' sovereignty as the "ruling principle" of a liberal society that might be "more efficient and less restrictive" than communism as well as requiring no "revolutionary upheaval."

The other eight articles in part I of the book continue the theme of "The Battle of Ideas for the Good Society." Two more early papers, from 1938 and 1940, warn (in the first) of the dangers of dependence on "the favours of the State" and (in the second) of the incompatibility of collectivism, as advocated in this case by H. G. Wells, and political liberty. In a 1955 paper Seldon reviews six lectures on the contribution of economists to policy, pointing out—in an early statement of the views he later developed about the welfare state—that rising incomes mean there should be increasing private provision of services such as health and education. He concludes his review by noting the deficiencies of contemporary economic analysis. Because the "eternal verities of the classical economists" have been forgotten, "we are poorer materially and spiritually than we need be" (p. 27).

A 1958 article again praises the "fathers of English classical political economy," who would have understood the error of welfare statists who wanted to supply everyone with a state pension. Seldon generalizes his argument into a critique of the welfare state—"a vast State machine for taking from some who need it in order to give to many who do not" (p. 30)—and of the ideas of Richard Titmuss, one of the intellectual founding fathers of Britain's welfare state. In a 1968 piece on "The Perpetual Welfare State," Seldon launches another powerful attack on Titmuss for his lack of understanding of economic forces and his inability to adjust his ideas from wartime conditions to the freedom of peacetime.

Part I of the book is completed by another 1968 article that criticizes the

3. See volume 1 of these Collected Works.

British Conservative Party for its failure to be radical in restoring freedom and, in particular, for its unwillingness to accept classical principles of liberty, decentralization, and limited government; by an attack, made in 1979, on governments for supplying goods and services which could be supplied privately; and by a 1980 analysis of the "prevailing ethos" of British higher education, which then was (and to an extent still is) Left inclined, in which Seldon proposes that competing centers of classical teaching be established.

In part II Seldon shows how classical economic thinking can be applied to a variety of practical issues. It begins, appropriately for someone who started his career as an economist in the brewing industry, with two articles from the 1950s that argue for reform of the restrictive British licensing laws for the sale of alcoholic drinks that hindered the industry from adjusting to market forces.[4] A 1963 article then comments on the failure of a consumers' advice magazine, pointing out that the consumer's "best friend" is "choice in competitive markets free from inflation" (p. 76).

An article about the welfare state, from 1966, which foreshadows Seldon's later work on charging for "public" services,[5] describes the rising costs of "welfare" and argues that markets in welfare should be established, beginning with government charges for such services and choice for consumers in the form of vouchers that would be provided for low-income families. In similar vein, a 1971 article puts the case for abolishing "national insurance" contributions, which paid only a small proportion of state pensions, most of which were financed by taxation. The "collectivist anachronism" of the state pension should be abolished and people should be encouraged to save for retirement in ways that best suited them.

Inflation, which impoverishes savers and distorts price signals, is a more serious problem than unemployment, says a 1972 article. After an article on charging for police services, written in 1977, Seldon returns to the unemployment issue, then perceived to be near the top of the political agenda. "The Truth About Unemployment" (1982) argues that the total number of people in unemployment is less important than its duration: governments could, in any case, reduce unemployment by, for example, attacking mon-

4. Seldon was economic adviser to an association of brewing and food-catering companies, chaired by Air Marshal Lord Tedder, deputy to General Eisenhower in the wartime invasion of continental Europe. During this period, Seldon wrote reports on the industry, which later yielded material for articles in *The Economist, The Times*, and other journals, about Britain's restrictive licensing laws.

5. In particular, *Charge* (1977), in volume 4 of these Collected Works (forthcoming).

opolies (including trade unions), reducing social benefits and rent subsidies for "public" housing, and reducing taxes on earnings.

The final paper in part II, written in 1986, sets out Seldon's views—by then well formed—about the problem of over-government.[6] The British government, he says, has unintentionally created an "underground" economy by overtaxing its citizens. "Tax rejection has become part of the culture" (p. 100). Legal repression will not work; only sizable tax cuts will restore the law-abiding nature of the British.

The next three parts of the book, parts III through V, consist of twenty-five articles addressing problems of the welfare state and the reforms required. Long before most other commentators, Seldon saw the incipient tensions in the government welfare system and criticized the flaws in the then conventional wisdom about state welfare. Clearly and forcefully, over many years, he emphasized the advantages of replacing this universal regime—which required ever-mounting taxes to provide state handouts for the middle classes as well as for the genuinely needy—with a system that provided choice for consumers of health and education services, pensions, and other aspects of "welfare." His critique of the state pensions system, dating back to the 1950s, is perhaps his greatest contribution. Only recently, with the system widely perceived to be approaching the kind of "crisis" Seldon predicted nearly fifty years ago, have British governments begun efforts to reform the pensions system and to increase private provision for it.

Many of the other aspects of state interventionism attacked by Seldon and authors writing for the IEA fell before their intellectual onslaught: privatization of state-owned industries, reform of labor laws, and abolition of exchange control were all features of the programs of the Thatcher governments of the 1980s. But, for many years, the British welfare state seemed impervious to criticism and immune to reform. Governments recognized the intellectual strength of the criticism but were unsure whether the electorate would punish them for attempts at reform, especially if it involved privatization. Conservative governments in the 1990s took some tentative steps, for example, toward increasing the role of private pension provision; however, only since the advent of the New Labour government in 1997 and the growing evidence of serious problems in health, education, pensions, and welfare generally, have there been signs that reform is beginning, albeit grudgingly.

6. For his later papers on this subject, see volume 5 of these Collected Works.

The two articles that begin part III, from 1957 and 1958, address the pensions issue. "A Private Welfare State?" examines whether private pension rights should be transferable on a change of job, concluding that "we may, in fact, see a private Welfare State grow within industry not to avoid taxation but to reproduce the differentials which high taxation has tended to wipe out" (p. 105). "Why State Pensions?" shows that these pensions are being financed more and more from taxation, suggests that their basic rates should be frozen, and proposes a largely privatized pension system. "State pensions are a part of [the welfare state] that could gradually be wound up as the conditions that gave them birth pass away" (p. 109). Two other articles on pensions, written in 1960, also propose that the government should encourage private pension provision: there is no need to force people to "do the wise thing *through the State*" (p. 118, italics in original).

Articles from 1961 and 1962 on the social services echo the argument in the 1955 paper referred to above (p. xiii) that, with rising incomes, people will be more able to provide for themselves and that state spending on welfare should decline. High state spending has weakened personal responsibility, raised taxation, and impaired incentives; universal provision of benefits has hindered the ability to help the genuinely needy. In another paper, written in 1962, Seldon points out the dangers—only widely accepted early in the twenty-first century—of making the universities dependent on state finance and therefore subject to increasing state interference. In a 1963 article Seldon reverts to social insurance, explaining the errors of William Beveridge, the architect of Britain's postwar social insurance scheme.

Part III ends with two papers, from 1963 and 1964, about state intervention in the housing market. Seldon criticizes the rent controls that, at the time, more or less paralyzed the market for rented residential property and, more generally, describes the welfare state as "a vast machine for shovelling out equal benefits" (p. 151). He also castigates the building societies for their lack of entrepreneurship. At the time, these societies provided most of the finance for household mortgages and were paternalistic institutions that ran an interest-rate cartel.

Part IV contains some of Seldon's articles on the welfare state in the period 1965–70, when, as he says, the attack was mounting. A 1965 article in a popular newspaper sets out the argument for welfare vouchers, provided by government, so that people could choose between buying from the State or from private suppliers, thus enabling the private suppliers to come forward in competition with state services. The building societies are again criticized in another 1965 article in which Seldon says they have been too ready to accept political supervision and have shown too little interest in competing. Welfare privatization is the theme of another 1965 article. Seldon argues that the political process should be reinforced by the profit motive to provide improved and better-directed "welfare" services such as vouchers, direct payment of fees, and the use of insurance.

In a 1966 paper, Seldon foresees the time when the people of the (then) Soviet Union would expect political freedom. The early Soviet economic reforms were just becoming apparent in the mid-1960s, but in Britain, says Seldon, politicians still persisted with their paternalistic attitude toward the population. People would not for much longer be willing to be treated as "servile, cap-in-hand supplicants" at state schools, doctors' surgeries, and hospitals (p. 178). They would demand choice. Another 1966 paper explains the indiscriminate nature of many state benefits and argues for the taxation of social benefits, whether provided in cash or in kind. A 1967 article on a similar theme makes the case for selective social benefits, concentrated on the needy, and proposes adoption of a reverse income tax. A paper written in 1969 claims that workers are rejecting state welfare: again Seldon urges giving them choices through tax rebates, grants, or vouchers.

The final article in part IV, entitled "Roll Back the State," encapsulates much of Seldon's economic philosophy. He quotes Tocqueville on the dangers of "benign" government and argues that state provision of goods and services has gone far beyond the necessary provision of public goods and minimal redistribution of income to aid the disadvantaged. In a controversial statement for the time (1969), Seldon says state industries should be privatized, the "fraud" of national insurance should be wound up, industrial subsidies should cease, and private welfare provision should be encouraged. The state should concentrate on the provision of genuine public goods and help for the truly disadvantaged. The result would be a leap to safety out of the then economic and social quagmire.

Part V turns to the first tentative steps in reform of the welfare state (which in Britain is only hesitantly under way even in the early years of the twenty-first century).

First, there is a 1970 article about "The Great Pensions Swindle," the title of a book by Seldon[7] in that year, which like the article, argued against the then prevailing view that private pensions could never cover more than a minority of employees. The reverse income tax reappears in a 1971 article as a

7. See volume 6 of these Collected Works (forthcoming).

possible means, despite its difficulties, of concentrating aid where it is most needed. Another 1971 article describes some early measures to improve the operation of the welfare state and explains what more should be done; it asks, however, whether the British civil service will stand in the way of reform and whether there is scope for competing advice from outsiders. In 1972 Seldon was rebuking the Conservative Party—too intent on seeking consensus, too concerned about the media, and too much in thrall to the civil service—for its timidity in reforming the welfare state.

In an article written late in 1978, as the 1979 general election campaign (won by Mrs. Thatcher) was about to begin, Seldon chides the then Labour government for throwing taxpayers' money at problems that should be dealt with at a family level. The state was crowding out the natural tendency for parents and children to look after each other: the state has "replaced the natural paternalism of parents by the political paternalism of government" (p. 223). A 1980 article again makes the case for introducing market forces into higher education and reducing the universities' unhealthy dependence on state finance. A paper written late in the Thatcher years, in 1988, argues that despite the progress made during her governments the problem of over-government remains. Very little has been done to cut back the oversized welfare state, and radical reform is needed in education, health, pensions, and housing.

Part VI of the book consists of eleven articles on "The Excesses of Over-Government." In the first three articles (1969, 1972, and 1979), Seldon launches into hard-hitting criticism of civil servants, who claim to be pursuing a "public interest" that they have no means of defining and that they would have little incentive to follow even if it could be defined. They put a brake on reform: perhaps a new government should renew the top layers of bureaucracy with political appointees, as in the United States. The number of civil servants should be reduced because "half or more of what government is doing it should not be doing at all" (p. 253).

Giving more influence to parents in the education of their children is urged on the government in a 1980 article. It is, says Seldon, "immoral for government to misuse [taxpayers'] money by locking them and their children into State schools" (p. 259). Another 1980 article points to the deficiencies in opinion polls that ask questions about satisfaction with the welfare state without presenting alternatives or attaching prices to welfare services.

In 1983 Seldon was writing about the "New Right" and urging Mrs. Thatcher, who had already "begun to educate the nation out of its producer obsession" (p. 266), to proceed boldly rather than incrementally toward economic and social reform. The "New Left" figures in a 1988 article in which Seldon offers advice about a proposal, then current, for a left-of-center think tank modelled on the IEA: it should, he says, adopt the IEA's injunction to its authors to take each analysis to its logical conclusion, undeterred by thoughts about what might or might not be "politically possible."

A 1986 article summarizes *Corrigible Capitalism, Incorrigible Socialism*[8] and reiterates Seldon's prediction[9] that China will go capitalist, Soviet Russia will not survive the century, and Labour "as we have known it will not govern Britain again" (p. 275).

A short journal article, written in 1988, emphasizes the damage done by academics who temper their advice to politicians, restricting it to what they regard as "politically possible." Academics should model themselves on W. H. Hutt (the subject of Seldon's first paper, in 1937), who "was never seduced into offering politically easy solutions" (p. 286). The collapse of communism provides the starting point for a 1990 article that, like several earlier papers, draws the conclusion that over-government is a more serious risk than under-government. Government should concentrate on the "irreducible minimum of goods and services that cannot be supplied in the market" (p. 289).

The final article in *The State Is Rolling Back,* written in 1992, is a powerful indictment of government action, especially its creation of the welfare state in the twentieth century: people would have been better off if they had used their own money on health, education, pensions, and other services, now "public." Politicians still control more resources than the people do, even after "a decade of Conservative government that set out to roll back the State" (p. 291). Seldon ends the book with a plea, following Winston Churchill, to "set the people free—*laissez-faire*—to produce, to exchange their surpluses, to enrich themselves and one another" (p. 296). That plea admirably summarizes the principal message of the articles in this book.

Colin Robinson
17 March 2003

8. See volume 1 of these Collected Works.

9. See the General Introduction in volume 1 of these Collected Works.

VOLUME 2

THE COLLECTED WORKS OF ARTHUR SELDON

The State Is Rolling Back

I dedicate this book,
severely critical of the political process
in modern democracy,
to the politicians
who wanted to roll back the State

Rhodes Boyson
Ian Gow
Douglas Houghton
Geoffrey Howe
David Howell
Keith Joseph
Nigel Lawson
John Moore
Enoch Powell
Nicholas Ridley
Norman Tebbit
Margaret Thatcher

Elliott Dodds, Liberal
Desmond Donnelly, Labour MP
Ray Fletcher, Labour MP
Jo Grimond, Liberal MP
John Pardoe, Liberal MP
Brian Walden, Labour MP
Ray Whitney, Conservative MP
Woodrow Wyatt, Labour MP

PREFACE

For thirty years, as Editorial Director of the Institute of Economic Affairs, Arthur Seldon was instrumental in producing a stream of high-quality publications which changed the intellectual climate in Britain.

Beginning in the 1950s, when planning was in vogue, and continuing through to the Thatcher administrations which put into effect some of the ideas which Arthur had championed, his influence was remarkable. Arthur selected subjects, found authors, edited their work ruthlessly no matter how eminent they might be and told them when their conclusions were unclear or lacked logic. By the time he "retired" (he is, of course, still extremely active in the IEA), academic authors were only too delighted to have their work published by the Institute which had become a very prestigious publishing organisation. That contrasts with earlier times when academic colleagues would look askance at those of us who published with the IEA.

Throughout the period when Arthur and Ralph Harris co-operated to compete so successfully in the market for ideas, Arthur was a prolific author. Most IEA readers will be familiar with his longer works. They will also have read some of his newspaper and other shorter articles. But they will probably not have been aware, until the appearance of this book, of three important features of his output of shorter pieces: the first is how numerous they are, the second is how right he almost always was, and the third is how consistent they are from the beginning. Few of us can claim to have stated our views on such important topics (especially on the Welfare State) so clearly, consistently and forcefully over so many years.

To check for consistency, readers should turn to the first piece reprinted in this volume—an article from *The Clare Market Review,* commenting on Hutt's *Economists and the Public,* published in 1937 when Arthur was twenty, and almost twenty years before the IEA was conceived. It does, I suppose, show some signs of Arthur's youth—if he were writing it now I suspect he would edit out a few of the words! But otherwise, it deals with the same basic issues—such as the dangers of State coercion and the advantages of using markets—to which Arthur constantly returned, at a time when he would have had few supporters. Readers will instantly recognise it as a piece by him.

The Institute is particularly pleased to be associated with a collection of such distinguished and influential papers.

Colin Robinson
Editorial Director, Institute of Economic Affairs
Professor of Economics, University of Surrey
14 March 1994

FOREWORD

It is distinction enough to be an original and courageous thinker. But to combine such talent with being a fine journalist, as Arthur Seldon has done, is rare indeed. This book represents journalism as a vehicle not just for prophecy, but for securing urgently-needed reform. Clarity of expression is not something one inevitably associates with writers for the press. But in the same way that Arthur has clearly seen the truth of the relationship between capitalism, deregulation, private ownership and personal freedom, so too has he clearly communicated it to his audience. That is what comes through from re-reading these pieces, in some cases a quarter of a century after their original publication.

Arthur has fair claim to the status of prophet. He realised early on that, as Ayn Rand once said, the difference between a welfare state and a totalitarian state is a matter of time. He grasped the notion that one of the quickest ways for a society to seize up is to soak its productive sectors in order to bloat and subsidise its unproductive ones. He grasped the iniquity of politicians running—or, more accurately, trying to run—businesses; and how the only social justice worth having is found outside welfarism.

Above all, Arthur Seldon understood the basic values of humankind. He sensed the oppressive nature of the State when it seeks to control individuals, and has for years argued against such control. Once upon a time he was almost alone; then, thanks in part to the power of his own advocacy, he found himself surrounded by like minds. Market solutions are not, by any means, accepted as being the right way to proceed by all those in constitutional politics, however much the Labour Party may think it has changed. But at least, now, if a government ever seriously tried to roll forward the frontiers of the State again, Arthur Seldon has equipped us with the intellectual weapons and the philosophical justification to join the battle.

In his writings, Arthur Seldon pointed towards the inevitable victory of the individual over the worst manifestation of the State, the interventionist politician. He is the ultimate long-termist, despising the short-termism that torpedoes our politicians. In the articles reprinted here one catches the authentic flavour of his books *Charge* and (his masterpiece) *Capitalism*, books whose underlying message is what Elgar, in the superscription to his First Symphony, characterised as "massive hope in the future." Arthur Seldon is no dry ideologue; his doctrine teems with the passion of a man who seeks to redeem a society crippled by its mistakes, but far from beyond salvation. On some fronts he is still fighting; his arguments against the National Health Service highlight the cowardice of our politicians, who obstinately refuse to listen to him.

To men and women of my generation, old enough to be Arthur's children (or even his grandchildren), these are inspirational messages. We regard them not with the complacency of those who have won a certain victory, but with the care and watchfulness of those who may yet have to fight all over again. Freedom of ownership, freedom of choice, freedom to retain what we earn, freedom to spend it as we choose, all these are essential parts of post-socialist society's liberation. Arthur Seldon has been one of our foremost liberators, and these articles are a crucial part of his testament.

Simon Heffer

FOREWORD

This book assembles Arthur Seldon's huge output of shorter articles, not easily found in libraries, on the policy issues he treated in books and papers. They show for how long he has been explaining the case for the market as superior to government where it was thought impregnable. The argument is detailed, tailored to each subject. It is not "ideological," restating principles without justification, but informed by a coherent view of the world.

The writing is eminently accessible. Some scholars used to think that the right tactic was to blind with (too often pseudo-) science. It is easy but irresponsible to avoid real debate with politicians and the informed public by taking refuge in technicalities. The sort of writing Arthur Seldon largely pioneered in expounding advanced economic reasoning to the general reader in plain English is important not only for public discussion and debate with politicians; it also clarifies economists' suppressed premisses on the "politically possible."

The Seldon pen has consistently flagged up the issues that continue to dog us today. We owe much to his efforts before and at the IEA that Parts I and II on the free society and the free industrial market have been taken on board in this country—and elsewhere as I heard Vaclav Klaus of Czechoslovakia movingly testify.

The instinct to protect and intervene is, as de Tocqueville observed 150 years ago, deeply rooted in democratic systems. No sooner routed, they perpetually recur in novel guise: witness President Clinton's "managed trade."

Yet it is on the Welfare State that our problems run deepest and reforms still have far to go. We have been mesmerised as a nation by blandishments in health, education and social security. The Seldon Papers on welfare started before 1950, from the very start of Attlee's Welfare State. They foresee the concerns of today: the waste of resources when services are free at the point of consumption, the lack of market testing of suppliers, the undermining of incentives by taxation . . .

As with trade the welfare hydra produces new heads: "managed internal markets," schools paid for by taxation but "opted out," and the rest. The essays repeatedly remind us that the monster ceaselessly mutates.

We battle on, and should be deeply grateful to him for defining the task, starting it by his advocacy, and in part setting it on its way.

Patrick Minford

FOREWORD

Arthur Seldon brings together a blend of articles and essays tackling the big issue of our day. Some are perceptive, some are argumentative, some are brave: all have something to tell us about how we live now, all have views on how much government we want, need and is good for us.

The battle for ideas in a free society is to me the most fascinating part of politics. What is zany or unthinkable in one year may become avant garde government policy a few years later and conventional wisdom within the space of the same decade. When I first wrote of the power of the marketplace in increasing customer choice and economic success in the 1970s, the ideas I espoused on introducing competition and new ownership into nationalised monopolies were thought daring or even silly. They are now ideas whose time has come, adopted as policy by an increasing number of governments around the world. Those communities that cling to the pretence that government knows best and that government intervention and investment decisions are what is required to power their communities to greater prosperity are finding themselves in the slow lane of world development with little behind them in the rear mirror, peering ahead to see where the leaders have gone.

Arthur Seldon has over many decades spoken out for the unthinkable and stoutly defended true freedom in a world that often looked to State-based solutions for every problem. His collection of essays and articles brings home the importance of this central debate and reminds us of his staying power during the post-war period. The essays and articles assembled show that there have always been some thinkers who have seen the fundamental connection between freedom and limited government. They also show how the voices became more intense in the 'seventies and 'eighties as people began to recoil from an all embracing State spending almost half the national income and often performing badly in important areas, especially in areas where the free competitive marketplace could deliver the goods and services better to a higher standard at a lower price.

As the emphasis of the book reveals, attention is now turning from industry to the Welfare State. In Clinton's America radical new thoughts are being expressed by a democratic administration. The President has said that welfare should be a second chance and not a permanent way of life and he and his colleagues are marshalling the private sector to help in all sorts of new ways.

In the United Kingdom bold decisions have been taken to give most people the chance of a good second pension backed by assets they or their employer have saved and placed into a trust fund. Many more people have been brought into home ownership through the discounted sale of public property and the development of a large number of attractive new housing estates and housing developments. The public services themselves are experiencing fundamental reform as functions are put into separate more accountable agencies and as activities are subject to market testing to ensure high levels of service and productivity.

The articles are a reminder of why these things were necessary, an incitement to debate about where the true boundaries of the State and the private sector should lie in a successful, free, enterprising society. Arthur would agree that the State does have an important role to play, that it should be the champion of the oppressed, the disabled and those who cannot help themselves. But he would also agree that it is Parliament and government's job to strengthen individual responsibility and self-reliance wherever possible and in business to allow a competitive marketplace to drive forward improved customer choice and higher standards. The State needs to have authority and it needs to be strong to do those things that only government can do. As these articles reveal, it can overstretch itself and if it becomes too large not only does it start to do things badly, or mess things up, but its authority too can be questioned by those who resent the all-embracing tentacles.

These essays are a timely reminder of a timeless dilemma faced by all practising politicians. Many come into politics to right wrongs using political power benignly. They also have to learn that there must be limits to the use of political power if freedom is to survive and enterprises to flourish.

John Redwood

ACKNOWLEDGEMENTS

Of 231 essay-articles from 1937 to 1992 on the classical liberal view of politico-economic life, 47 were given a home by W. F. (later Lord) Deedes, Colin Welch and (later Sir) Peregrine Worsthorne in the *Telegraph, Daily* and *Sunday:* these were radical thoughts long before Conservative governments began to roll back the state. Of the selection of 54 in this book 17 were published in the *Telegraph.*

Such thinking had no natural home in Left-inclined publications, though *New Society, Encounter,* and Peter Preston of *The Guardian* were hospitable.

The Times, The Financial Times, and, in all, 74 newspapers and periodicals enabled the essays to reach large readerships, from policy-makers to the general reader who benefited or suffered from their policies.

I invited forewords from three younger men in journalism, academia and politics whose scholarly minds will have much influence in their lifetimes. (For readers overseas: Simon Heffer, Deputy Editor of the weekly *Spectator,* founded in 1828; Patrick Minford, Professor of Economics at the University of Liverpool; John Redwood, Member of Parliament, Fellow of All Souls, Oxford, 1972–87.)

Marjorie Seldon designed the jacket, Geoffrey Hobbs executed it, and Alistair Hodge of Carnegie Publishing gave patient advice.

Ralph (Lord) Harris, my close colleague for many years, made suggestions for sharpening the lessons for today. David Green brought me up to date on some latest developments.

The essays began in 1937 at the London School of Economics, continued in the early 1940s, were echoed in Army Education talks in Italy to the troops preparing for peace, followed in *Store,* a retail journal in the late 1940s, in *The Economist* and *The Financial Times* in the 1950s, and were developed at the Institute of Economic Affairs (IEA) from 1957.

The Liberal Lord Grantchester, influenced by classical liberal thinking, published several essays in *The Owl* in the early 1950s. (Sir) Antony Fisher fertilised the IEA when it had few friends. Many academics helped to build its intellectual armament. And some far-sighted businessmen contributed funds without influencing its scholarly work.

In local government the message was carried tenaciously by Cecil Margolis for seventeen years as a Yorkshire councillor in high-spending county and borough councils.

My deepest debt is to the Scottish and English classical economists and their heirs—in England Lionel Robbins, Arnold Plant, Frederick Hayek, John Jewkes, Colin Clark, Graham Hutton, and in America James Buchanan, Gordon Tullock, Milton Friedman, Ronald Coase, George Stigler, F. H. Knight, Armen Alchian, Israel Kirzner, Murray Rothbard and, wherever he worked, Ludwig von Mises.

A.S.

15 March 1994

PROLOGUE

The economic and political problems of the 1990s and the opening years of the twenty-first century cannot be understood, the failure of government to solve them analysed, or the required remedies devised without the thinking of the classical Scottish and English economists and political philosophers.

The essays reprinted here, based on classical thinking, appeared as articles in (mostly) British newspapers and periodicals over fifty-five years from 1937 to 1992. The fifty-four, selected from some 230, form a running commentary on the economic and political history of our times. They appear as originally published, with minor omissions to remove repetitions except where necessary to maintain the argument for readers interested in particular subjects. The short introductions indicate the historical context, the core of the argument at the time and, following the asterisks, present judgment on the subsequent adequacy of government action to remedy its failures.

Criticism of government by political scientists and historians often dissects the personal strengths and weaknesses of politicians. The classical approach refined by the modern school of "public choice" focuses rather on the political process in which strong and weak, good and bad men, and more recently women, have to work. Yet the mood and the style of the essays change from the severely clinical in the early and middle years to the impatient and in a few cases, I confess, the mildly contemptuous as they survey the repeated excuses and subterfuges of intelligent and informed politicians to explain away, rather than explain, their failures.

Although most essay-articles dealt with current or impending events, they analyse the underlying long-term causes and consequences underestimated by government preoccupied with three- or four-year electoral timescales. Their original titles, composed by sub-editors to emphasise the "topical pegs," have therefore mostly been replaced by shorter titles to indicate the essential underlying causes or solutions. Readers who wish to trace the original articles and titles will find the sources and dates at the end of the introductions.

The prime minister who said "a week is a long time in politics" divulged the thought-process in the minds of politicians but revealed a chilling truth about the consequences of a political process that puts the short-term benefits for government before the long-term interests of the people. In British history there have been politicians—"statesmen"—anxious about the long-term effects. Yet so far no political party, except in the short decade of the 1980s, has attempted to heed the lessons of classical thinking on the fundamentals of policy-making. They have been repeatedly deferred in British representative government. They have been rejected by socialist thinking in all parties on the power of government to correct the spontaneous activities of the people trading in markets. The lessons of classical thinking have been derided by Labour, fitfully acknowledged by the Liberals, paid lip-service but by-passed by Conservatives until the 1980s, and again now diluted, compromised or deferred.

Of the most fundamental lessons three point to intensifying yet unresolved tensions in democracy. First, the government of Abraham Lincoln is further away than ever. In Britain it is not of the people, by the people, for the people. With a risk of over-simplification it is, between infrequent elections, of the busy politically active, by the bossy party managers, for the bully organised.

The second lesson is that shopping in open markets offers the ordinary non-political people better influence and rewards than voting. David Marquand's notion that government can be made "accountable" to "participating" citizens by transformation into "every man [and presumably every woman] a politician" is to escape from reality into a desperate attempt to save big government, in its guise of "social democracy" or "market socialism," from inescapable intellectual disrepute.

The third lesson is that the search in all schools of thought for optimum government, by identifying the irreducible minimum or the desirable maximum, is vain. Even if it comprised saints and seers government would not reach its goal; it would aim too high or too low. The choice in the world of *Realpolitik* is between too much State ownership or too little, too much regulation of private industry and welfare or too little, too high taxation or too low, too high inflation or too low. In short, the choice is between too much government or too little.

The alternatives the political parties should offer in a democracy that claimed to be of the people, by the people, for the people is a balance of evils and risks. If the people want to avoid the evils of over-government that all parties have created by inflating the State, it must accept the risks of under-government.

A democracy must consciously accept too little government. If we make mistakes in our private lives and activities we must learn, individually or collectively, to help ourselves. We must not expect government to attempt its well-known remedies that, as in the past will fail because they prevent us learning from our mistakes and they end by destroying our capacity to find better remedies. The lesson of the past century is that the State has suppressed the natural recuperative powers of a free society to develop spontaneous remedies as the forces of supply and demand provide new opportunities.

These opportunities require a new direction in historical research. Too much is employed analysing the nature and consequences of the past on which historians agree. Too little dwells on the past that could have developed if humans had decided otherwise but were suppressed by human error—notably political misjudgment, myopia, or self-interest. These are the so-called "counter-factuals" of history that could shed new light on the possible future. In view of their neglect they may now have to be "heroic" if historical research is to yield its lessons for the future. The recent view of an economist that the people, not least the poor, would have suffered if the Welfare State had not been created is a *non sequitur* that is belied by the history of private welfare before the Welfare State. The numerous studies of the historical welfare state that earn M.Sc.s and Ph.D.s have shed little light on the better alternatives that were emerging in the late nineteenth century.

But here is the tortuous dilemma. Politicians cannot embrace the classical remedies, refined for present-day conditions by the schools of economics that study individual ("micro-economic") motivation and behaviour, because they expose the limitations of politics. The classical remedies prescribe minimal government confined to the services that individuals cannot provide for themselves by mutually advantageous "contracts" to buy and sell their specialised abilities. They therefore demand large-scale withdrawal of government from its enormous growth in the past century. The politicians would be confessing the failures of politics. They would be prescribing their redundancy in many human activities. They would have to preside over the dissolution of large tracts of their empire.

There is therefore a conspiracy of silence. The politicians attack one another across the House of Commons but they implicitly assert that only the political process can solve the problems. If there is an abuse, an excess, an error in spontaneous, voluntary, mutual arrangements between individuals or private groups, politicians agree and assert that control and regulation, if not outright expropriation, by the State, is the only remedy. They do not confess the imperfections of their political remedies, their reluctance to withdraw when circumstances change.

Hence the piling of politics on politics. The teachings of the classical economists and political philosophers reveal, as no other school of thought reveals, the limitation of the democratic political process. The lessons will have to be applied in the years ahead if the excesses of over-government are to be overcome.

The failure of post-war government has been the inability to keep pace with the new opportunities created by changing supply and demand—the technical advances and the rise in real incomes—that can be exerted only in markets. Government—in industry and trade, welfare and culture—has lagged far behind. It has not been able to move as opportunistically as markets. Still less has it anticipated them.

The essay-articles were addressed mostly to the general public. They are now in the 1990s offered as essays in persuasion to academics who create and refine ideas, to opinion-formers in the press prepared to recognise the grievous excesses of over-government, to people in industry who could produce better services than the State, to politicians who create the constraints within which they are produced.

The title of the collection reflects the fundamental U-turn in the long academic, political and public faith in the benevolence or capacity of government. It is difficult to think of any philosophy in the past that has suffered such a fate. All the political doctrines that rested on the supposed power of government to right wrongs—communism, socialism, social democracy—have collapsed like packs of cards in a few years. They are now the dogs that no longer bark. There are few plausible thinkers who deny that the faith in the State as a principle of policy has rolled back, or believe the State should be rolled further forward.

The critics of the 1980s governments deny that the State has rolled back. They plausibly quote their long charge-sheet of high taxation of incomes, not least on the middle classes, the continuing State over-regulation of industry, the meagre efforts to liberate the control of education and medical care, the five million homes with perhaps eight million occupants remaining in the ownership or control of government, the painfully slow withdrawal from State pensions, the continuing free supply of services to the increasing numbers who could and might prefer to pay in prices, which convey the power to reject and escape, rather than taxes, which do not.

The indictment of pre-1980s Conservative politicians is formidable. Yet to "roll back the State" has become the new and acceptable culture of the last decade in the twentieth century. *The State Is Rolling Back* was decided as the title on two counts. The first is the general political acceptance of rolling back as desirable. No political party now scoffs at markets. Even Mr. Neil Kinnock has discovered them. It merely claims to run them better than other parties.

The second reason for the title is that the power of politicians to suppress the market should decline, is declining, and will continue to decline. The politicians are no longer in charge of economic life. They no longer control the services they are loath to lose. They can no longer enforce controls and regulations. And they can no longer impose taxes at will to pay for their long-enjoyed control.

The inconvenient truth has slowly and painfully insinuated itself that the market is not only more desirable than most politicians have understood for a century. It is also stronger than they thought.

The market has become more powerful than politics in economic life. However tenacious the posture of government, the power of the market is above it. The so-called "forces" of supply and demand, which politicians thought they could command, control, influence, or keep at bay, are proving resistant and insurmountable. Supply has been transformed by technological advance that accelerates the pace of obsolescence beyond the power of centralised bureaucracies to manage with the efficiency of decentralised, smaller-scale, adaptable firms under the constant impetus of competitive markets. And supply has been widened by the freer trade in Europe and the world. Exporters do not have to accept the *diktat* of home governments. Capital can move overseas to escape domestic controls. People—labour—can escape conservative trade unions or exclusive professional associations.

The waning authority of politics to run economic life is powered by the multiplying escapes from over-government. There are three. The first—even in welfare—is to private suppliers. Second, there are escapes for education, medical, employment and investment to overseas suppliers. And third, not least, people in all social classes can escape to the underground economy. And they are escaping in large numbers and are producing, with unrecorded barter as well as deals paid in cash, perhaps nearing 20 per cent of the national output, approaching the even larger proportions of Southern Europe.

Moreover, persistent over-government has turned the moral argument against itself. It has induced the reaction from the normally law-abiding British that what government makes illegal is not necessarily immoral. And that counter-reaction has turned a beady eye on over-government. What it makes legal is no longer regarded as moral. Its Welfare State has weakened the spiritual authority of parents. The family would have done better if welfare had remained a family concern as it was developing from the 1850s or earlier.

The essays chronicle the long, fifty-year defensive rearguard action of the State to hold its preserves. In view of the misunderstandings about the growth of spontaneous individual activity several essays explain that it is not a life of selfish "individualism" but of decisions to co-operate by trade with one another as individuals, or in groups and communities. The people form communities of mutual interest and assistance when they sense shared requirements—for medical costs or income on retirement—and identify others with like interests. Hence the spontaneous friendly societies and the mass of communal mutual aid. The notion, resurrected by the socialist mind in all parties anxious to find a role for the State, that only government can create communities is disingenuous. It was government that almost destroyed the spontaneous communities when it built the Welfare State.

In each century the scholars' thinking took many years to be understood and applied in everyday life. But in time they have altered the relations between government and people. The classical scholars of the mid-to-late eighteenth century mostly did not live to see their teaching bear fruit in the liberalisation of economic life from 1830 to 1870. The scholars of the late nineteenth century, the Fabian "social democrats" or the "social liberals" in all political parties, were rewarded earlier by seeing extending government applied in their lifetimes from the 1870s. The scholars of the mid-twentieth century, the classical liberals who echoed and refined their eighteenth-century forebears, have been even more fortunate in seeing their thinking accepted recently in their lifetimes.

Some may insist that the reaction against the State in everyday life would have appeared whatever the weight of intellectual judgment for and against government. For those who believe that sooner or later ideas influence minds and affairs, interest lies in the means by which they are transmitted from the study and the laboratory through the text-book and the lecture hall to the political tract and the popular press and finally to political programmes and legislation.

The thinking of contemporary classical liberals required to be marshalled and focused on current political policies if its relevance was to be demonstrated to the millions of potential beneficiaries. These scholars were more inclined than other schools to address their work to their academic peers and less to the general public and the makers of policies in government. The

Mont Pelerin Society, the annual world conclave of classical liberals, had since 1947 fortified the liberal academics of many countries. But it had little or no direct effect outside the universities.

It required the further stage of marshalling their superior expertise and focusing their work onto current government policies before the groundswell of public opinion could influence those who discussed, advised or made government policy. The new Institute of Economic Affairs in England made this its task from the 1950s. Its influence was exerted largely through the general press when its relevance for the man and woman in the street was recognised by reviews and articles on its "academic polemics."

The selection here begins twenty years before the Institute was formed, continued for a further twenty years to the mid-1970s when its groundwork inspired the founding of other think-tanks round the world, into the subsequent fifteen years. Their purpose was to explain the benefits that were being persistently denied to the people by the obstinate continuance of government power.

They have stood the test of time. Their criticisms of the record and failure and especially myopia of government have been vindicated by events.

The indications of reforms in these essays may have seemed "before their time." The value of proposals based on analysis of long-term consequences is precisely that they provide the salutary corrective to the debilitating short-run thinking of the political process. If "academic" proposals are "too soon," in the not disinterested judgement of Ministers, political reforms since the 1939–45 war, and earlier, have been inherently "too late." The state has failed to keep pace with the opportunities created by the free market. The winding up of outdated state pensions was proposed here in 1971. In 1993 the political process summoned up the statesmanship to announce the winding up to begin forty-six years later, in 2017.

Human beings act in 1994 much as they did in 1894, 1794 and 1694. The difference is that government has changed in the amount of freedom it has allowed individuals in their everyday lives. When individuals have been free to live their lives as they wished they have enriched themselves by enriching one another. When they have been directed by political power they have impoverished one another and, in the extreme, have waged a war of all against all.

A.S.

25 February 1994

PART I

The Battle of Ideas for the Good Society

CHAPTER 1

1937

The State *v.* the Market

Socialism *v.* Capitalism

> Fellow-undergraduates at the London School of Economics, then dominantly left-wing and hopeful of the Soviet Union, were challenged to consider the power of the liberal vision. * By the 1990s the USSR pack of cards had collapsed and China is going capitalist. The lingering faith in the State remains among social science academics. The battle of ideas has been decisively won by the market, but the politicians are slow to translate it into reality.
>
> (*The Clare Market Review,*
> LSE Students journal, March, 1937.)

The past two decades have been the heyday of the collectivist writer. With the exception of Professor Robbins' *Great Depression,* and several other lesser known works, every politico-economic treatise, from the planned monopoly capitalism of Captain Harold Macmillan's *Reconstruction* to the unadulterated Marxism of Mr. John Strachey's *Nature of Capitalist Crisis,* has advocated economic and social policies which would effectually curtail the freedom of the individual in his economic relations with his fellows. All are agreed that Competition is a damnable system: no one has a kind word for it. The appearance of Professor W. H. Hutt's *Economists and the Public* must therefore have been a rude shock to serious writers in this field. To defend—indeed to *advocate*—a system of Competition when one man in seven is workless, when thousands are living in hovels, when . . . !

What then is the system of Competition which Professor Hutt so vigorously advocates in his book? What are its social objectives? and the means of which it makes use? What is the rôle assigned to the individual and to the State? Above all, how does it compare with other systems of social and economic organisation?

The communist ideal is a society where the "proletariat" is dictator; theoretically the proletariat as a whole decides the use and distribution of economic resources. Since all are proletarians all are "dictators" but since all cannot dictate to everyone else, in the final resort, no one, qua individual, dictates to anybody. The only element of dictatorship is expressed through some sort of central supreme council which embodies the collective will of the proletarians. All elements of privilege, whether arising from inherited wealth or social standing, are eliminated; there are, therefore, no social or economic class distinctions. The proletarians are equal in their opportunities, but not in their incomes, since distribution is based on the principle "to each according to his needs." Finally, the function of the central representative body is to interpret and supplement the wants of the proletarians.

How far does Hutt's ultra-liberalism compare with the principles underlying this form of society? In the ultra-liberal society the individual will receive from the common pool what he has contributed to it, i.e., the principle of distribution is the same as in the first (or "socialist") stage of communism, *viz.*, "to each according to his labour."

This, then would appear to be an outstanding contrast between the two forms of society. Yet, on closer examination, it is seen to be illusory and to be based on a difference of assumptions. In the communist society, it is claimed the individual will voluntarily work according to his ability and production and will therefore be so greatly augmented that he will be able to take from the common pool the amount of goods and services which he believes will satisfy his needs. But this conclusion rests on two vital assumptions which are, as Lenin gives them: (a) "a productivity of labour unlike the present," (b) "a person not like the present man in the street." It follows that the principle "to each according to his needs" will be capable of application only in so far as these basic assumptions become realities, and not before.

Two questions are therefore involved. To what extent can these assumptions be expected to be realised? and: how soon is it likely that they will be realised? As regards the first, Marxists have no doubt. Under socialism, when once production has been freed from the shackles of the profit motive, it will be only a matter of time before the conditions of scarcity are virtually abolished (for this is what assumption (a) involves). Mr. Strachey calls this process the creation of "super-abundance," and adduces the fact of scientific advance in support of the claim that it is a technical possibility. Now it is a commonplace of "bourgeois economics" that scarcity is a concept of relativity. A vast increase in physical production may amount to the abolition of scarcity *if wants and needs are relatively stable,* but one of the reasons why wants and needs are not static is precisely the fact of technical advance. It is therefore suggested that this movement of the system of wants *pari passu* with increased efficiency in production is under-rated, and that it seriously prejudices the validity of this assumption.

But conceding for the moment that it is technically possible to abolish the conditions of scarcity, how long will the process take? Lenin, in *State and Revolution* writes: ". . . how rapidly this development will go forward . . . we do not and *cannot* know."

And Mr. Strachey in his *Theory and Practice of Socialism,* writes:

> It would be futile to guess how long it will be, after the abolition of capitalism in Britain and America, before the technical basis necessary to give everyone as much of everything as they like (*sic*) can be established. It may be that a hundred years will be too short an estimate: it may be that it would be much too long. Moreover, it is not particularly worth while even to attempt such a guess, for the second condition [assumption (b)] . . . will almost certainly take longer to achieve.

The principle of distribution "to each according to his needs" is therefore dependent on the validity (primarily) of the "no-scarcity" assumption. Only when (and if . . .) "super-abundance" has been created will communism become practicable. As long as scarcity remains, the individual will receive in the main not what he needs, but what he is worth (or what the supreme council thinks he is worth) to the community. But this is just as true of any other system. It is just as true of a liberal society. It can be claimed that when production has been freed from the shackles of parasitic vested interests, monopoly and restrictionism, output will be so greatly increased, that *if wants and needs remain as they are,* conditions of "super-abundance" in respect of these wants will have been created: but the assumption is highly unrealistic and the consideration has only theoretical interest. It is therefore suggested that the principles underlying the systems of distribution of the communist and the liberal society are fundamentally alike.

What, then, is this "liberal ideal"? The ruling principle of the liberal ideal is "consumers' sovereignty"; society is moulded in such a way as to make the decisions and preferences of consumers (or rather of individuals in their capacity as consumers) the guiding and regulating force in the use of the material resources and human talents of the community. To this end, elements of economic privilege (monopoly and vested interests), irrespective of the economic category by which it is enjoyed—manual worker, business administrator, etc.—are swept away; the abolition of economic privilege and the restoration and maintenance of competitive institutions is indeed the positive function of the central authority (i.e., the representatives of the consumers). Competition is no respecter of persons, or of groups of persons. The individual, qua individual, is therefore impotent: neither is he able by combining with his fellows to coerce the rest of society. Moreover, the central authority (the "State") has no power to direct the use of economic resources. The only controlling and guiding force is the "social coercion" of the unfettered demands of the totality of consumers. Since all privilege—economic, social, or otherwise—is eliminated, ability and "usefulness" (as determined in the market by the impersonal force of demand) constitutes the only claim to income; therefore all will contribute to the social dividend, and through their power of changing their demands, every member of the community will have a voice, although a very small voice, in "dictating" the use of economic resources. Finally, the basis for this super-structure of the free market and competitive institutions is the equality of opportunity which it is the function of the State to ensure. The features common to Professor Hutt's society and to the communist society are thus revealed. Both are classless, equalitarian societies, with like principles of distribution; in both the individual begins life with opportunities similar to those of his fellows, but as an individual he is powerless. Both societies envisage the enthronement ("dictatorship," "sovereignty") of the impersonal voice of the people ("proletariat," "consumers") to the detriment of inherited or contrived privilege.

In these respects the liberal society and the communist society are then essentially alike. What of the means by which these objects are to be attained? It is here, in the structure of their economic institutions, that the distinction between the two forms of society is to be found. Professor Hutt's diffused private property, absolute freedom of choice of consumption and occupation, complete economic and political liberty, the restoration and maintenance of competitive institutions by appropriate State action—all this contrasts sharply with the public ownership of property, the inevitably more restricted choice and the centralised decision-making of the communist society.

What of the relative efficiency of these economic mechanisms? If the validity of assumptions (a) and (b) are accepted, then there are no problems of breaking down economic privilege ("vested interests") in a communist society when the wants of the proletarians change, since owing to the divorce of reward from effort there is no "interest" in doing one kind of work rather than another.

It is suggested, however, that too much has been read into assumption (a) (the "no-scarcity" assumption), that its meaning is that there will be no scarcity of "necessaries" only, but that problems of pricing and value will remain in the "higher" forms of production. But even this interpretation does not answer the objection that it involves too static and objective a view of what are "necessaries." Further, this means that the principle "to each according to his needs" will not be capable of universal application, but will be confined to the "lower" forms of production. Third, if the problem of the disposal of scarce resources persisted in the "higher" forms of production, there will also remain the objections which have long been raised against a centralised system of economic organisation, viz., that not only will the central authority have no accurate machinery by which to gauge the wants or needs of consumers, but also that there will be excessive reluctance to change, that is that the interests of the proletarians as consumers will be subordinated to their interests as producers—in short, that the problem of "vested interests" will be as great as ever it is under a system of monopoly capitalism, and worse still, that it will be unrecognisable.

Professor Hutt, on the other hand, makes the more reasonable (implicit) assumption that scarcity and its concomitant, the problem of dislodging vested interests, will persist in a liberal society. Economic privilege is, however, subjected to the tender mercies and the vagaries of consumer demand. The State will not support decaying industries: the right of an industry to stand or fall is determined by its capacity to satisfy the interests of the people as consumers: that is the sole criterion.

This system appears to be open to two important criticisms. First, some may say, Professor Hutt pleads for the absolute sovereignty of consumers' choice, yet he demonstrates (*passim*) that much of this choice is emotional and irrational. Does it not therefore follow, it may be said, that it is not in the long run interest of consumers to allow their demands free play? I think the answer is No. Just as the case for political democracy does not rest on the assumption that the electorate is rational and unemotional, so (I think) the assumption of rationality is not a condition precedent for a liberal economic society. The "liberal" case in this regard is, to put it very baldly, along the following lines: (1) that only the individual knows best what his wants are, and that if he finds that his unaided action is leading him into error, he will voluntarily seek the advice of the "expert"; so that the remedy will come from below; (2) that to force the individual to follow "expert" advice from above is bad because (a) it is a dangerous precedent, (b) it is essentially undemocratic, (c) it tends to make man a puppet, (d) what is rational for one man is not rational for another, (e) the "expert" is not infallible, (f) the "expert" may be serving a vested interest.

The argument of consumers' irrationality is a criticism not of the economic system which gives effect to the demands of consumers but of the demands themselves. Evils arising from faulty or misguided valuations of consumers ("faulty" in the opinion of others who possibly are, or who more often only think they are, better informed) are erroneously attributed to the economic mechanism, the soundness of which can be judged only by the degree of success with which it translates these valuations—faulty or otherwise—into reality.

The second objection has more weight. It will be urged that the State in a liberal society may not be able to resist the political power of sectional entrepreneurial or labour interests, if these are threatened by "social obsolescence," i.e., by a fall in demand for their products. This consideration may well be regarded as the *sine qua non* of a liberal society.

But Professor Hutt might reply that given the institutional environment he envisages, it is improbable that any sectional interest will be able to hold the rest of society to ransom, especially if the State has the backing of an enlightened consumer body alive to its interests. However, Professor Hutt's critics will ask for elaboration of this point.

There are also several other gaps in Professor Hutt's analysis, which he will perhaps fill in his next work. First, Professor Hutt does not deal adequately with the complexities involved in State intervention to ensure equality of opportunity. It appears that short of abolishing the institution of the family (which Professor Hutt would not do—see p. 346) a compromise between the ends of absolute freedom of consumers' choice and equality of opportunity is unavoidable. Second, Professor Hutt does not touch on the subject of the cost of the State action contemplated. Supposing that the "liberal ideal" is practicable, is it economic? May not the cost be too great? Finally, Professor Hutt omits to deal with the problem of the Trade Cycle. At least one student of Professor Hutt's work eagerly awaits elucidation of these considerations.

It is impossible in one book to describe in detail a new form of society, to examine and defend the principles which underlie it, to give an exhaustive account of the structure of its social and economic institutions, and to anticipate and reject objections which might be urged against it. Still less can this be done when half of the book is taken up with an extensive denunciation of past habits of thought and past political and economic practice.

It is not therefore surprising that Professor Hutt has as yet not fully established his case: gaps will need to be filled and parts of the analysis modified. Yet Professor Hutt here offers us a glimpse of an equalitarian society of the future which might fulfil the more desirable ends envisaged by theoretical communism, yet which may be shown to be more efficient and less restrictive, and which may be attainable without a revolutionary upheaval and without the (at any rate, temporary) deprivation of individual political liberty.

CHAPTER **2**

1938

Liberalism and Liberty

The Diffusion of Property

Extracts from the Report written for a Liberal Party Committee advised by economists Arnold Plant and Lionel Robbins, restating political liberalism in terms of classical thinking on private property. (The connecting passages are from a 1952 article.) * The Report foresaw the results of war-time government regulations, but the Liberal Party later returned to the social democracy of Lloyd George which produced big government in the Welfare State.

(*The Owl*, May, 1952.)

The Committee established in 1937 to enquire into the ownership of property in Great Britain and the means by which it could be diffused was headed by Elliott Dodds, who had emphasised the central importance of a widely diffused private ownership of property in a liberal society.

The notion of a broadly based private property was not new in Liberal thinking. It is implicit or explicit in the thinking of the liberal economists, philosophers, political scientists for centuries from Adam Smith or earlier. But it was not always to the fore in political action. Nineteenth century Liberal governments were busy establishing political liberties. The Liberal governments of the early years of the twentieth century were pre-occupied with improving the living conditions of the masses. The diffusion of ownership was discussed by the authors of the outstanding piece of British political thinking of the 1920s, the Liberal Industrial Inquiry, known as The Yellow Book, the work of a group of leading members and advisers of the Party, including J. M. Keynes. But the idea was, in the context of the 1920s, not a dominant motif of the Inquiry.

It may have been the increasing concentration of power accompanying much of the legislation of the short-lived Labour government of 1929–31 and then of the Conservative-dominated "National Governments"; it may have been the ugly results of the illiberal regimes on the Continent; it may have been the increasing awareness of the need for a restatement of the distinctive basic tenets of Liberal philosophy; it may have been the thinking of a man who sees a truth. Whatever the reasons, the Committee produced a Report that filled a gap in the Party's programme, and supplied it with a stirring restatement in modern terms of the central principle of the Liberal creed: that peace, liberty and social justice were most firmly based on a social and economic system in which power and property were widely diffused among the populace.

The Dodds committee was advised by economists, and the economic reasoning in the Report was inspired by their thinking and their writings. It owed much also to Walter Lippmann, whose book, *The Good Society,* appeared while the Report was being drafted, and to the many liberal economists in other countries who were helping to build the body of modern liberal thought to which, with the exception of this Liberal Committee, few in the 1930s (as Professor Hayek said in the last issue of *The Owl*) were paying much attention.

The keynote of the Report was put by Elliott Dodds in his Introduction:

> . . . "new" fashions (in political thought) are . . . not new . . . they are a reversion to heresies which . . . it was thought civilised peoples had discarded.
>
> Autarchy . . . may wear a new name; but it is merely mercantilism writ large. State control and direction . . . may trick itself out as overhead planning; but it is only the technique of the Middle Ages in another dress.

The Liberal Party itself was not free from what Walter Lippmann called the "gradual collectivism" that had infected non-socialist thinking between the wars. Perhaps the infected were victims of the vulgar, ignorant or malicious misrepresentation of the free economy as "*laissez faire* individualism," or of the socialists who had befuddled clear thinking by implying that those who advocated free economy stood for the capitalism of the '30s which was prostituted to serve industrial and agricultural interests.

Ownership for All recalled the *raison d'être* of property from David Hume's explanation as arising from scarcity. It contended that if the ownership of property were widely diffused, and its deployment subject to the "social coercion" of the market, it would be used to serve the interests of the community.

The report urged that such an economy would make not only for productive efficiency but also, by decentralising power and responsibility, for virile free institutions, for personal liberty and independence.

When the Committee came to examine the ownership of property in Great Britain it found gross inequalities; even when allowance was made for technical difficulties in the estimates, for small savings, and for the social services, the degree of inequality remaining was far greater than could be accounted for by unavoidable differences in natural ability, prudence and chance. Some differences were due to avoidable causes that political action could remedy: inheritance, inequality of opportunity, monopoly, and retrogressive indirect and concealed taxation.

To diffuse bequeathed property the Report advocated that the rates of death duties should vary with the size of the bequest and the wealth of the inheritor. In the circumstances of the 1950s when penal taxation had almost choked off private saving so that capital investment requires huge budget surpluses, measures to disperse inheritance are less relevant.

It was for monopoly that the Committee reserved its severest strictures. The way in which monopoly causes inequalities of property was "by limiting the avenues for exploiting ideas, originality and ability."

> It is not commonly appreciated that the process of competition is a great levelling force. Where there is relative freedom of entry into all kinds of work, professions and industries, glaring inequalities cannot be outstanding for long; but where there are barriers to men and resources . . . these differences may be very wide and may persist for long periods. It is mainly because it prevents the operation of the equalising force of mobility that monopoly contributes to inequality of wealth and property.

In the 1930s the notion that monopoly was a necessary part of capitalism, which could not long remain free but which would sooner or later be overgrown with monopoly, was being urged strongly by socialist writers. The Committee would have none of this. It replied:

> . . . technical reasons are by no means sufficient to explain the volume and extent of monopoly in Great Britain today.

The advantages from large-scale organisation and technique are reached relatively quickly; firms attain their "optimum" size at a fairly early stage in their growth . . . the size to which they would grow from the operation of . . . technical factors alone is not such as to warrant the belief that the present extent of monopoly is a necessary characteristic of the economic system. Moreover, there are increasingly significant factors such as electricity and the internal combustion engine which should make for a greater decentralisation of industrial activity.

> ... the cause of the growth of monopoly is to be found not in any inherent technical necessities of the system, but in false political and economic ideas and the pressure of vested interests. In Great Britain monopoly is largely a legacy of War. The loss of export markets, the growing industrialisation of other countries, monetary deflation and the restrictions on international trade created the need for widespread structural readjustments in industry. Because the period of adjustment was prolonged, the opinion grew that the competitive system worked too slowly and too harshly. Moreover, the war inculcated habits incompatible with the functioning of a free system—the centralisation of the control of industry, the grouping of industrial concerns into combinations, the authoritarian fixing of wages and prices, and so on. These practices hindered the normal functioning of the competitive system, but . . . the competitive system itself was blamed. Gradually . . . the view spread that the necessary adjustments would take place more smoothly and more quickly if undertaken either by government or else by industry itself in the form of self-imposed or government-encouraged monopolistic authority.

The Report divided monopolies into three kinds. First, there were the "natural" monopolies where the number of producers was limited by technical conditions (gas, electricity, etc.). Here public control or operation was desirable. "It should be borne in mind, however, that control tends to spread easily from one industry to another, that it may involve serious abuses in other spheres, and that it may create more evils than it cures." These warnings are now in the 1950s timely in Britain when the nationalised railways have been kept alive by suppressing competition from private enterprise road transport.

The second type of monopoly arose from the defective state of the law, which permitted restrictive practices; here the Committee strongly urged the establishment of a body analogous to the Federal Trade Commission in the USA. British Liberals have shown themselves dissatisfied with the Monopolies and Restrictive Practices Commission established by the Labour government in 1948.

British company law also permitted agglomerations (such as the holding company) under which abuses were possible.

> It may well be asked whether the law of public companies should encourage concentration of so much power in so few hands (in some cases under the sway of one dominating personality); whether the multiplication of directorships of associated (and virtually self-appointed) boards is

> in the interest of society; whether the immense power wielded by such corporations may not be used to exploit, to oppress, to hush up, to prevent effective competition, and by extortion or waste to enhance the cost of commodities or services, or . . . arrest development and hold back new processes and methods.

The Committee emphasised that "The joint stock company is the creation of law, and society has the right to insist on very stringent safeguards as the condition of the privileges it has conferred." It called for revision of the 1929 Companies Act. A new Act was passed in 1948, and it met the Committee on some points. But the gulf between the control and ownership of joint stock companies remains.

The law also allowed monopolies to be built on the basis of the law of patents. Here the Committee endorsed the remedy proposed by Professor Sir Arnold Plant that all patents be endorsed "Licences of Right" so that they could be used by anyone on agreed terms or on terms fixed by the Comptroller. This ". . . would spread the use of new methods . . . prevent the exploitation of the consumer, and . . . remove the basis of many industrial monopolies."

The third type class of monopoly was that encouraged or even insisted on by government:

> . . . this is the most remarkable . . . feature of post-war economic history. Governmental policy in this sphere has created a revolution in our economic system.

The Committee embarked on a forthright denunciation of artificial government-fostered monopoly in many industries. The "most blatant" was in iron and steel. Here its conclusion was that "planning" was "a covering for sectional monopolistic privilege." The coal industry "has . . . been established as an *imperium in imperio,* and vested interests have been built up in favour of a tighter form of monopoly." It pointed out that protection and subsidy for agriculture meant higher prices for the consumer, and that the Agricultural Marketing Boards were squeezing out the smaller farmers. "If the small man is going out of business it is not because of the 'natural' superiority of the big firms but because he is being forced out by governmental action."

The Report pointed to the origins of the licensing system in the transport industry, and showed that it conferred monopoly privileges on the firms that happened to be in the industry before licensing was introduced. Further:

> We do not accept the view either that monopoly in transport generally is an inevitable development or that large-scale control and operation is essential for efficiency. Particularly in both passenger and freight motor transport are these views unfounded.

Capital costs of entry (the cost of vehicles) and operating costs were low and personal service favoured the small firm. But "recent legislation has discriminated against [the small firm] and conduced to the maintenance of the position of vested interests."

How much truer is all this in 1952!

> There should be a general framework (of law) which should specify certain requirements or standards as regards safety and kindred matters, but all should be free to enter the industry . . . Would not "consumer representation" prevent exploitation? The Committee was contemptuous of this sophistry. And, again, events have justified it.

How was the growth of artificial monopoly to be halted? The Committee faced the difficulty that monopoly conferred sectional gains on employers and employed in the favoured industries. The public must be made to see that "although some sections may gain here and there at the expense of the rest of the community, consumers in general are being mulcted."

If this was ineffective, a more effective appeal to public opinion might be to show

> that Government-fostered monopoly means the degeneration of democratic institutions . . . Pressure by particular groups, sometimes of a dubious character, lobbying and other methods are used . . . Industries vie with each other to gain the ear of the Government . . . forgetting that theirs is a job of production to satisfy the wants of consumers. The unholy alliance between trade and politics must be dissolved.

The Committee considered there was need for a body that would uncover monopolies, and it proposed a Royal Commission "to investigate the whole question of trustification." But the main need was "to create by every device a public opinion alive to the sinister features of monopoly."

The Committee concluded:

> . . . the Liberal view is that it is the function of the State "to create the conditions of liberty," but not to direct the economy or to attempt to do what individual citizens can do better for themselves and for the country . . .

> . . . the Liberal way . . . involves a complete reversal of present tendencies, a wholesale challenge to the reaction which, here as on the Continent, has marked recent years. Rejecting the heresy that it is the function of Governments to "plan" the lives and activities of their citizens, it seeks, by destroying privileges and equalising opportunities, to set men free to develop their faculties and thus contribute, each to his utmost, to the general good. Instead of concentrating property, it would distribute it; instead of erecting barriers, it would demolish them; instead of entrenching monopoly, it would destroy it; instead of deifying the State, it would exalt the citizen . . .

This was in 1938. The general principles of the Report were endorsed by the next Party Conference, although some found the whole-hearted denunciation of "planning" and the forthright advocacy of a free market economy strong meat.

Then came the War, and the Aftermath, which brought pressing problems that seemed to leave little room for basic issues. The greatest compliment paid to the Dodds Report was the imitation that came from the Conservative Party which began to speak of a "property-owning democracy." Perhaps *Ownership for All* was good "politics" as well as good economics and good morals.

Six years of Socialist planning have confirmed the analysis and the warnings of *Ownership for All.* Much of the improvement in the social conditions of the common people has meant increasing dependence on the favours of the State. The free market has given way even more to hard bargaining between vested interests and to special pleading with government officials behind closed doors. Monopoly has become rampant, and new men with new ideas are shut out. The individual is less than ever master of his fate; he may depend for his very livelihood on membership of a trade association, a professional organisation, a trade union. The history of the British people does not indicate that this is the kind of life it takes to kindly.

CHAPTER 3

1940

The New World Order—H. G. Wells' Myth

A rejection of the notion that "human rights" could be safeguarded in a collectivised world society with centralised sovereign states. A "Declaration of Human Rights" would remain a dead letter. * The Wells vision is still shared by many academics. The task now is to free the world from the nationalism of sovereign states which are too small for the prevention of economic friction and too large for regional cultural development.

(*Free Europe,* May 1940.)

The war has released a flood of intellectual energy which is generating vigorous discussion of the political and economic problems of the peace. To an eager, receptive world Mr. H. G. Wells offers a restatement of his political thinking to date. He begins by examining the two disruptive forces which, he says, are at work in the modern world: the abolition of distance and the increased scale of human activity. The first makes the political organisation, and the second the economic organisation, of the world out of date. The only remedy is collectivisation; political collectivisation to supersede the sovereign state, and economic collectivisation to supersede the independent business unit. The trend towards collectivisation is in any event inevitable; the only question is how we can influence the form in which it will come. The collectivisation must not be "Easternised" or Bolshevik ("class war Communism only replaced one autocratic Russia by another") but "Westernised" and liberal. To achieve this "New Liberalism" a new Revolution is required in which the text book will replace the sword and the time bomb. And to ensure that collectivism will not degenerate into autocracy, a new Declaration of the Rights of Man is to be adopted.

In the course of this analysis Mr. Wells finds himself discussing a number of concepts and propositions: the parallelism between the sovereignty of nations and of business units; the planlessness of the private property system; the relation between federation and collectivism; the inevitability of socialism and collectivism; and, most vital, the retention of political liberty in a collectivist economy.

Mr. Wells' declamation against "the institutions of the private appropriation of land and natural resources generally, and of private enterprise for profit," is not uncommon. It is possible to go far with Mr. Wells in the first of these. Economists have long been aware of the problem of exploiting resources which for technical reasons cannot be appropriated; the problem is to devise the most appropriate legal institutions to minimise waste, and to decide in particular cases whether private agents are best replaced by social exploitation. But Mr. Wells' complaint that private business conducted for profit is "unco-ordinated" is out of date. Few economists now deny that the private property system has a co-ordinating mechanism, the price system. Whether the mechanism is efficient or works justly is a different matter. But, more important, unknown as yet to the generality of socialists, there has in recent years grown up a school of socialist economists who not only recognise the existence of a price mechanism, but also concede its utility; their problem now is not that the price mechanism is a bad co-ordinator but that it is so indispensable that a means must be found of incorporating it into any socialist economy.

The parallel between the sovereign state and the "sovereign" business unit is therefore misconceived. The nation state is a sovereign entity; the private business unit is not. There is no effective international law—no "co-ordinator"—between nations, but there is a co-ordinator—the price system—between business firms. It is true that the greater the degree of monopoly the less is the business unit subject to the dictates of the market. A competitive system, however, is not one in which there is no monopoly, but in which monopoly is of relatively short duration. How long, in a world of rapid technological and psychological change, would monopoly persist if government assistance were removed? and if the endeavours of government were designed not to create and fortify monopoly but to prevent and destroy it? This, and not the fact of monopoly, is the important point; it should at least be considered. If our concern is to devise principles for a Great Society that will endure, it is to take too narrow a view to look at the economic structure of England between 1931 and 1940 and conclude, without analytical evidence, that the features it presents are inalienable, immutable, inevitable.

The absence of such analysis leads Mr. Wells to proclaim the inevitability of socialism and collectivism. "In the world now," he says, "all roads lead to socialism or social dislocation"; and the war has increased the tempo of the process of socialisation. It is of course true that the war years and the reconstructive post-war years will see an extension of government direction and control of economic affairs. But the reconstructive period will not last for ever; and a world which has seen the barbarities of Continental collectivism is not likely to look kindly on a super-collectivism because it is advocated by well-meaning and liberal-minded men.

Meanwhile, as a collectivist, Mr. Wells' view on international organisation is that Federation is not enough; it must be supplemented by collectivism. "The USSR is a federated socialist system which has shown a fairly successful political solidarity during the past two decades." But a federated system—if it is to remain federal—cannot be socialist, and if socialism is imposed on a federal system it will not long remain federal. The USSR is not a federal system; it is a unitary state: the national units have no real independence; they are no more than administrative areas of the central authority. Neither is it correct to impute the political solidarity of the USSR to its socialist structure. Authoritarianism does not cure social and political ills; it suppresses their symptoms. The authoritarian state does not "abolish" unemployment; it stifles it. It does not "cure" the trade cycle; it disguises it. And it does not engender political cohesion; it enforces it.

Mr. Wells' central preoccupation is the most vulnerable part of his analysis. Like other writers in recent years, Mr. Wells recognises that freedom is not ensured solely by the satisfaction of material needs; the well-fed slave remains a slave. There can be no freedom without political, civil, spiritual and intellectual liberty. Mr. Wells also recognises, as have other political writers, that the Soviet system has not given political liberty. But, he says, "these valid criticisms merely indicate the sort of collectivism that has to be avoided. It does not dispose of collectivism as such." This is true; *but neither does this absolve collectivists from the obligation to demonstrate that collectivism is compatible with political liberty.* Ask an admirer of Soviet Communism why there is no political liberty in Russia and he will hunt up all sorts of reasons: the existence outside the USSR of hostile capitalist countries; the possibility of capitalist agents within the USSR; the political adolescence of the Russian peasant; the unfortunate character of Stalin or of those he has gathered round him—any reason except the fundamental one. There is no political liberty in Russia for the very good reason that there can be no political liberty in any system in which all power is centralised—even if those who wield the power wear pink shirts and call themselves "New Liberals." "The more socialisation proceeds and the more directive authority is concentrated," says Mr. Wells admirably, "the more necessary is an efficient protection of individuals from the impatience of well-meaning or narrow-minded or ruthless officials and from all the possible abuses of advantage." Yet how all this is to be guaranteed by a formal legal document, a Declaration of the Rights of Man, is not explained.

Nowhere in the book does Mr. Wells pause to consider the political implications of collectivist economy. His case *for* collectivism rests on his case *against* the private property system; nowhere does he attempt to show that collectivism is *good,* but only that it is *inevitable.* If Mr. Wells could show that collectivism can preserve political liberty, his case would be impressive. Until he has done this, those who, as he does, value liberty cannot follow him.

CHAPTER 4

1955

The Contribution of Economics to Policy

A discussion by six British and American economists. Politicians had to run government, but were not good at running industry. Their task of leadership was largely to persuade the electorates of the necessity of unpalatable but necessary policies. * Nearly forty years later the "democratic" political process still leads benevolent government into short-term expediency. The few partial exceptions have been in post-war Germany, the USA, Britain led by Erhard, Reagan, Mrs. Thatcher.

(*The Owl*, October 1955.)

Never before have economists been used as widely as today in government and industry in Britain, America and other Western countries. War was the forcing house: it speeded up what would have come anyway but more slowly. Modern economic thinking dates from 1776 with Adam Smith's *Wealth of Nations*, but it remained for long largely an academic discipline: as a practical profession it is still young. The public does not realise the extent to which its life is affected, directly or indirectly, by economic advisers and administrators in government and business. Their influence is growing, if more slowly in conservative Britain than in America. And how they see the value and limitations of their science in formulating policy must be of general interest.

Economists with experience of private business have not yet written widely on their work, perhaps because they largely remain in business. It is easier for academic economists, perhaps with experience of public service, to write freely on the application of economics to government policy; and in Washington last year six distinguished economists, Professor Arthur Smithies of Harvard, Professor Joseph J. Spengler of Duke University, Professor Frank H. Knight of the University of Chicago, Professor John Jewkes of Oxford University, Professor Jacob Viner of Princeton University, and

Professor Lionel Robbins of the University of London recently delivered lectures on how economics can contribute to public policy and where further knowledge or thinking is necessary.

Professor Smithies sets the lectures in historical and intellectual perspective by reminding us that economists since Adam Smith were, naturally enough, concerned with the problems of their times. Adam Smith, Ricardo and other Classical economists emphasised the importance for welfare of accumulation. Marshall and the Pigovian economists were more concerned with the means of distributing resources in order to maximise satisfaction. Hicks, Kaldor and other Paretian economists tackled the same problems with different theories. And Keynes and his followers concentrated on the maintenance of full employment.

Today all these theories, and more, are needed to help achieve a synthesis or a compromise between several aims: economic growth, high and stable employment, a steady price level, equitable distribution of income, a market economy for allocating resources, and conservation of cultural and natural resources. And this is where the political trouble starts.

For the politician is apt to promise *all* of them. And it is left to the economist to risk unpopularity by showing that you cannot have everything: that if you want more growth, you must have more inequality; that if you want very full employment, you cannot have stable prices. No wonder the economist often earns the reputation of a dismal Jimmy who prevents the people from coming into their inheritance. It remains perhaps the greatest truth that economists contributed to modern thought that the central condition of man's existence is scarcity, that scarcity means choice, and that choice means abandoning some objectives that are desirable in themselves in favour of even more desirable objectives. In the Great Depression of the 1930s it seemed possible to have increasing employment, increasing investment, increasing incomes, greater equality of incomes, *and* stable prices. But that was hardly a normal condition of modern industrial society; and full employment has confronted the world with the problem of choice in its starkest forms: it is now a matter of higher wages *or* stable prices, more factories *or* more houses, greater social security benefits *or* development of the colonies. For the politician full employment is not entirely a bed of roses.

But how large does the role of government loom in economic policy? Politicians are apt to puff themselves up: they take the credit if things go well, and blame the weather or the foreigner if they go badly. Present-day discussions of economic policy are so concerned with what governments should or can do that we are apt to forget that they furnish only, or largely, the framework for the individual effort and decision on which economic systems rest. Professor Smithies administers a cold douche to political pretensions. He refutes

> the impression that the economy is always ready to veer widely off its course and only the skill and the sagacity of government can hope to maintain its direction . . . The normal process of growth [he is speaking of the USA] has continued, and extraordinary stability of employment has been maintained, despite the vicissitudes of demobilization, post-war reconstruction, partial mobilization, and partial demobilization. These results must be ascribed more to the inherent forces of stability and growth than to the wisdom of economic policy.

Professor Robbins also denies that "it is all a matter of fluke that the system is not always either at the zero of deflation or the infinity of hyperinflation." But he believes that stability must be partly contrived by deliberate policy, particularly in money and credit. Now, monetary policy could be conceived as part of the legal framework of a free economy. But Professor Robbins argues that a market system also requires legislative and even administrative discretion to maintain a high level of demand and to provide indiscriminate benefits (defence, etc.). This would now be widely accepted among liberal economists. But he argues strongly for discretionary intervention on a more novel and controversial ground: namely, in order to avoid or minimise the disruptive effects of rapid change. Some liberals might fight shy of such a wide-ranging proposition. To suggest that the State should protect people from the consequences of change may seem highly dangerous. In a free society, although insurance against unemployment can be nationalised, the individual must be left with much of the risks (against which he cannot insure privately) of the consequences of unforeseen change. The depressing effects on incentive and initiative of State-guaranteed security needs no emphasis.

How much discretionary intervention will be needed? Professor Robbins says ". . . probably most of the instances of alleged distress caused by change are best left to the existing apparatus of general relief." If electronics, automation, and atomic power are to refashion economic society, many expectations will be upset, many industries will shrink, and many industrialists and employees in the fuel, transport, textile and ancillary industries will change their interests and occupations. The public weal may require a rate of shrinkage in railways, coal-mining, cotton and other industries greater than would accompany the wearing-out of machinery and the death or retirement of older workers. Britain's vulnerable competitive position in the world economy will dictate an early and urgent adoption of the newer methods and materials. And opposition to change, especially in the congealed nationalised industries, will need to be met by courage and foresight from governments.

What are the chances of such statesmanship? Professor Smithies remarks that economists have too readily assumed "that the politicians to whom we recommend action are dominated by rational considerations of the common good. We have ignored the fact that they themselves are at the mercy of the political forces that have placed them in power." Yet if the economist can assist in maintaining full employment, the courage to face facts, to speak plainly and to act quickly may become more common. When a Member of Parliament can tell cotton manufacturers that "if there was nothing they could do to lower costs they ought to see what else they could do with their money by investing it elsewhere" there is hope for the future. There is still more hope when businessmen see the truth for themselves, as the cotton manufacturer who said

> . . . it is in the best interests of Lancashire that the textile industry is not being built up by special Government support beyond the point where it is economic in present-day world conditions . . .

The duty of the economist to society and to the individual businessman is to point to the still more evil consequences that would follow if adaptation to new conditions is not made quickly: for society industrial stagnation, for the businessman bankruptcy.

Professor Knight discusses an allied problem that must trouble economists.

> We . . . must look at problems objectively, impersonally, intelligently, and not in "moralising" terms. For believers in democracy it is surely stupid to denounce or criticise public officials in power for giving the public what it wants and demands. Or to abuse those who are trying to get positions of power for using the arguments that will and do win votes as long as it is done in open competition . . . It is stupid to denounce business for producing the goods that are in demand, or selling them by the arguments that will and do have these results . . . Freedom to persuade the consumer, in free competition with other persuaders, is of the essence.

This is the classical argument with which liberal economists have traditionally been associated. There are too many arrogant autocrats who would foist on the people their own tastes and standards—in household goods, advertising, or art and culture. They forget that the "good" taste of today may be scorned tomorrow, as indeed they are apt to scorn the tastes of yesterday. Tastes are not objective or absolute; they are subjective and relative. If you disapprove of other people's tastes, teach them "better," but leave them free choice.

Yet such a position may offend some as too simple and as an abdication of responsibility. For democratic politicians must lead as well as follow the public. The free market system is the most effective device that has come down to us, or that has been conceived by man, for giving the consumer what he wants. But the politician may be concerned with the quality of the demand. What should the liberal economist advise? Should he be satisfied with refining a neutral mechanism for translating demands into reality? Or should he also be concerned with the objectives of social policy? The benevolent autocrat and the Socialist Planner alike could use horror comics as a pretext for general censorship. The liberal is reluctant to invade the province of the family nightly. The social worker will tell him that many parents are even now not mature enough to entrust with the welfare of their children. What then?

There can be no fixed rule. Professor Robbins quotes Mill on the underlying assumption in the case for the free economy: that people know their own interests, with children and backward peoples as exceptions. Yet the general prejudice in favour of liberty must involve risks. We cannot enslave all because a minority of parents are irresponsible or immature. There are too many laws that have not changed with the social and economic advances of the last half century, and that are "justified" by dogmatists or cranks on the ground that they are necessary for 0.05 per cent of the population. This issue will sooner or later confront the whole structure of the Welfare State itself. State-subsidised education was necessary when incomes were too low or the sense of parental responsibility too weak to leave education to individual family decision. When neither of these conditions is true of the great mass of the people, State-subsidised education is as out-of-date as the horse-carriage. The purpose of the social services was to make themselves superfluous. As Mill put it: ". . . government aid when given merely in default of private enterprise, should be so given as to be as far as possible a course of education for the people in the art of accomplishing great objects by individual energy and voluntary co-operation." But standards in education, health services, etc., continually rise. As incomes increase should not more be left to *private* enterprise, *private* provision, and *private* insurance? For those who care for human liberty and dignity there can be only one answer. It may be necessary for some time to extend some kinds of provision, and even to devise new ones. Professor Robbins believes that "in the present position of most western societies some provision of this sort is desirable and creative of greater eventual freedom." Equally, parts of the Welfare State that are passing from paternalism to injustice and could become tyranny should be dismantled. Few economists have as yet given their minds to this aspect of public policy; and one who has, Mr. Colin Clark, has earned little support from others. Yet economists may be overtaken by events. The Welfare State may have started to crumble from natural causes. It is true that the inhabitants of rent-subsidised Council houses often buy luxuries before necessaries. But in time middle-class incomes should bring middle-class standards. And already the more self-respecting working people are beginning to send their children to private schools, to insure for private medical services, in short, to reject paternalism as soon as they are able. Again, the human spirit may save the day.

Whatever the future may bring, should economists attempt to forecast it? Professor Jewkes elaborates the *Lloyds Bank Review* article in which he argued a strong case against prediction on the ground, *inter alia,* that there were too many unpredictable variables to make prediction scientific. His argument was impeccable. But it was an austere doctrine; it seemed to suggest that economists should be concerned only with the past. Certainly the ambitious (and faintly ridiculous) annual economic surveys of the early post-war years have been replaced by more modest documents. Yet governments and businessmen are concerned with the present, and still more with the future. Everything they do now must be based on assumptions about the future. And they rightly look to their economic advisers for guidance. Professor Jewkes himself later in his lecture comes near to stating what may have been in the minds of many who shied from his original statement. He argues that economists should have "a sense of history." By this he means "a knowledge of the kind of things that *can* happen, a feeling of what fits with what, a comprehension of how a multitude of tiny interlocking events make up the whole." This is the same kind of talent as economic judgment, and is what Keynes meant when he said

> the theory of economics does not furnish a body of settled conclusions immediately applicable to policy. It is a method rather than a doctrine, an

> apparatus of the mind, a technique of thinking which helps its possessors to draw correct conclusions.

"Economic judgment," says Jewkes,

> is bound up with a sturdy disposition not to allow current affairs to bulk too large, . . . the caution that comes from the knowledge that everything under the sun is both old and new, . . . the power to absorb other men's experiences, . . . [and] a confidence about what will probably not happen which remains unshaken although the future is a dark mystery.

The possession of economic judgment, so defined, transforms the economics graduate into a fully-fledged mature economist. And it is these purely personal qualities, particularly the "confidence about what will probably not happen," allied to the economist's theoretical equipment and experience in handling economic quantities, that the politician and the businessman look for in seeking advice on preparing for the future. Professor Jewkes has incisively delineated the qualities in the economist that make him a valued adviser.

Economics is a living and growing science: refinement, elaboration and new methods of application to novel situations will undoubtedly come in the future. Yet as regards the fundamental tenets of the science, little has been added to Adam Smith and his followers. It was partly because we forgot or ignored the eternal verities of the classical economists that we are poorer materially and spiritually than we need be. And it is by applying them to the technical and political conditions of our day that we shall realise the potentialities of science and the flowering of the human spirit.

CHAPTER 5

1958

Citizenship—The *Cul-de-Sac*

The leading post-war advocate of State welfare, the sociologist R. M. Titmuss, thought the lessons of war-time social services could be applied in peace with a "badge of citizenship" in sharing peace-time social benefits—free, equal, universal, permanent. This essay-article in the liberal monthly edited by the historian G. P. Gooch dismissed the notion as naive and outdated. * It was revived in the 1980s by social democratic academics and politicians to reconcile "participating" citizens to the "accountable" socialist State. "Every man a politician" (David Marquand) is an adroit attempt to validate big government.

(*The Contemporary Review*, May 1958.)

The Labour Party's plan for National Superannuation was published with the modest, scholarly appeal that it be used as a basis for discussion. In response economists and others have examined its long-ranging estimates and actuarial theories. Some of its critics, including the Minister of Pensions, have demonstrated inaccuracies or chancy guesses in its statistics. Debating points have been easily scored on whether the total contribution needed for the new pensions would have to be 10 per cent of income, as the plan envisaged, or more, as the critics contend, or whether the estimates of income, outgo, or accumulated funds by 1980 or 2030 were two or three hundred million pounds out. This concentration on statistics is a pity, for it has distracted attention from what should have been the prior question of the political philosophy underlying the Labour proposals. Much of the discussion has put the cart before the horse by putting detail before principle. It has concerned itself with how the scheme would work, or whether it would work well, before asking whether it was desirable and should be worked at all.

The broad philosophy behind the new pension scheme has for some years been persuasively argued by Professor R. M. Titmuss, who, together with Dr. Brian Abel-Smith and Mr. Peter Townsend, is its architect. In brief, the view is that pensions are one of the social services which the Welfare State ought to supply to everyone, freely, equally, permanently. They would then confer on the whole community the protection of the State and give to every man, woman and child a mark or "badge of citizenship." It is not difficult to see how the notion evolved. Professor Titmuss is the author of the much-praised *Problems of Social Policy,* the Official War History of the social services. The upheavals of war produced emergencies that could not readily be handled by the market—evacuation, re-housing the victims of bombing, the distribution of iron rations, makeshift schooling, medical services. Only central or local public authorities with powers to override private rights and personal liberties could organise people and resources swiftly enough to meet rapidly changing needs. If these rights and liberties could be discounted for the duration, it is possible to argue that the State and its organs built up an apparatus of social provision and assistance—orange juice for babies, rent tribunals for parents, pension adjustments, allowances for this, grants for that, and so on, in bewildering variety—that were suited to the needs of a centrally directed, singly-motivated, siege economy. The wartime social services were, in many respects, a humanely administered and technically efficient umbrella under which all could shelter and be assured of basic requirements and protection from unexpected catastrophe.

It is easy to romanticise all this into a community working in selfless, happy harmony for the good of all: a big family in which the strong help the weak, the healthy the sick, and the fortunate the unfortunate. But this conception of society is a highly idealised simplification of a much more complex pattern. The wartime social service economy had its darker side, which cannot be passed over lightly in a realistic appraisal of social institutions and their suitability for the human beings they are to serve. The war and post-war controls drove into conflict the private purposes and the general advantage that are substantially harmonised in a free society. Even in this land of law-abiding, kindly, conscientious citizens they produced, however mildly, the string-pulling, the suborning of officials, the abuse of power, the jobbery, and the rest which on a much larger scale today disfigure every directed economy inside and outside the Iron Curtain. The "badges of citizenship" worn by some citizens in wartime Britain were sadly tarnished. They are no recommendation for a social service State. These lapses took place in spite of the all-compelling purpose—defeat of the enemy—that unified the nation and must have raised the general level of behaviour and intensified the sense of public service inspiring everyone's activities, civilian no less than Service. Personal hopes, ambitions and freedoms were surrendered to the immediate national purpose. How much more tarnished would the "badges of citizenship" be in peacetime when the normal human instincts and motives hold sway?

We must not be cynical, but we must employ a proper and wholesome scepticism about human frailties and fallibilities. The same people act differently in different conditions. Some institutions evoke their best qualities, others their worst. What then is the quality of the "badges of citizenship" worn in the post-war Welfare State? Why is the time of doctors wasted by people who come to them with trifling ailments?—and wasted so much that doctors often cannot attend properly to those who are really ill? Why do people live in subsidised houses who can afford to pay market rents? Or accept "free" State education when they can run a motor car? Or, being able to support their aged parents, throw them on to State assistance? Why are young people who call for higher State education grants in order to avoid dependence on their parents prepared to accept dependence on other people's parents? If a family means test for pensioners is degrading because it involves dependence on children, why is it less degrading to accept money from other people's children? Is this what the Welfare State has done to people who in other circumstances can display, and have displayed, the most noble qualities? Whatever the merits of the Welfare State which have made it desirable in spite of its defects, we must not overlook the defects. The notion that supplying "free" services to all and sundry confers on everyone an honourable badge of citizenship breaks down because it strains human nature to breaking point: it brings out the worst, and often suppresses the best, in man.

The sad truth is that the "badge of citizenship" is a badge of dependence. It is based not only on a misreading of human nature but on a misunderstanding of the purpose of the Welfare State. The only circumstances in which assistance from the State, that is, from one's fellows, is compatible with self-respect are those in which one's own efforts cannot yield the basic requirements of life; assistance is then necessary to ensure them. Such help can be received with dignity and given with pride. Like Portia's mercy, it is twice blessed;

> It blesseth him that gives, and him that takes.

But to erect a vast State machine for taking from some who need it in order to give it to many who do not deprives the act of grace and makes it a cause of cynicism, bitterness, and social disruption. Let it be accepted that to relate State assistance to need involves the use of a test of means. Without it the end result can only be chaos. If assistance is to be given as a right without reference to need, everyone must receive every form of assistance so long as any one person can establish evidence of need for it. So we must all receive "free" State education as long as any one family suffers not only from Seebohm Rowntree's "primary poverty" of inadequate income but also from his "secondary poverty" arising from inability to dispose of it wisely. The logical conclusion of such a principle is universal subsidisation that must collapse sooner or later when it collides with the need to maintain competitive trading strength in a world economy.

The error of applying these principles to pensions is evident. Fifty years ago it was right for the State to help old people in need; very many of them were in need since they had had little opportunity to save during their working years, and their children also were hard put to it to earn a tolerable standard of living. But now no one aged under 35 or 40 has known mass unemployment, slumps, doles, hunger marches, or the soup kitchen. There is no reason for continuing a system of State pensions to support in retirement those who can afford to save for it out of income. Certainly we should go on supporting the older generation that had no chance to save, and let us be as generous as we can. But let us recognise that the circumstances in which there was a need for State assistance are passing away. To continue subsidised pensions for those who do not need it is to make the "badge of citizenship" a mark of sponging on one's fellow-citizens.

The fathers of English classical political economy understood these matters much better than some of us today. They displayed astonishing prescience in the role they assigned to State assistance. Mill laid it down that:

> . . . government aid . . . should be so given as to be as far as possible a course of education for the people in the art of accomplishing great objects by individual energy and voluntary co-operation.

In a memorandum on popular education to the 1861 Royal Commission on Education Nassau Senior put the classical philosophy with uncanny clarity:

> We may look forward to the time when the labouring population may be safely entrusted with the education of their children; . . . the assistance and superintendence . . . of the government for that purpose . . . [is] . . . only a means of preparing the labouring classes for a better but remote state of things . . . *in the latter part of the twentieth century* . . . when that assistance and superintendence shall no longer be necessary. (My italics.)

In 1893, when Alfred Marshall was asked by the Royal Commission on the Aged Poor what he thought of "a universal scheme of pensions," he replied that he was opposed to them because

> their educational effect, though a true one . . . would be indirect . . . and they do not contain in themselves the seeds of their own disappearance. I am afraid that, if started, they would tend to become perpetual.

How right he was! Those who would now erect a colossal new structure of State pensions in which the enterprising would subsidise the slothful or income would be transferred from right-hand pockets to left-hand pockets (with a large chunk for administrative drones lost on the way), would fix for all time a crutch that was designed to help the maturing members of a free society to stand on their own feet. Increasing income, a developing sense of responsibility, and growing awareness of the need to take thought for the future are making it possible to dispense with this crutch. National Superannuation would beat it into a shackle. There are signs that shallow political thinking would be defeated by the elemental groping towards independence as civilisation matures. The most self-respecting of the beneficiaries of the Welfare State are already beginning to throw off its comforting but degrading supports. They are paying for education and medical services; they are taking out life assurance; they are buying their homes. They are learning, with heartening speed, to stand on their own feet. In the end they will predominate, for the exhilaration of independence is more compelling than the deceptive solace of the crutch. Walter Lippmann's prose deserves to be written in blank verse:

> . . . the will to be free
>   is perpetually renewed
> in every individual
>   who uses his faculties
> and affirms his manhood.

CHAPTER 6

1968

The Perpetual Welfare State

> A critique of R. M. Titmuss. The notion of free, everlasting State welfare was founded on good intentions but confusion about the means of producing the required resources. * Its simplistic thinking still influences many in public life, not least academics in universities subsidised by the working classes who derive the least benefit.
>
> (*Social and Economic Administration,* University of Exeter, July 1968.)

The doyen of post-war academic social administration has a formidable literary output. One day it will be assessed for its strengths and weaknesses. Whether he arouses agreement or disagreement, admiration or condemnation, Professor Titmuss will leave his mark on the teaching of social administration for many years, on social policy, though it seems not for so long, and on the fortunes of the Labour Party that until recently sat at his feet.

This book comprises twenty-one lectures, addresses, essays, articles and a foreword, most from the period 1963 to 1967, two or three going back earlier. Although his writings convey the impression of a modest, humble thinker, he allows himself a dash of vanity in explaining that they are published because "students of the subject are said to have great difficulty in locating [them]. Naturally they complain about this, and the patience of my secretary . . . is sometimes over-strained by the flow of requests for offprints, typewritten copies and the like." Now their anxieties are assuaged. (*Commitment to Welfare,* Allen & Unwin, 1968.)

The pieces illustrate Professor Titmuss's wide range of interests: from teaching and research in social administration (four pieces) through "the health and welfare complex" (five) and medical care (four) to income redistribution (eight). (The third and fourth groups are reversed in this book, but this seems the more logical sequence.) Some are straight-forward addresses with a formal academic flavour, others are more combative—contentions, dissections and dismissals, with varying degrees of acerbity, of ideas, people or institutions that displease him. In the article from the *New Statesman* he is impatiently angry with almost everybody from the CBI through the *Economist* to Mr. Douglas Houghton for suggesting there may be something in the reverse income tax, which as a possibly potent instrument of selectivity he rejects with contumely. He has so little regard for economists (except the two or three he quotes in support—Arrow, Boulding), and is so certain in his "commitment," that he would presumably not be influenced by the 1,200 economists in the USA, from Friedman of Chicago through Tobin of Yale and Samuelson of Massachusetts to Galbraith of Harvard, who have jointly commended it as a device to deal with the removal of poverty. Professor Titmuss's collection reveals his increasing displeasure with the Institute of Economic Affairs and with individual British "liberal economists"—Professor John Jewkes, Professor A. T. Peacock, Professor D. S. Lees, Dr. E. G. West, and even the undersigned. He deploys a battery of qualities, faculties and facilities—high mindedness, good intentions, wide reading, ample funds for research, experience of service on official committees (to which he has been appointed by Conservative and Labour governments), wide international contacts, shrewd debating skill, courage in tackling a strong case he wishes to destroy, not least an identification with the poor, the under-privileged, the deprived, the unfortunate, the handicapped, the disadvantaged—to erect and defend the principle and philosophy of the universalist welfare state. The analysis is not infrequently interrupted by prose cloying with the cadences of compassion, and indeed the title of the book aptly indicates the mixed normative and behaviourist content; but it comprises a convenient collection of the arguments for universalism that will give both acolytes and critics material for reflection on the principle and the thinking behind it.

For the economist interested in welfare this impressive performance provokes unease as well as awe, because if this collection reflects the degree of economic understanding with which the students left the department it cannot have been very much. Emotion is no substitute for analysis, nor compassion for cost consciousness. Professor Titmuss delivers eminently sensible judgments: that universities should teach (*passim*), that the benefits of education for society are more questionable than for the individual (p. 63), that institutions tend to become impervious to the public they are presumed to serve (p. 75), that for the first time in history poverty is confronted by (relative) abundance (p. 153), and so on. And he is acquainted with the terminology of economics: he uses "scarcity," "choice," "cost," "competition," "consumer," "market" freely. The doubt is whether he uses them as an economist: he writes of "markets" as though they are primeval devices for subjecting helpless humans to the uncertainty of the unknown, or at the very least the rapacity of commerce, especially private insurance organisations. There is nowhere evidence of understanding that a market is a device that can be fashioned to subject the use of resources to the preferences or indeed idiosyncrasies of individuals as consumers rather than as producers, politicians, officials, academics or even kindly (but often bossy) social workers. His criticisms of markets are couched invariably in historical terms, often going back a surprisingly large number of decades, rarely, and even then inadequately, in analytical terms.

It may be an accident that the incidence of tax refunds on private insurance premiums is misdescribed as "impact effect" (Chapter XV, p. 181), but it further strengthens the impression of amateurishness in the deployment of economic terminology. The prose is generally clear, concise, astringent. What is less clear is the analytical framework of "social administration" within which the varied subjects—income maintenance, means tests, medical care, housing, education, the difficulty of reaching people "in need"—are examined. The nature of "social administration," its characteristic methods or principles, its differences from public administration and business administration are not clearly defined. Is it a science or an art? Is it a social science or social work? Is it really an intellectual discipline with distinguishing characteristics? If "social administration" is concerned with serving social welfare, community benefit or "need," its teachers or practitioners must analyse the essential, underlying problem of the measurement of "need," the degree to which it can be met, and the obstacles to meeting it as generously as every civilised person, inside or outside the Department of Social Administration, would wish. Well-researched evidence on tax avoidance or tax evasion, topped up by easy moralising or demonstrations of inconsistencies and anomalies in the law (as on cohabitation and divorce, p. 195), does not help social workers or professional welfare advisers or civil servants or ministers to see that there is no agreement on the definition of "need," or the use of available funds for "the needy," and still less on the readiness of law-respecting, compassionate, public-spirited people to yield income or assets in taxation, social insurance or gifts in amounts sufficient to produce the resources for "the needy" at the level Professor Titmuss or anyone else would like. Parts of the collection suggest he would not be satisfied until everyone were living near the average and had as much of welfare as everyone else. At these points the flavour of social science is replaced by that of romantic mysticism.

It may be that the Department of Social Administration has suffered from "over-agreement" among its staff and students. The difficulty of conducting an intellectual debate with Professor Titmuss is that he makes his adversary feel not only wrong but also wicked. His Achilles heel is that he knows (or, more accurately, feels) he is right, and that doubters, sceptics and critics are to be ignored or cast into the outer darkness. Although occasionally couched in tentative terms, the collection gives rare space to acknowledgement of doubt, qualification or criticism. And the published products of the department rarely question one another. Such an intellectual environment must have a far-reaching debilitating effect on thinking and administration in the welfare services.

Professor Titmuss makes a strenuous and ingenious effort to escape from the dilemma confronting him, as the leader of the universalist school, that universal benefits are no longer considered fiscally feasible, politically acceptable or individually humane. He has been evolving a formula that appears to reconcile his philosophic preferences for universality with the growing recognition among Labour as well as Conservative and Liberal thinkers that social benefits must increasingly be selective. The formula appears at several places in the work. Instead of the unqualified advocacy of universalism as recently as in the political euphoria of December 1964 (Chapter XVI), with no reference to selectivity at all, there is more recently (April 1967, Chapter XI; September 1967, Chapter X) to be an "infrastructure" of universalist services to provide "a framework of values and opportunity bases within and around which" can be developed acceptable selective services based on the needs of categories, groups and areas. This solution is presumably intended to combine the best of universalism and selectivity; but it abandons his case against the "social divisiveness" of selective benefits while acquiescing in the acknowledged waste unavoidable in basing benefits on groups. There is no case for assisting people in "categories"—council tenants, widows, heads of large families or the inhabitants of deprived areas—unless their incomes are too low to enable them to pay for welfare services considered desirable or essential. The problem is not social or biological or regional but financial and individual; compassion is for people, not for "categories."

There is much else in these addresses and articles that provokes reflection on whether measures required to succour the subnormal can be erected into principles for a great society; how far social integration would be achieved, and alienation prevented, by enabling the poor and the needy to enter the market for welfare on an equal footing with the 80–90 per cent of the community who have no intention of exchanging their status as consumers for that of beneficiaries; how far social workers should be concerned with fostering and accelerating independence as well as with ameliorating deprivation; how far universal State welfare is compatible with individual self-respect, with the family as a social unit, with choice in political institutions; and much else. By forcing them to reach judgments, Professor Titmuss has served his readers.

The addresses and essays of the later years adopt a more defensive but not less confident posture. They reveal Professor Titmuss's growing disenchantment with politicians, or perhaps theirs with him. But the collection as a whole indicates the early strengths and the recent weaknesses of Professor Titmuss's position and influence. His post-war academic standing derived largely from his widely-praised official war history, *Problems of Social Policy.* From his experience of the social services in wartime he drew conclusions for peacetime: but the transition was made without allowance for the economic, social and psychological transformation. The experience of common dangers and fears produced a sense of "community" that could yield a "badge of citizenship"; but the "badge" looked tarnished and as incongruous as other war-time relics when fathers of families were out of uniform, military or civil, and resumed concern for the education, health, housing and income of their families, or could be enabled to satisfy the natural urge to assume family concerns. Wartime gave Professor Titmuss his chance, and he seems out of his element in the freedoms, aspirations, diversities and spontaneities of peace. His compassion for individuals is consummated only when he sees them in communities; like other collectivists he cannot see that man in the mass too easily becomes inhuman. War—or social disruption—would restore the chance of creating a badge of citizenship. At least Professor Titmuss might share his critics' hope that they will never return.

CHAPTER 7

1968

Conservatism and Liberalism

A candid talk to Conservative activists presented classical liberalism as the economic order more moral and more efficient in raising living standards than societies dominated by the socialist political State or resting on conservative hierarchical status. * The 1980s' Conservative Governments applied modified liberalism to industry but less confidently to welfare. Their 1990s' successors are moving more slowly than the market in creating new freedoms.

(*Swinton Journal*, 1968. Reprinted in Richard Cockett, *Thinking the Unthinkable* [Harper Collins, 1994].)

My qualifications—and disqualifications—for writing this piece should be stated simply to be judged by the reader.

I am an intellectual with ten years' experience of industry—and its commercial attitudes, salesmanship and profit-making that often offend intellectuals. For nearly ten years I have been an entrepreneur in intellectualism as editorial director of the Institute of Economic Affairs. And I have no party allegiance (although I usually vote Liberal) but a social philosophy that, if I must have a label, makes me a radical conservative, or a conservative radical.

The third qualification—or disqualification—explains much of what follows. My origins are working-class or *très très petit bourgeois* (my foster-father was a self-employed cobbler in a working-class area). I developed Labour politics as a youth, rejected them under the influence of an economic historian in the sixth form, reinforced by the teachings of and talks with Arnold Plant (to whom we all owe a debt we can never repay—so much for social cost/benefit analysis) and Lionel Robbins, spent my undergraduate years as an ardent Liberal in frustrating, futile protest against Hitler, Mussolini and Stalin, Hoare and Chamberlain, worked for the Liberal Party on and off till the middle 1950s. I have emerged with a passionate desire to raise the working man to dignity, independence and self-respect but with confirmed apprehension that his Labour leaders espouse or pursue policies that will deny him these urges, conditions and rewards of social progress, and a growing conviction that in the end he will achieve them, even if he has to reject his class allegiance.

Hence my radical conservatism. I would conserve—and refine and strengthen—the *conditia sine qua non* of what Walter Lippmann in a lucid interval called "The Good Society": personal liberty (I would take risks with licence if the alternative is over-cautious repression), individual and corporate initiative, decentralised authority, and government limited to services that cannot be organised by spontaneous contract in the market. This is the classic formulation, of what I shall insist on describing as liberalism, by Adam Smith, Abraham Lincoln, John Maynard Keynes and the younger Robbins. But I would be radical about reforming the legal institutional framework in order to preserve these principles—the laws on property, contract, industrial organisation, sale and purchase of goods and services.

Hence also my love-hate relationship with Conservatives for not understanding or for failing to re-create conservatism. This is the dilemma that has both nurtured and soured the relationship between intellectuals and Conservatives in my adult life. Two denigratory half-truths have periodically been levelled at Conservatives (but not necessarily at conservatism): "the stupid party"; "you can't trust the Tories." The first was valid sometimes, less often in recent years. The second has been true even in recent years, but not of some individual Conservative leaders.

The ambivalence of public opinion is paralleled by what seems ambivalence among intellectuals. Professor George Stigler has said "the professional study of economics makes one politically conservative." Professor F. A. Hayek added a post-script entitled "Why I am not a Conservative" to his book *The Constitution of Liberty.* Professor J. R. (now Sir John) Hicks of All Souls College, Oxford, said in a war-time essay:

> Our economic system has developed out of the relatively free enterprise of the nineteenth century . . . What had not happened before was the association of free enterprise with a framework of ideas . . . which have fallen into such disrepute that . . . there are few to do them honour; yet they deserve to be honoured. Manchesterism was not a mere demand by the successful businessman to be allowed to prosecute his own interests in his own way without interference—the caricatures drawn alike by the young Disraeli, by Marx, and by Goebbels. It was a demand for an economic policy based on moral principles; although those principles are not in all respects the same as ours, and in any case the deductions we should draw

> from them are widely different, the thread which comes down from that old liberalism is still discernible. It is a noble heritage . . .

But what is this "conservatism" or "liberalism" that intellectuals who reject, fear and resist centralised political authority both support and reject it? Professor Stigler defines a conservative in economic matters as "a person who wishes most economic activity to be conducted by private enterprise, and who believes that abuses of private power will usually be checked, and incitements to efficiency and progress usually provided, by the forces of competition." Professor Hayek rejects conservatism because the philosophy for which he stands—he describes himself as a liberal or an Old (i.e., pre-French-Revolution) Whig—although sometimes described as conservatism, is different from conservatism as it has developed in practice—a negative resistance to change (which is laudable if change is undesirable) but not an alternative to current undesirable etatist tendencies which can prevent their continuance, so that it has "invariably been the fate of conservatism to be dragged along a path not of its own choosing." And what is, or should be, the conservative or liberal alternative? Sir John Hicks' statement of "the moral principles of Manchesterism" will satisfy me: "the first was Freedom: the right of the adult human being to be treated as an adult, to have the power to choose and the opportunity to bear responsibility for his own actions. The second was Equality or Fairness." The second principle means not the egalitarianism of the present-day universalists who want equal social benefits for all, even in unequal circumstances, but the treatment of all citizens as equal before the law and objection to privilege—as in the levying of taxation on the few, because they are few, to benefit the many, or customs duties levied on the many to benefit the few in protected industries. Other liberals would put the content of liberalism differently; I want to emphasise that liberalism is not merely an economic system that yields commercial opulence, but a moral order.

And there's the rub. Conservatism in our day has too often appeared to be a negative opposition to change, a stubborn adherence to the status quo, with nothing to put in its place. Conservatives have not yet resolved the dilemma whether it stands for the established order because at least it works and because change may be bad, or whether it stands for a body of good principles which it will introduce in place of the bad principles it inherits from its opponents. Of course, there is a good case for continuity, for caution in replacing what is perhaps not so good but is at least known by something that may be better but is unknown. But that is no case for continuing what is being done even though it is thought bad. This is conservative conservatism; it preserves the institutional framework as well as the principles, good or bad. It has refused over a large part of society to change the legal and institutional framework and in so doing risks and further weakens the principles of liberty, decentralised initiative and limited government. This is what the Conservatives did in 1931 when they took over ideas on transport licensing, agricultural marketing, coal organisation, public boards and other forms of quasi-socialism left over from Labour. They were rather better when they followed Labour in 1951, although even Labour might have continued to dismantle the apparatus of wartime controls if they had stayed in office. But the Conservatives did nothing, or almost nothing, to denationalise the State-controlled fuel, transport or welfare services introduced by Labour. The most disappointing case was that of Enoch Powell who taught the virtues of individual liberty and freedom of choice between alternatives in markets, yet did almost nothing to restore them when he was Minister of Health from 1960 to 1963. Perhaps he needed more time, or his colleagues were obstructive, or he wanted more evidence of public support for change. But the record stands.

This is the dilemma of Conservatives that mystifies antagonists or repels intellectuals. Are they no more than pragmatists without principles who run the State machine rather more cleverly and more subtly than Labour by better timing, more influential connections, more persuasive power ("leadership") or the divine right to rule? Quintin Hogg's book on conservatism came perilously close to arguing the superior virtue of political flexibility over fixed principle. Or do Conservatives stand for an identifiable philosophy that is different from Labour's? Do they propose to run the nationalised sector, now nearly half of the economy, rather better than Labour? Does all their raillery against "socialism" mean no more than that they think, arrogantly and with no support from experience, that nationalisation is nauseous except when run by the right chaps in old school ties?

This is the impression created by Messrs. Maudling on income policy and planning, Boyle (and Kathleen Ollerenshaw) on education, Boyd Carpenter (when in office) on social insurance, among the seniors and Raison, Howell, Watts, Spicer, and now Rhys-Williams among the juniors. And the outsider has some difficulty in reconciling their views with those of Powell, Joseph, Thatcher, Maude, Macmillan (the Younger), Howe, Biffen, Braine, Jenkin and others who offer a distinctive philosophy and distinctive principles.

Conservatives speak with two voices: there is no doubt which must prevail if they are to regain the respect and encouragement, but never, never, never, the slavish subservience of intellectuals.

I have argued, like Tibor Szamuely, that the Conservatives should present a coherent structure of principles so that the electorate will not only have a choice between two systems of principles but also know what will guide the Conservatives in office. They are now offered a choice of men. That will not suffice. Conservatives will have to work their passage back to a position of trust that they partly forfeited during the thirteen years in which their praiseworthy but inadequate acts of commission were outnumbered by their failures in acts of omission. If a choice of men is not enough, I am not asking for a choice of measures, for no opposition can or should anticipate the acts it will have to perform in office. But there is a third choice that can be offered. Not men, for that is not enough; not measures, for that is too much; but method, principle, philosophy.

Four years out of office should have given time for refinement of radical Conservative principles. They rest on a philosophy that Labour has ignored, rarely mentions, and in practice frustrates: the philosophy that sees the prime mover of social and economic vitality and advance in the individual and his family. This is not to erect self-interest, or selfishness, as the mainspring of human conduct. It is to recognise that, except in short bursts of war or emergency, men can work only for the people and the purposes they know, and understand, and love: their families, their friends, their personal, local, causes, clubs, churches, hospitals, schools. Edward Heath is the first Conservative Party leader in my lifetime who has echoed this theme, and more distinctive and systematic repetition would cause the heart to beat faster and the spirit to lift.

The primacy of the individual and all that flows from it—the role of the family as the social unit, freedom for individual and corporate initiative, the essential morality of independent business enterprise, commerce, salesmanship and advertising in competition contrasted with the sickening mendacity and sanctimonious humbug of the politician who pretends to serve "the public interest," the supremacy of the consumer in the economy, freedom for and encouragement of local, voluntary effort in welfare, social and cultural activities, the subjection of the official and the bureaucrat to the taxpayer and the recipient of social benefits, not least freedom from political influence in education, research, learning and scholarship—these are what intellectuals should, and I think overwhelmingly would, support.

And the last is not the least. It is incredible to me that intellectuals have supported social and economic policies that require central control or direction by the State, which must in time entail restriction of freedom in literature, the arts, and the sciences. Happily the recent reaction has come only a few years after the government began to extend the power of the State in 1964. Whatever their individual views on the desirable form of society, intellectuals must increasingly yearn for freedom from political control of universities and colleges. Professor Edward Shils, no conservative or liberal (in the European sense), spoke in the first number of *Minerva* of the "governmentalisation" of learning, and there is a growing reaction by intellectuals of all schools against the increasing control of British universities through the University Grants Committee. Little wonder that some are turning to the idea of establishing independent universities financed by a multiplicity of private sources. And businessmen will see that the money they have contributed to the foundation of universities in Sussex, Essex, Kent, Warwick, Aston, Bradford, Strathclyde . . . has established institutions that increase the power of the State to make mistakes and the power of politicians to play politics.

The experience of the Communist countries under their Stalins, and their efforts in recent years to restore liberty in Yugoslavia, Hungary, and now Czechoslovakia and even Russia itself, must be showing many intellectuals that where economic freedom is suppressed, there literary, artistic and cultural freedom cannot breathe. Even in the USA, which has been going down the wrong road back to statism for some years, there are signs of reaction against the State. Mr. Robert Kennedy, regarded as a "liberal" of the wrong (American) sort, made a remarkable speech last summer in favour of private enterprise. And in September, Mr. Daniel P. Moynihan, Director of the Institute for Urban Studies at Harvard University, also a "liberal" of the collectivist school, warned against the trend to political centralisation in Washington, and urged alliance with political "conservatives" (i.e. liberals in the European sense) "who recognise that unyielding rigidity is just as much a threat to the continuity of things as is an anarchic desire for change," and that

> we must begin getting private business involved in domestic programmes . . . what aerospace corporations have done for getting us to the moon, urban housing corporations can do for the slums. All that is necessary, is to enable enough men to make enough money out of doing so . . . The task of liberals is to make it politically worthwhile and possible for the (Washington) administration to disengage.

And not only intellectuals will support a party that offers to restore freedom. The emerging masses, even more than the suppressed middle classes, will want freedom to spend their rising incomes. Professor John Vaizey has recently pointed to "the grave internal contradiction" in "the ideology of equality" that it cannot at the same time concentrate what resources the State can command on the less gifted or fortunate in the name of equality and on the more gifted in the name of excellence. The dilemma of the egalitarian must be increasingly painful. Should he give his child the advantages he has inherited directly in wealth or indirectly in ability and so sacrifice his principles? Or should he share the State service that is no better than the State can supply for everyone and sacrifice his child? This is not only a conflict between public profession and private performance. A Wedgwood Benn can salve his conscience by the reflection that you do not have to practise to be a good preacher. The dilemma of the egalitarian is far more intractable. It is that, as long as incomes are unequal and the family is not abolished, parents will want to spend their money on something that benefits their family: there is not much sense in forcing them to spend it all on colour TV, cars, hair-dos and fun fairs; they will want better schooling, doctors and hospitals, houses and pensions: and these are freedoms that the State denies, but will sooner or later have to yield.

The yearning for intellectual freedom must be described by the name it has been given by political philosophy down the years since the eighteenth century: liberalism. It is a noble word that has been prostituted by etatists in North America, but I agree with Professor Milton Friedman that we should not let the devil get away with misleading labellings. "Democratic" has been defiled in the communist "democratic people's republics"; "selectivity" is being made a new shield for progressive taxation; "micro-economic" is being naively applied to arbitrary, discriminatory, capricious government favours to individual industries or even firms. All these words should be rescued from captivity. They have been misappropriated because they describe ideas that their misappropriators sense express underlying understanding of what is good, true and civilised. Let the devil sing his own malevolent songs.

But the Conservatives are not the only party to whom intellectuals can turn. Some businessmen turned to Labour in the early 1960s for the wrong policies. But Labour could adopt the right policies for a host of reasons from cynical expediency to a belated recognition that the ordinary people in a western society want more freedom. As the defects, incompetence and dangers of State control spreading from economic to cultural life become more apparent, Labour could change its policies, as it might have done under

Gaitskell, and the Social Democrats have done in Germany, away from State socialism to acceptance of competitive capitalism and private enterprise.

I should be more at home with some Labour men or Liberals than with some Conservatives. In politics, as elsewhere, competition is essential for good order, responsibility and sanity. If the Conservatives want the advice and encouragement of intellectuals they had better lose no more time in saying where they stand and giving an earnest of their intention to act on it when they return to office.

CHAPTER 8

1979

Individual Liberty and Representative Democracy

Digest of a paper in celebration by twenty-six international economists of Hayek's eightieth birthday: political democracy represented less individual/private consumer preferences than politically organised producer interests. Its social tensions could be avoided by the emerging economies of the East if they put the market before politics. * The East has been advancing faster than the West. China risks the dilemma of retarding economic advance if it suppresses the market in Hong Kong.

(*Ordo,* Germany, 1979.)

As incomes rise and become more equal in competitive societies, individuals can pay for more goods and services in the market: yet British government has since the last world war, and further back for a century, increased its supply. Some of the expansion has been in defence and other public goods, but most of it has been in private/personal/family benefits: education, health care, housing, pensions, transport, fuel, and other services. These tendencies have recently become evident in the market oases of Asia as well as in industrial countries of the West.

The nine arguments for expanding the government supply of goods and services—poverty, irresponsibility, equality of access, parity of esteem, economies of centralisation, natural monopoly, external benefits, external detriments, demand management—have been increasingly seen to be vulnerable and unfounded. But liberal economists could have used two general arguments against State supply: first, that the hypothetical case for government provision was at most an argument for experimentation, not for comprehensive national supply; second, that even if experimentation had indicated that State supply has advantages, they did not justify monopoly. To allow private production and distribution in the market was the only way to demonstrate the superiority of State supply. Exclusion of possibly superior private alternatives was too high a price to pay for the supposed advantages of exclusive State supply.

In practice, even in Western countries with "liberal" traditions, State supply has been increasingly exclusive and has led to deterioration in the quality of State services. The evidence is most clearly apparent in British medical care and education.

The extension in the Western democracies of State services from public to private goods has increased unnecessary social conflict. The majority/committee procedures necessarily used by government have suppressed individual preferences. The resulting tensions and conflicts are increasingly seen in Britain. The existence of suppressed preferences is evidenced by field studies that demonstrate a wide gap between the small private sectors in medicine and education that are "allowed" to exist by the side of State medicine and education and the much larger market supply that would result from the creation of unbiased choice through reverse income taxes and/or voucher systems. These developments in Britain and in other industrial countries in Europe, North America and Australasia show undesirable economic and political consequences that the market oases of Asia could avoid.

State economy maximises group conflict and individual frustration; markets minimise them. Further field surveys in Britain suggest that the social welfare function was a figment of the State planners' imagination or wishful thinking.

The defenders of State supply have resorted to the false claim that democratic "representative machinery" can make it accountable to the citizen. This machinery is less egalitarian than the market: the inequalities that arise in the market from inequality in income and wealth are less difficult to modify than is the inequality of cultural, "social," economic or political power which decide access to services in State economy. State "representative machinery" is usually manipulated by articulate activist individuals or groups, usually more literate and moneyed than the average, and is therefore inegalitarian as well as arbitrary and "unjust."

The further claim that public preferences are respected by the machinery of party politics in representative government is no more convincing. In Britain the party in government has not represented majorities of electors since the 1939–45 war; there has often been little or no choice between their policies; and there has been no opportunity for the citizen to record preferences on single services.

The task of confining government supply to public goods will require not only macro-economic "expenditure ceilings" or "cash limits." It will require also micro-economic market pricing or charging, which would be more refined in reflecting individual citizen preferences and be more certain to contract government since it would transfer unpopular political decisions from government to individuals in the market.

Taiwan, Hong Kong, South Korea and Japan have made the fastest postwar economic advance because they have based their economies on open markets and have, so far, avoided the errors of the West in expanding the functions of government from public to private/personal/family services. The recent advice reaching their governments from officials, academics and politicians that, as their national incomes rise they can "afford" to spend more on "social welfare," etc., is an error based on a misconception. There is still time for them to avoid it. The proper relationship between government expenditure and national income is not direct but inverse: as national income and therefore personal incomes rise, government expenditure should fall.

If the market oases of Asia follow the errors of the West they will confront new problems of resistance to government, a weakening respect for law in general, increasing tax "avoision," undermining of the family unit, retarded economic growth, decelerating living standards, weakening national security.

CHAPTER 9

1980

La Trahison des Clercs

Subconscious philosophic bias moves scholars in all schools. Ten reasons for the especially deep-rooted and persistent antagonism in British universities to classical liberalism. * The dependence of universities, with the Open University, on consumer finance has been increased but the subsidy from government largely remains. A solution lies in creating competing centres of classical teaching.

(*The Times Higher Education Supplement,* January 1980.)

Is the prevailing ethos of British higher education predominantly Left? What are the consequences for British intellectual vitality—and ultimately for the strength of the economy?

There has been a substantial shift in some faculties since the mid-1960s, especially in economics, in many universities. Then why is the Left predominantly, stubbornly and anti-intellectually resistant to change and *conservative?* In sociology, political science, history and the arts it remains labour, social democrat, socialist, communist, Marxist or Trotskyist despite the evidence, despite the changing balance in argument, and despite the change of opinion in people of intellectual stature outside the universities though with closely-linked influence on the nation's thought, teaching, scholarship and public philosophy.

Short of a lengthy comprehensive answer, my attempt draws on impressions since my undergraduate days at the LSE to over twenty years at the Institute of Economic Affairs where I have worked with three hundred academics, mostly economists but also political scientists, historians, lawyers and sociologists in Britain and overseas.

British academics were much less hospitable to the market approach of the IEA in 1957 than they have become. Keynesian deficit financing seemed to be assuring full employment, Beveridge's Welfare State, with Bevan's National Health Service, was only nine years old, Titmuss's "badge of citizenship," which had worked for communal co-operation during the war, sounded promising for peace. It was not easy to persuade academics to write for the fledgling Institute that seemed to go back on the prevailing preoccupation with macro-economics and wanted to resurrect Hayek, Böhm-Bäwerk, Nassau Senior, Adam Smith and even older economic jokers, as some early critics thought. Higher education was high-church orthodoxy; the IEA must have seemed very low-church non-conformity. That contrast is still largely true outside economics. That is why I dub British university higher education predominantly conservative even when it is strongly Left, and IEA higher education predominantly dissenting radical even when it is considered Right.

Much has changed in two decades. The Institute publishes some twelve studies a year, some by several authors, many of national or international repute. And there is no lack of new writing, particularly from younger men and women with names to make. Whether their sympathies are left, centre or right, they are commissioned because they are sophisticated in micro-analysis and aware of the limitations as well as applications of macro-economics.

The main reasons for the tenacity of left conservatism seem to be broadly ten. First, the conservatism of human nature itself: a university teacher who absorbed and, until his or her late thirties or early forties, has taught a Marxist or social democratic interpretation of economics or history must find it torment to acknowledge error and lose years of intellectual capital. It is difficult to count the "converts" in more than dozens who have recalled uncritical acceptance of post-war leftist orthodoxies in favour of State action to solve problems and achieve objectives in all spheres.

Since university higher education is properly and closely linked with broadcasting, from instant punditry and trendy Reith lectureships to regular teaching for the Open University, it is relevant to remark that many producers and directors show their intellectual origins and continuing links by the opinionated Left-inclined academics they invite to the microphone and screen. BBC and ITV hierarchs in their forties/fifties seem often to be the products of post-war university teaching in the euphoric heyday of the Keynes/Beveridge/Titmuss consensus. It is otherwise, as the latest example, difficult to explain the attention lavished on Peter Townsend's *Poverty,* a work of attenuated analysis and superabundant sentimentality.

The second reason is the reigning fashion of compassion. There is poetry in poverty, no romance in productivity. An able economist who had written a combative Fabian appraisal of IEA writing in 1968, and who, despite reluctance, had found some analysis to applaud, was reduced to justifying his general assault by the accusation "but you don't care as much about poverty as Titmuss does." The confusion between motive and consequence largely explains the sentimental attachment to left conservatism, especially in sociological faculties but also among economists whose hearts confuse their heads.

Transparent though it is, the sentiment that to mean well is to do good reigns in the social sciences despite the evidence of remote and recent history. Adam Smith knew better when he taught that the butcher's benevolence was not the most certain source of the customer's supper. But the Left has always confused self-interest with selfishness, and cannot see that it is validated by self-knowledge, which includes the personal circle. The do-gooder wants to do good to others without knowing their preferences.

The economist often seems a cold-hearted creature because he is, or should be, forever prating about opportunity costs. He is even known to say that the relief of suffering, or even saving life, cannot justify the resources required if they could be used to better effect elsewhere. It is the sociologist or social worker who is often the callous profligate in the use of resources. The notion that the study of economics excludes concern for human compassion helps to explain the persistence of academic left conservatism.

A third explanation is the sheer intellectual arrogance of much technocracy. It infects both the social scientists, with their characteristic contempt for the idiosyncrasies and susceptibility to advertising of the consumer, and the natural scientists, with their disdain for the wasteful taste of the populace that frustrates the tidy, uniform arrangements of the engineer, the architect, or the town planner.

An allied influence is the subconscious understanding that statism creates jobs for intellectuals. I should add that dismantling statism, to accelerate its disintegration by market forces, will also require a large input of academics.

The fourth explanation is the commitment to egalitarianism, seen as requiring redistribution by the State of benefits in kind and therefore irredeemably conflicting with the market. This dichotomy has always seemed to me inexplicable. As one of working-class origins who reacted strongly in my childhood against demeaning charity in kind, I have increasingly seen history and analysis establish the market as the supreme emancipator of the masses in western society. Galbraith saw, but did not understand, the contrast between private affluence in food, clothes and homes and public squalor in State education, medicine and accommodation cubicles.

The contract of the market had to replace the status of State mercantilism for mobility to produce increasing equalisation of opportunity, access to resources, and income. And that transition has been retarded by socialism. Redistribution through the State in kind—as in State education, the NHS, subsidised council housing—has subjected the common people to the arbitrary processes of cultural influence, political pressure and economic power that individuals possess in widely different degree according to birth, temperament, character. The Achilles heel of the vainly egalitarian Left is that these cultural and other influences in a State economy are more difficult to correct than are the differences in income or wealth that determine access in a market. To equalise differences in income or wealth by devices from reverse income taxes to vouchers is child's play contrasted with the coercive, authoritarian measures required to offset differences in accent, family background, social connections, occupational pull, political strings. The conservative-left university egalitarian continues to plump for the State against the market. The more reflective thinker—from Professor David Marquand through Evan Luard, who still abhors the market, to the Christian-Socialist Eric Heffer and the aspiring prime minister David Owen—is beginning, at last, to talk of socialism without the State. But it remains talk: an escape from reality into conjecture without support from history or logic.

The fifth explanation is the elemental anger at "capitalism" and the instinctive rebound to its opponent—State economy in one form or another from social democracy to Marxism. The underlying error is the million-mile leap in logic from capitalism with warts to socialism sublime. The rejectors of "capitalism" escape into a funk-hole. Socialism is the opium of the intellectuals.

This is a shocking episode in university anti-intellectualism. The defenders of capitalism examine its limitations—"inequality," "poverty," monopoly, externality, instability—and have worked to devise means of removing or reducing them, though without losing the dynamism that, as Marx saw, had created unprecedented productivity. Yet socialists make a series of empty claims for socialism, the twentieth century's South Sea Bubble of cornucopia, and change their ground when they have to concede criticism. "True" socialism, they doggedly insist, exists nowhere: not in Sweden (though Mr. Denis Healey has lately taken to quoting Austria), not in "liberal" Yugoslavia, certainly not in Soviet Russia. Thus is socialism made immune from criticism. The university leftist engages in wordy guerrilla warfare and then vanishes in dialectical smoke when asked for evidence from tested hypotheses. A belated case for the political advertising council? University left-conservatism rests on a will-o'-the-wisp more elusive than Baroness Orczy's Scarlet Pimpernel. To mix the metaphor with a dash of Lewis Carroll's Dormouse in the Mad Hatter's tea party:

> They seek it here, they seek it there
> Those faithfuls seek it everywhere;
> They find it heaven, others hell;
> That damned, enticing, treacle-well.

One implication of the political unrealism, the wishful thinking, in left-conservatism, is that the right ideas will unfailingly be put into effect by the right people when they acquire power. The result is its neglect of a realistic analysis of government, democracy and politics. The wisdom of the classical economists that created their scepticism about the ability of political authority to serve the public weal has been re-created in a new branch of economics pioneered since the late 1950s mostly by the American economists J. M. Buchanan and Gordon Tullock, although one of its earliest texts was by the British (Scottish) economist Duncan Black. There is an active branch of the Public Choice Society in Europe, but no chair in the economics of politics in any British university, though Professors Rowley, Peacock, Wiseman and Littlechild (Newcastle, Buckingham, York, Birmingham) keep the flag flying with occasional writing and lecturing.

The university leftist is the arch-conservative who will not, or cannot, recognise argument or evidence. The Bourbon journals of the conservative left, much read by university teachers and students, are the *Guardian,* the *Observer,* the *New Statesman, New Society, Tribune,* the *Listener.* Even *The Times Higher Education Supplement,* after years of square yards on or by Marxists like Thompson, Hobsbawm, Miliband, Saville and socialists like Williams, Tunstall, Townsend, Hoggart, Eric Robinson, Glennerster, Peston, Halsey, recognised the existence of the IEA in barely fifty square inches by Peston—but not until 1979. All these journals still reflect the economics of the Keynesian/Beveridge/Titmuss consensus as though the world has stood still since 1946. The myth still rules: government can solve problems if it has enough power, taxes and bureaucrats. Failure teaches nothing: it merely creates louder demands for more power, taxes, bureaucracy.

The national newspapers that make more room for radical thinking are ironically the formerly true-blue *Daily Telegraph* and the *Daily Mail.* And it should give political, psephological and social observers in the universities furiously to think that three mass newspapers catering for "working class" readers, the *Sun*, the *Sunday Mirror* and the *News of the World*, print "right-wing" editorials or publish columnists that do not antagonise Labour loyalists. The university Left is a long way behind the masses in their disillusion with the Welfare State, nationalisation and bureaucracy.

The "quality" Bourbons attract the student by their literary and art criticisms and thus entice them into their political treacle wells. Yet good sense forces its way into the best of their writers. Mr. Peter Jenkins in the *Guardian* recognises the strength of the liberal critique of socialism. Mr. John Cole, deputy editor of the *Observer*, a self-confident socialist who scoffs at "laissez faire" but intellectually the equal of some academics, is more perceptive of economic realities than are some Tory journalists. Lately logic has drawn him to ultimate truth: he now recognises (*Observer*, 30 December) that the power of politicians is only marginal: the "fearsome truth" is that "improvement will come only through a million decisions taken . . . well away from Westminster, Whitehall, or even the TUC and CBI." That "fearsome truth"—that decisions are best made by individuals (which must mean *in markets*—where else?)—is the truth the radical right has resurrected from British classical economic philosophy but which the conservative left continues to deny.

My sixth reason for the continuing influence of the conservative left, despite its waning intellectual vitality, is the authority that students attribute to its teaching when it reflects acquaintance with the corridors of Whitehall sfollowing sometimes justifiable preferment. In my lifetime governments have been advised mostly by intellectuals to the left. The supreme example is the use made by Labour of Titmuss, Abel-Smith and Townsend. And the knowledge they acquired then led the Conservatives to use them almost as extensively. Other examples are plentiful: Lord Young, Lord Vaizey, Lord Wedderburn, Lord McCarthy, Donnison, Atkinson and others. Perhaps because of the more intense intellectual curiosity on the left, the Conservatives have rarely used sympathetic academics as advisers, or even confidantes. By 1970 Sir Keith Joseph was beginning to understand why he was a Conservative, or rather an economic liberal, and appointed Professor Dennis Lees to the National Insurance Advisory Committee. Is that because the liberal don is generally less distinguished than the socialist? Differential patronage makes it appear so to the student. Yet among the great names of British scholarship which will live in history—Laski or Hayek? Dalton or Robbins? Tawney or Popper? And, in the United States, Galbraith or Friedman?

There is an allied difference in the attitude of Labour and Conservative politicians. At an IEA seminar on the economics of politics in 1978, at which honours for the heads of nationalised industries were discussed among the reasons for accepting the jobs, Lord Robbins discounted honours as giving "half-an-hour's private satisfaction." Yet if Keynes rather than Marx was right to put ideas before interests as the prime influence on affairs, intellectuals may be right to share the human desire for recognition with politicians, bureaucrats and businessmen. Mrs. Margaret Thatcher is the first prime minister to acknowledge the new radical right.

Seventh, left intellectuals are generally more dedicated, committed, embattled and angry than, with exceptions, right intellectuals. Left-inclined academics tend to evolve as members of a conspiratorial cause; they attract young acolytes by exciting lofty condemnation of the established order. Rightists tend to regard themselves as individuals and resist labelling; nor do they easily join in dissent against suppression of intellectual liberty. Professor Julius Gould is a rare exception. Left intellectuals are more likely to engage themselves as activists. They are the players. The rightists tend to be the gentlemen. They do not spring to their pens to write to *The Times*, or appear on television, or support good men on political platforms. There may be a chicken-and-egg relationship in the relative scarcity of radical-right equivalents of the *New Statesman, Listener, New Society, Tribune*, no British counterpart of *The Public Interest* or *Commentary*, both written partly by former intellectuals of the United States Left.

My eighth reason is that academics of the Left tend to appoint like-minded academics to their departments. All academics are human, but the Left is more human than the Right. I have yet to hear of a sociological faculty headed by a left intellectual who has appointed a right-wing sociologist. Robbins and Hayek appointed A. P. Lerner, who became one of the most formidable exponents of market socialism. My impression is that this diverse tendency remains, and is dangerous for the quality of British intellectual life.

My ninth reason is the State financing of British universities. Except for the dwindling private endowments of Oxford and Cambridge, and the private University College at Buckingham, British higher education, especially in the red-brick universities, is almost wholly financed by "public" money, or rather *private* money taxed and channelled through political authority. And more *private* money is subscribed by industry, private foundations, even individuals to State universities under political influence.

The difference that should alarm scholars is that, in financing university higher education indirectly through political authority, the diverse private sources yield influence to politicians exercising monopoly. In sharp contrast, much more private money for higher education in the United States goes directly to private universities, colleges, etc., where administrators and teachers are less likely to take off into the intellectual stratosphere and indulge breast beating at the monstrosities of "capitalism." There may be the opposite tendency to romanticise business, but it is not so dangerous when competitive business funds are further diluted by research grants, student fees, and private bequests.

More private millions are channelled to conservative left academics through the Social Science Research Council and other conduits, not with intentional bias but because social scientists are still largely conservative left.

Tenth, and for the time being lastly, the Left remains conservatively collectivist because it has misled itself into a paroxysm of hatred against the market and "market forces." When I asked a former Labour chancellor where in the history of socialist thinking the antipathy to the market had originated, he asked another guest, also a former Labour minister, "Can you answer that?" He did not. The fulminations of university leftists, from compassionate sociologists to autocratic technologists, serve to conceal the inadequacies in their sparsely analysed alternatives to capitalism.

Despite the shift in economics the intellectual imbalance in British higher education is both cause and consequence of the relative doldrums in the British intellectual climate.

The weekly outpouring of conservative-left thinking in the weekend journals and the Sunday press, even those in right-wing ownership (not least the *Observer,* owned by Atlantic Richfield of the United States), is a regular booster to university-left morale. The obvious antidote would be equally vigorous radical right literature. The *Spectator* blows hot and cold. *Encounter* finds room for the periodic right-wing counter-blast, but infrequently. The most hopeful development is the news magazine *NOW!,* where long features emerge with mostly right-wing conclusions, despite some left-wing writers. But students read leftist Goldthorpe/Halsey sociology reviewed by the left Hoggart in *The Observer* and the leftists Kellner and Wilby in *The Sunday Times.* Where is the academic stimulus if the left is reviewed by the sympathetic left and the right is ignored by the hostile left?

The urgent task is to redress the imbalance and reinvigorate British intellectual debate. The main obstacle is that the right does not read as much as the left. Otherwise market forces would produce profit-oriented entrepreneurs who could make money by publishing a right-wing *Listener, New Statesman, New Society, Guardian* or *Observer.* The Mainstream Bookclub, a Whiggish venture fathered by Lord Blake, Jo Grimond, Alan Peacock and John Patten, may help if amply financed. The IEA has been thinking of establishing a quarterly to provide a platform for running commentaries on current economic affairs by its now long list of university writers, and is hoping to find a publisher who can work fast enough. Perhaps the project might commend itself to Lord Hartwell of the *Telegraph,* Sir James Goldsmith of *NOW!,* or Victor Matthews of the *Daily Express.* Meanwhile what can be done to reverse the engines that have created the conservative-left dominance?

With notable exceptions the conservative-left establishment is in the saddle in the media. Perhaps Conor Cruise O'Brien, editor-in-chief of the *Observer,* Peter Preston of the *Guardian,* and Harold Evans of the *Sunday Times* can make more room for radical-right writing, even if only to reduce the predictability of their general flavour. But there is at least a wide variety of newspapers.

The serious blockage lies in broadcasting and in paperbacks. Perhaps a new chairman of the BBC will be strong enough to persuade his producers and directors that virtually excluding a source of non-conformist thinking is unacceptable in the public service BBC. And perhaps the rich conservative-leftist Lord Bernstein will see that a lopsided left-inclined diet is not good television for Granada. In radical right paperbacks the chicken must come before the egg (or vice versa): a publisher will have to take the same long-term risk that Allen Lane did with the left-inclined sixpenny Penguins. Perhaps cheap radical-right reading will produce the readers.

The "compassion fashion" is passing as the failure of the Welfare State is recognised in Britain—fifteen years after the failure to abolish poverty by State paternalism in the United States of the 1960s. A market-oriented talk on welfare to staff and post-graduate students in Professor Rudolf Klein's department of social policy at the University of Bath in October was received with little hostility. At a weekend conference on poverty in December at Cumberland Lodge, where I argued against Frank Field and Peter Townsend for replacing benefits in kind by cash or vouchers, which implies a revolution from the Welfare State to the market, the audience of left-inclined social workers were more receptive than I had expected.

The failure of state technocracy is also increasingly acknowledged. But the gospel is spreading more slowly by intellectual conviction in the universities than by instinct among the common people. Perhaps sociologists will be appointed increasingly for their analytical power, not least in economics.

The commitment to egalitarianism is weakening before the evidence that the State is inegalitarian. The cynical "working" of the welfare system by what the Americans call "limousine liberals"—the middle classes, often university teachers, who corner the best state schools and hospitals by outbidding the lower orders for local housing—is also revealing the humbug of university leftists who advocate comprehensive schools and NHS treatment for the masses outside their cosy middle-class *enclaves* with private schools and hospitals.

The hatred of the market, even of dread "capitalism," is waning before the evidence that the communist economies are lost without it. A sabbatical study month every three years in Eastern Europe might teach that economies resting on central coercion have to use honest individual market incentives even in medicine to help get the world's work done.

A long lecture to the Centre for Ecological Studies at the University of Edinburgh in October, with the aggressive title "Corrigible Capitalism; Specious Socialism," would not have been received as passively two or three years ago, said the chairman, Dr. John Loraine, and several self-confessed Labour academics in the audience. There has been similar reaction in the Oxford and Cambridge unions. The student is father to the teacher.

Political preferment is easily remediable. There is no shortage of radical-right intellectuals with whom to strengthen the House of Lords as a "second opinion" on the Commons.

The dedication of the conservative-left intellectual will not be matched until the radical-right intellectual recognises the danger to intellectual freedom. Since by nature he is more of an individualist than the conservative-left collectivists, reform will take time.

Philosophic preferment will be as difficult to remove in academia as it was in the Church. The main safeguard is knowledge of its prevalence to disinfect its influence.

Private patrons of scholarship could direct funds to more Buckinghams and less through the UGC to fewer redbricks. Switching from State universities might suffice. One less redbrick would be no tragedy. One strong Buckingham would be a beacon of independence from politics in British scholarship that academics of all schools should demand for the vitality of higher education.

The false denunciation of the market as obstructive of compassionate social policy will wane, but very slowly in the lifetime of present left-inclined heads of departments and their acolytes. Again the short-term antidote is publicity.

Elitist leftism in British higher education is financed by the taxpayer yet is cavalier about his sentiment. The radical right emphasis on the market mechanism is more consumer oriented and respectful of popular sentiment. The conservative-left ethos has strayed too far from the populace it is supposed to serve. And the ultimate solution must lie in reconstructing the financing system.

It must be a cause for alarm to Mrs. Thatcher, Denis Healey and Jo Grimond that for thirty years the academic life of Britain has been dominated by university teachers caught up in a lopsided, left-inclined, fashionable consensus producing policies designed to frustrate the public philosophy. It is even more damaging to British intellectual vigour that they will survive in the universities and other centres of intellectual influence for perhaps thirty years or more after their out-dated consensus has been revealed as an almighty flop, and the public policies it continues to produce do lasting, severe damage to the national economic, social and political life. The national interest lies in nurturing the best thinking. But it will not emerge until there is more radical-right competition to the prevailing conservative-left ethos.

The solution may have to lie in multiplying the platforms and the spokesmen for market-oriented solutions outside rather than inside the universities.

Within the universities there are two solutions. The long-term corrections would come from students themselves as grants are replaced by loans perhaps eased in the early stages by vouchers. Britain has too long suffered from a university ambience in which industry and commerce, and therefore education for them, have been under-estimated with contempt or contumely by the conservative-left. Too much talent has been diverted to the non-commercial professions. More financing of students by themselves or by private firms would increase the emphasis on engineering, management or marketing education for industry that has helped Germany and France to overtake Britain.

The interim university solution is to emphasise faculties that produce graduates in engineering, applied science, languages, marketing and economics. The universities will have to accept that, as long as they accept taxpayers' money through Parliament, they cannot spend it without accountability to the taxpayers' representatives in Parliament. The theory of the UGC, that it makes universities independent of political influences, is defective because unrealistic and undemocratic.

But there is little prospect of early redress in the imbalance of intellectual influence. The conservative-left will long continue its dominance in the social sciences. The solution is to create more platforms for the radical-right outside the state universities.

This means the press, television, book publishing, the Open University (or rather largely "shut" to radical-right teaching), the House of Lords, and perhaps in new forms. And the example of the IEA should encourage academics in other faculties to question their conventional consensuses. If British intellectual life is to regain vitality and quality in the next five or ten years, while there is still time, to challenge the conservative-left ethos, it will have to be redressed by a stronger radical-right voice outside the universities. If we wait for the slow, long-run solution of intellectual conviction, it will be too late.

PART II

Classical Market Thinking Applied to Industry

CHAPTER **10**

1950

The Brewers' Dilemma

Government regulation prevents industry from moving with the market, illustrated from long-established brewing and inn-keeping. The long-term decline in consumption with rising incomes and growing amenities required the tie to be loosened: retailing and production would develop better separately. * The later liberalisation of the licensing laws has strengthened the market inducements, but restrictions remain unnecessarily repressive.

(*The Economist,* December 1950.)

For half a century the brewing industry has been confronted with a persistent decline in the demand for beer. It spent some £75 million upon improvements to public houses between the wars. It has directed co-operative and competitive advertising at the public, and more concentrated campaigns at successive Chancellors. But all these policies have had a persistent flavour of the defensive: the industry is reluctant to admit that lower beer sales might have part of their origins in fundamental changes of social behaviour. It has not accepted any need for radical revision of its own policies or outlook, and it explains the fall in beer consumption and brewing profits—during a period of brimful employment—almost solely in terms of excessive taxation. This explanation is simple; is it also the complete answer?

Until the First World War, the industry's marketing problem was clear. Brewers made beer, and their prosperity depended on maximum sales. The marketing of beer was governed by a licensing system that forced brewers to own or control public houses and other licensed premises in order to ensure retail outlets. Such vertical integration might in any case have offered some economies, but it was primarily the licensing laws that determined the modern structure of the industry. The result is that some 80 per cent of the public houses in England and Wales are brewer-owned and three-quarters of the industry's assets are in licensed premises. In order to increase the number of selling outlets, amalgamation has been pursued until the number of brewers producing "for sale" has been reduced from several thousand in 1900 to 602 in 1949 (the *Brewers' Almanack* for 1950 records some 450 independent firms). Brewers are substantial owners of real estate, not for its intrinsic profitability, but primarily to guarantee selling outlets for their beer.

Until the first decade of this century, such an attitude could easily be justified. But this close association of beer and the public house has since been weakened by changes in social behaviour that have followed the placing of a host of new recreations, amusements, and amenities at the disposal of the working classes. Today the public house no longer has a monopoly either of beer sales or of the working man's leisure. Apart from increased consumption of beer in clubs, the list of new contenders for the public's leisure and money is familiar and still growing; it ranges from open-air sport to the dance hall and the cinema, from the "dirt-track" and the skating rink to television. What has the public house to offer to retain the patronage of both sexes and of all ages and social classes against these counter-attractions? It has long provided bowling greens, skittle alleys and dart-boards; it has experimented with paintings, poetry and plays; it has attempted, not very successfully, to revive interest in traditional "pub" games; but it can hardly add a greyhound track or a swimming pool. And where the installation of further attractions is possible—television might be one—it is still a question whether their provision increases the sales of beer to new customers more than it reduces sales to regular customers distracted by them from drinking. It may be that sales of beer in the public house and the general profitability of the public house are, in the mid-twentieth century, becoming conflicting objectives.

The industry unites in blaming the decline in consumption of beer on high duty and, in recent years, on low gravities. But the evidence for this case is not conclusive. Beer consumption rose generally throughout the nineteenth century as population and income grew; the peak of consumption per head seems to have been reached in the 1870s. In the present century the trend has unmistakably turned downward, though periods of artificially high or low consumption have resulted from abnormal causes—notably unemployment and war. Consumption since the war has been higher than it was immediately before the war, but has been falling fast this year, and there is no clear evidence whether it has settled down to a post-war norm. If the beer duty is responsible, it has to be remembered that it rose to 8*d.* or 9*d.* per pint only after 1939. In 1938 it was only 2½*d.* against ¼*d.* early in the century;

yet consumption was 33 per cent lower in 1938 than in 1900, in spite of increased population and purchasing power. More recently the failure of the 1*d.* cut in price following the 1949 Budget has convinced the industry that only a slash of 3*d.* or 4*d.* would revive the demand. This plea, unfortunately, harks back to days that may never return, of vastly different Budget commitments for social services. And the argument of "diminishing returns" in the revenue derived from beer is bound to be lost on any Chancellor who is not absolutely convinced that high prices are the one factor responsible for falling consumption.

The part played by lower gravities, again, seems difficult to prove. Average gravity was reduced during the war by government order from 1040.78 degrees in 1938 to 1034 or 1035 degrees; but it had already been voluntarily reduced by the industry from 1055 in 1899 to 1041 degrees, partly to lighten the burden of successive increases in duty and partly to cater for the emerging taste for lighter beers. To argue from this past experience that the industry had discovered that 1040 degrees is the exact strength below which further reductions in gravity automatically reduce demand would surely be too charitable. Less has been heard of the gravity argument since the 1950 Budget, for although that made possible a three-degree rise in gravities (and a reduction in the index of retail prices), it produced no consequential rise in consumption save perhaps in bottled heavier beers.

What the public house is losing in importance in the distribution of beer, it is trying hard to gain through its other attractions. In the nineteenth century it was predominantly a shop for the sale of beer; in the twentieth century it is, at its best, a social centre valued for its atmosphere, company, comfort and recreational amenities. Have changing conditions in the supply and demand for beer, in the character of the public house, and in other competing attractions undermined the basic reasons for brewer-ownership of public houses? The public house is no longer the only method of selling beer, and it may not necessarily be the cheapest method. Beer and the public house are becoming divorced in the economy of the brewing industry. Public house operation is less important to the brewer for the distribution of beer because other outlets have grown; selling beer is becoming less important to the public house in the maintenance of its clientele and profitability. The two factors must now be considered as potentially separate; not end and means but distinct entities—a commodity and a service that need not necessarily be provided jointly, but can be separately offered to the public on their individual merits. Beer will continue to be sold in public houses, but conceivably more may in time be sold for consumption elsewhere. Many firms have been able to expand their sales of bottled beer and powerless to prevent a contraction in their sales of draught beer. Many of them have made considerable enlargements of their bottling capacity. Public houses will continue to derive an important part of their revenue from beer, but conceivably sales of other beverages and food may eventually overtake it.

If these developments occur, neither need be considered calamitous by the brewers. But if they are to plan profitably for the future, they might pause to consider whether the methods of marketing their two products do not need to be conceived and executed independently. They may need consumer research and selling efforts consciously directed towards different social classes and age-groups, and towards different buying motives. Beer will need to be sold wherever the public chooses to spend its leisure time and spare money. Bottling and packaging must be adapted to cater for the needs of consumers wherever they may be—at home, at the club, or out of doors. In the middle-class economy of the future there should be an opportunity for expanded sales for consumption at home. There may be a lesson in the work of the United States Brewers' Foundation whose group advertising has made good use of cosy domestic scenes with the caption "Perhaps no beverages are more at home on more occasions than good American beer or ale." Again, should brewers be inhibited by over-sensitivity to the interests of licensees from developing door-to-door delivery? Here may be the only means of generating sales to middle-class and women consumers.

The public house may also need to develop a distinct selling technique if it is to free itself from its main preoccupation with beer. This might involve supplying any services it can economically provide that are demanded by its clients, not least food. It must extend its facilities, amenities and amusements and raise its standards as a place of social resort for both sexes (it is still largely a man's institution) and all classes (it is still mainly a working-man's haunt). Whether in this kind of development it can retain its *raison d'être* and distinctive place as an English social institution remains to be seen.

Some go-ahead brewers have read the signs of the times. One is marketing a "TV" pack; others offer door-to-door delivery; several are advertising beer for home consumption and appealing to women consumers. But only a handful would concede that radical economic changes are affecting their business. Even where modern selling policies are being adopted, it is not clear that the changing relationship between beer and the public house is accepted. At least the unchanged policy of advertising undertaken for the industry by the Brewers' Society does not suggest as much. In the 1930s, total beer consumption slumped to 18.9 million barrels and average consumption per head to 14.3 gallons *per annum*. The Society's director conceived it necessary not only "to declare that England's is the best and healthiest beer a young man can consume" but also to show "all the good will and contentment the public house imparts in England." But the "Beer is Best" campaign was designed above all to increase the consumption of beer; and the public house was still only the instrument. Consumption revived to 25 million barrels in 1938, largely for reasons that had little to do with the slogan. But the latter had won a place in the affections of the industry, and after the war it was resuscitated—in entirely different conditions of low gravities. Indeed, after the 1950 Budget permitted beer to be strengthened, Beer became Better after many years of being Best. Advertisements publicising the attractions of the inn have appeared since the end of the war, but they usually end with the old slogan; the man in the street has not yet been invited to patronise the public house for its own sake.

If the sale of beer in bottles for consumption elsewhere should begin to overtake the sale of draught beer inside the public house, the smaller local brewer will face intensified competition from national (or regional) brewers with their advertised brands. There is nothing a brewer likes less than to sell another's beer in his houses, but he cannot exclude interlopers from the neutral territory of home, club, or dance-hall. The local monopoly of the small brewer, formerly maintained by the high cost of transporting beer, will no longer protect him. For a time it may be preserved by the conservatism of local tastes, but improvements in transport and packaging will in time further increase the penetrative power of advertised brands.

Such competition may lead some small brewers to sell out to the larger: others may attempt to make their houses profitable by turning themselves into inn-keepers and hoteliers owning chains of "free" houses and selling the beer in greatest demand. Beer would then be supplied by a smaller number of specialist brewers who had disposed of their houses (the largest brewers already own few houses or none) or regarded them as an ancillary interest. The industry would then tend to separate into its two parts as the economic conditions in which the licensing system led to their integration faded away; the controversial "tied" house system might in time come to be recognised as a phase arising from the peculiar social and economic conditions of the nineteenth century. But such a division of beer production and distribution would take several decades to develop, particularly because of the brewers' massive investment in bricks and mortar. In the immediate future the marketing problem of the brewer is to adjust his selling methods to the divergent needs of the two products that past conditions beyond his control have left in his hands. He may prefer to remain a brewer, but fate has made him also an inn-keeper. He is responsible to the nation for passing on to the future a social institution that until now, at least, has had no parallel in the world.

CHAPTER **11**

1957

Reform the Licensing Laws

The changing markets—increasing competition in drinks, food and social amenities—made the licensing laws both too strict and ineffective. Yet another demonstration of government failure to keep pace with changing market conditions of demand and supply—reflecting public preferences and technical advance, still less anticipate or move ahead of them. Seven years later social advance made the licensing laws even more ineffective and superfluous. * By the 1990s further legal relaxation lags behind the market.

(*The Times*, June 1957.)

1950–58—These developments were further analysed in eleven articles in *The Economist* and some fifteen in *The Financial Times.*

A quarter of a century ago, in the middle of the Great Depression, the Royal Commission on Licensing under the first Lord Amulree published its report. Its majority, sixteen of the nineteen commissioners, largely approved of the existing licensing controls, although they suggested that the administration be, in part, moved from the local justices to a national body.

Since then, deflation, Hitler, the Kremlin, and inflation have precluded attention to more than particular problems and anomalies—the transfer of licences from bombed cities to new areas, young people in dance halls, international airports, and the like. In recent years abuses or grievances have agitated magistrates, tourist organisations, local authorities, temperance bodies, licensees, and the owners of licensed premises. Home Secretaries are reluctant to touch a "controversial" question. Yet is it really impossible to reach agreement on the licensing system appropriate to our day and age?

The 1931 commissioners hoped their proposals would "meet present and future requirements, as we see them." But they did not see—how could they?—that their report would be followed by twenty-five years of tumultuous change. They could not have foreseen television, wide-screen cinema, the seven-fold increase in soft drinks consumption, the accelerated redistribution of income, persistent inflation and over-full employment, the new wave of women's emancipation, the working-class motor car, the migration from slum to council house. And they did not foresee the result: the transformation of the licensed trade.

The better fed, better clothed, better housed, more discriminating customer spends a smaller proportion of his income on alcoholic drinks than in 1931. Poverty has vanished, except among the old. Drunkenness has become even more a lapse from good manners. No less significant, the licensed trade is much more at the mercy of the market. In 1931 drink and the public house had few rivals. In 1957 they face the unending counter-attractions that scientific ingenuity and economic advance lay at the feet of the moneyed working man.

Licensing laws were designed to protect the public from itself and from monopoly. In 1931 the commission thought that "the present restrictions should be maintained." In view of the profound social and economic changes since 1931 it could not possibly have sustained that view in 1957.

The clearest evidence that the licensing system is out of tune with the times is the persistent growth of clubs registered for the supply of alcoholic drinks. Their growth, of course, expresses a preference for their intrinsic merits as well as the state of the licensing laws. But their large degree of freedom in formation, premises, membership, conduct (hours, services, amenities, etc.), and taxation must have played some part. What part it is impossible to say, given the difference in the conditions governing them. The Amulree Commission pointed to their increase in England and Wales from 6,500 in 1905 to 13,500 in 1930, and concluded: "if the law remains unaltered, it is, theoretically at any rate, possible that by the multiplication of clubs the effective administrating of licensing law may be seriously prejudiced." The possibility is no longer theoretical. They have increased to about 22,000. In 1905 there was one club to sixteen on-licences; in 1931 one to six; in 1957 there is nearly one to three. In all, the clubs have increased the proportion of alcoholic drinks they handle from about 1 per cent in 1905 to 11 per cent.

These national figures indicate the trend, but they mask the varied situation in different areas. In some towns in the industrial North and Midlands and in South Wales the clubs probably handle 25 per cent or more of the drink; and they are already half as numerous as on-licences. Since the justices have no control over the number, and almost no control over the conduct, of the clubs, licensing in such places has largely broken down. It no longer effectively controls the supply or consumption of alcoholic drinks. It cannot work if there are plentiful escape routes. This is the dilemma of the licensing law.

Justices have now in many places an almost impossible task. And some have argued for control over the clubs. This view found an echo in the debate on Mr. Black's Children and Young Persons (Registered Clubs) Bill on 24 May. Certainly it seems logical. But it faces three difficulties. In the first place, the club is a private meeting-place, an extension of the home. Licensing law has no business in it. Secondly, because of the minority of ill-conducted clubs the vast majority of the well-conducted suffer reflected criticism. Lord Merthyr's Bill might have removed abuses by the guilty, but it would have imposed undeserved controls on the innocent.

Since there can be no question of clamping down on the well-conducted club, the solution must lie elsewhere. Thirdly, inhibiting the club would not prevent avoidance of the law. The club movement is, in part, a revolt against restrictive licensing just as the theatre club is, in part, a protest against excessive censorship. Repression of the club would drive people elsewhere, perhaps even farther removed from public attention.

This dilemma will not be resolved by obliterating its symptoms. The system is self-frustrating because it attempts to foist on licensed establishments conditions it is powerless, and should remain powerless, to foist on the clubs. The more restrictive it is made, the greater the urge to escape from it. The solution must be sought in relieving the pressure to escape.

Clubs are not the only escape route. Where summer extensions in hours or music, or games, or other facilities, are not permitted, people go to adjacent districts where they are allowed. On Sunday Welshmen, locked out of their own pubs, sail or drive to England; Scotsmen, barred from their locals, take to the roads to qualify as *bona fide* travellers, sometimes with undesirable results. Laws that proliferate such devices cannot be the best we are capable of devising.

The question that faces those concerned to design an enforceable law is: what reforms would make it practicable and acceptable in our times? How can the urge to escape it be reduced? To indicate specific changes would require exhaustive study of the system as a body of law and as a department of public administration. But the general direction of reform is readily illustrated by considering the ways in which the law and its administration have fallen behind changing social habits and economic conditions.

For example, monopoly value (an Excise levy payable for a new licence) is still exacted, although the monopoly formerly conveyed with the licence has been largely eroded by competition. The licence duties also reflect the former monopoly aspect of the licence. The law on the physical structure of licensed premises and the administrative control of structural alterations still go beyond the requirements of safety and hygiene. The system of permitted hours is not always flexible enough to enable licensed houses to be available when the public wants them.

Games, music and other facilities under the control of the benches often differ widely in neighbouring areas that are similar in social development and between which movement by public or private transport is easy. Sunday closing in Wales (and in Monmouthshire in England) no longer stops Sunday drinking but drives it into clubs or across the border. The procedure governing the grant of new licences, removals, transfers, permission for structural alterations, etc., is sometimes lengthy or complex and prevents licensed premises from being promptly adapted to changing public needs. There is generally inadequate appeal against decisions (on hours, music, etc.) that conflict with public demand. The system of compensation for redundant houses often ironically holds up their disposal by encouraging the owners to hang on in the hope of cutting losses.

Revision of such controls would produce greater equity as between one district and another and greater flexibility in the service provided for the public; and it would reduce the scope for arbitrary interpretations of the law. It would leave the broad framework of the licensing system intact. Indeed, by making it less stringent and rigid, it would strengthen it by relieving the urge to escape from its controls. If, at the same time, solutions to pressing problems could be worked out, we should have a more flexible law and administration that mirrored social and economic conditions, was practicable and enforceable, and earned public respect.

What is at stake? Nothing less than the hope of maintaining a workable licensing system. On this there can be no difference between the legislators who make the law, the justices who interpret and administer it, the trade which works within it, the public-spirited people who want it to be effective, and the public on whose behalf it is erected and maintained.

CHAPTER 12

1963

Best Friends of Shoppers

Which? Or Competition?

> The best protection was not laws regulating industry or consumer organisations but competition between suppliers because it created escapes. * Competition has been released by government but too slowly to prevent it spreading increasingly into "black" markets.
>
> (*The Times,* June 1963.)

By subjugating the British consumer, war economy and over-full employment have finally made him a focus of political attention. All parties salute him on paper but frustrate him in practice. Some critics say the economy over-concentrates on consumption; but the dangers of a producer-dominated economy tending to degenerate into syndicalism or corporativism outweigh the risks of an economy resting on consumer preferences.

Apart from safeguards against fraud and misrepresentation in products, advertising, labelling, personal selling, etc., one of the main essentials is information with which the consumer can choose between alternatives in the market. *Shopper's Guide* and *Which?* were a natural and healthy response to the post-war sellers' market with its inflation, rising incomes, shortages, and producers' bad habits derived from rationing, licensing, and price controls. Independent testing and reporting organisations should have been welcomed by industry as well as by the consumer. If widely used, and if available for typical samples of the whole and up-to-date range of products, they would make more convincing the argument that advertising claims indicate significant differences in value, rebut suspicion that prices are needlessly high, enable new or smaller firms to compete more effectively against the established or large, and discourage the use of advertising appeals that suggest contempt for the consumer but recoil by earning the contempt of the citizen.

Until the other day two of the "best buys" in Britain were *Shopper's Guide* and *Which?* Now *Which?* is alone. The early impression of infallible pontification has receded, but even benevolence is not improved by monopoly. The demise of *Shopper's Guide* removes an independent corrective not only to advertising but also to *Which?* During the six years of competitive coexistence, *Which?* made *Shopper's Guide* less inhibited and *Shopper's Guide* helped to save *Which?* from the charge that its criticisms betrayed hostility to private enterprise. When their conclusions differed about electric kettles recently, confidence in them should have been strengthened as human, imperfect organisations that helped consumers to judge competing claims, rather than as final courts of appeal sitting in judgment on industry. Now the one can no longer correct or overhaul the other if it flags or nods. Can *Which?* extend its services nationally to many more consumers as well as subscribers to *Shopper's Guide?*

It has still to reach the mass of wage-earners, who presumably need it most. It is bought regularly by 330,000 members but claims to be seen by at least 3 million, some 10 per cent of the adult population, or 12 per cent excluding pensioners. Surprisingly, many subscribers fail to renew each year. Four requirements need attention for a wider circulation.

First, more advertising. That the membership of *Which?* is nearly ten times that of *Shopper's Guide* reflects in part the failure of the British Standards Institution to advertise *Shopper's Guide* effectively. *Which?* has advertised skillfully and increased its expenditure on promotion from £24,000 in 1960–1 (10 per cent of income) to £56,000 in 1961–2 (15 per cent). Advertising has helped to increase membership and thus by spreading overhead costs improved the service. Editorial publicity—usually sympathetic—must be worth much more than paid advertising. The BBC programmes are a mixed blessing: a periodic reminder of *Which?* but also a free distribution which may dissuade viewers and listeners from buying it. Increased expenditure on promotion, based on detailed research, is in preparation. But the cost of recruitment will probably rise unless distribution, presentation, and the "product" are adapted to consumer demand.

Second, impulse sales in newsagents' shops, bookshops, and station bookstalls might turn occasional into regular readers. Retailing would replace club subscription by commercial sale and impair the appeal of *Which?* as the spearhead of a crusade, but the gain might be larger than the loss.

Third, simpler presentation. One of the failings of *Shopper's Guide* was its indigestible detail. Some consumers—the enthusiasts for gardening, motoring, do-it-yourself, photography, etc.—become as expert as the expert; but probably most wage-earners want not so much technical information as the advice distilled from it. The aim of making the consumer informed and discriminating may conflict with his wish to be saved the time and effort of making a choice. Nor is he irrational. Unless we are to be jacks of all trades, advice from specialists is worth paying for. *Which?* may have to give less room to detailed reports and more to short statements of "best buys." Alternatively it may have to be divided into a *Which?* on information and a shorter *Which?* on advice.

Fourth, the product. There is a gradual improvement in removing the three technical difficulties—not every brand is tested, although local consumer groups may fill the gaps; the samples tested may not be typical; and they may not be the latest. But three further difficulties are more stubborn.

First, some reports seem to be written for the exceptional rather than for the typical consumer. Manufacturers often cannot be sure how their products will fare in ordinary use until consumers buy and try them. It may be better for consumers as a whole to market a product with the risk that some units will be faulty or misused by the less careful or intelligent than to continue testing and perfecting and so raising costs and prices beyond the pockets of many. Standards can be too high as well as too low. Consumers must ask for guarantees, after-sales service, or replacements, but product imperfection is unavoidable because techniques and consumers are imperfect.

Second, choice is ultimately subjective. Even the most technical equipment—washing machines, cookers, domestic boilers—may be chosen for beauty rather than for utility. Since consumers differ, there may be no universal "best buy." Laboratory testing is a fruitful but imperfect short cut to ordinary human use (no one runs a motor car for 10,000 miles in a few weeks). And we like to confirm even exhaustive laboratory tests by personal experience. The consumer informs himself better by buying and trying than by reading biased advertising or independent reports. Even with commodities bought infrequently, such as clothes and furniture, the recent personal experience of others is still a good check on laboratory testing. *Which?* increasingly reports the findings of user panels, which yield opinion rather than fact.

Third, *Which?* helps not only its members but all consumers by impelling producers to improve testing before marketing. Some consumers may feel it unnecessary to buy it.

Which? would be better if it had a strong competitor. There are obvious risks of political abuse in a State comparative testing organisation, but if the Consumer Council (rightly) is not to do it the problem of lack of a competitor remains. Yet even two, or twenty, or a hundred *Which?*s could not keep up with the rapid change in goods and services coming on to the market. A more pervasive safeguard for the consumer is required: the ability to reject.

"Best buys" imply more than one. But there is little or no unweighted choice in education, health services, fuel, rail (rail transport), transport, tele-communications, postal services, libraries, sound broadcasting, saving for retirement. Elsewhere choice is restricted by omissions and commissions of public policy on monopolies, restrictive practices, marketing boards, trade unions, tariffs, quotas. If we want consumer advice to work, government must create the conditions it requires. Industry can reduce the scope for criticism by more use of consumer panels before marketing. The Advertising Standards Authority could publicise offenders as well as purge objectionable practices. Not least, school teachers could explain the simpler problems of producing for free consumers and the uses as well as the abuses of advertising.

The consumer's best friend is not the politician or the missionary who makes the most noise but the manufacturer who makes a better product. Without choice in competitive markets free from inflation, consumer information and advice are cabined, cribbed, confined, or stillborn.

CHAPTER 13

1966

Markets in Welfare to Strengthen the Economy

> Another economic crisis had provoked emergency measures that left underlying weakness in the economy, not least the "free" services requiring high taxes. * Sooner or later the solution—priced welfare to stimulate competition between State and private suppliers—will have to be applied. A "clearing" system to cancel taxes and benefits would reduce taxes and widen choices.
>
> (*The Times,* August 1966.)

Another economic crisis has provoked emergency measures that leave almost untouched an underlying cause of weakness. About half of public expenditure, some £6,500 million, goes on State or local authority welfare services. Roughly half of this sum is capital and current expenditure on free or subsidised education, health, housing or other services, much or most for people who can pay the full or at least some price. The other half goes on allowances, benefits, grants and other cash payments, much or most to people who do not need them.

Where there is need, we should be much more generous. But in the name of equality most of the services are available for everyone; and most of the cash goes to everyone who qualifies whether he needs it or not. People tend to think of the State services as all they want; they do not think of spending more on education, health services, housing, saving for retirement pensions, although many easily could. And, because millions of families receive millions of pounds they do not really need, the State and local authorities have to raise vast sums in taxes, rates or social insurance to spend on services that release money available for spending on consumption—much of it imported.

It has become all the more urgent to consider new ways in which to finance and organise welfare services. The present method is to supply them free or subsidised: few know their cost, care in their use is not encouraged, supply is choked off, and they have to be rationed by officials. We should gradually work towards the time when everyone can pay the full price for them. The changes would be of two kinds.

First, State services would begin to make charges for services now supplied free or increase charges where they are now nominal or low. We should think not merely of restoring the prescription charges, or raising the charges for school meals. The government should also charge for tuition and medical treatment, abolish the housing subsidies and either gradually reduce the State pension to the amount earned by contributions or raise the contributions to the amount required to pay for the pension. School fees, for example, might begin at 5*s.* or 10*s.* a week; the full cost is more like £2 a week at a secondary modern school and more at a grammar school.

Secondly, we should enable everyone to pay the gradually rising charges by new allowances where incomes are low or families exceptionally large. These allowances might be in cash or in coupons—on the principle of luncheon vouchers.

The main effect would be that in time everyone would know what welfare costs. No one would go short of the minimum amounts judged desirable—the State would continue to lay down minimum standards and requirements. But no one would receive services he could pay for.

Everyone would have a choice between State schools, doctors or hospitals; council tenants would have a choice between council houses. The cash or vouchers could also be used to pay for private education or health services, where these were preferred, provided they satisfied the requirements. We would thus also have a choice between State education or health services as a whole and private schools, doctors, hospitals; between council and private housing; between a State pension and a private pension from an assurance company or any other source.

The new competition would stimulate interest in welfare and attract purchasing power from consumption. We would be able to pay a little extra, as we now cannot, for something better—perhaps 5*s.* a week for smaller classes, 10*s.* a month for more nurses, 10*s.* a week for more individual preferences in council housing, £20 a year for life assurance or other benefits with State pensions. Better welfare would be worth working harder for; total output and national income would rise faster than in response to national targets or political admonition.

We would become customers of whom the suppliers, State or private, took notice, instead of being "beneficiaries" waiting to be served or told what to do by public officials. We would in time learn to distinguish good value from bad in welfare, as we generally can in consumption.

Some people would switch from State schools, doctors, hospitals, pensions to private. The loss of customers would raise State service standards. Council tenants would have a new freedom to move instead of remaining often reluctant squatters, sometimes desperately offering their squatters' "rights" in exchange for others where they want to live. Some council tenants would buy their homes, or rent or buy private houses or flats; gradual abolition of rent controls would create a new supply of private housing to let.

There would be new suppliers of welfare: philanthropic or endowed, denominational or non-denominational, "mutual" or commercial. All would have to observe the standards. Anti-trust laws would prevent the creation of monopolistic, dominant private suppliers. In time competition would supply services of a higher than the minimum standard, and it would discipline private suppliers more effectively than the voter can discipline public officials through general or local elections.

The essential is to create or re-create markets and market prices for welfare services and enable everyone to pay them for essential amounts. One method is tax rebates on education fees or medical insurance, as we now have with mortgage interest and life assurance policies. But tax rebates reach only taxpayers. Extending the rebates to everyone would be better, but they would not create a vivid sense of customer choice. Grants to schools or colleges, as now to direct grant schools and universities, enable them to reduce or abolish fees with the familiar undesirable effects. Grants, loans or coupons to parents for education costs, to tenants or owner-occupiers for housing costs, to patients for medical costs, and to earners for retirement saving are the best methods, because they create the power of the customer to choose between competing suppliers and to discard the unsatisfactory. We should give the aid to consumers, not to producers. Loans, as for students, may be better than grants where non-repayable grants might not otherwise be available from tax revenue. And vouchers may be better than grants as a more certain method of ensuring that the services are bought.

Tax is not paid in Australia on payments for school fees, books, uniforms, fares for full-time education at a school or from a private tutor up to £150 a year for each child under twenty-one. No tax is paid also on occupational education—uniforms, tools, books, and technical equipment. In Holland students of required standard and income may receive loans up to £120 a year which are repaid in ten years, beginning two years after the examinations and, if desired, by monthly instalments.

In health services Australia does not tax the payments for medical costs or insurance premiums.

Germany, Denmark, France, Sweden, and Switzerland (Zurich, Basle

Lane and Basle-Stadt) have various forms of housing allowances for tenant and/or owner-occupier families varying with their income and the number of children or dependents. For example, in Germany a tenant or owner-occupier is expected to pay from 7 to 22 per cent of the family income on rent or owner-occupancy costs; if the market rent or owner-costs are higher, the difference is made up by housing allowances. In Holland and Austria broadly similar schemes are being considered.

The common purpose or effect of all these methods of state aid for consumers is, in varying measure, to create or widen choice, not to deny it. Applied in Britain, they could enable or help the citizen to pay the market costs of welfare services and thus gain the advantages of competition, improved quality, economy, and the incentive to spend more. In particular they could enfranchise the wage-earner by giving a choice to the family of lower income which has little or no choice if it is given free or subsidised State services it does not use as well as fees for private services it may prefer.

Not least, the use of market prices for State services would reduce public expenditure and in time taxation. It could switch large sums out of consumption into education, health services, housing and saving for retirement pensions—perhaps £1,000 million out of the £18,000 million now spent on consumption.

The new charges and allowances and the increase in public revenue could begin soon. The new markets would take more time to develop. All the more reason for preparing them without delay. But the new approach would not require higher taxation or cuts in roads, fuel, telephone, local authority welfare or other essential services. Humanity and sanity point to the same fundamental reforms.

CHAPTER 14

1971

Wind Up National Insurance

> The new government was revising State and private systems. Private pensions were being retarded by the Inland Revenue. The Conservative minister was advised to avoid expanding "national insurance" and wind up State pensions by allowing the forty-five to fifty-fives to opt out of State to private pensions. * In 1993 the Chief Secretary to the Treasury announced the winding up would begin in 2017.
>
> (*The Spectator,* June 1971.)

Following Mr. Richard Crossman's abortive attempt in 1979 (after fifteen years of preparation), Sir Keith Joseph will shortly show how the Conservatives will reconstruct State pensions and the rules governing private pensions.

His thinking began after the Tory defeat of 1964. His respect for the academic and an ear close to the ground should make him see that his proposals will have to be radical. Patching up the forty-five-year-old National Insurance system by perpetuating the myth of "insurance" will be politically tempting, but it will belie the new hope of self-help and individual responsibility.

Experience abroad will warn him. He will see what happens when money for pensions is raised by graduating contributions. In Sweden State pension funds increasingly dominate saving and investment. In Germany contributions take almost a fifth of pay and may be escalating too fast to be contained except by savage surgery. In the US politicians avid for power and a misplaced intellectual compassion would inflate them out of control.

The system of graduated contributions for graduated pensions, begun by Mr. John Boyd-Carpenter in 1961, and intended for expansion by Mr. Crossman, has been half rejected but half accepted by the 1971 Conservatives. Graduated pensions are to be scrapped, but contributions are to be graduated.

Before overseas warnings are ignored Sir Keith should ponder. The insurance world has for fifteen years been driven into a shell, or frightened into appeasing hostile politicians, by jaundiced "social administrators" who know more about State pensions from Blue Books and White Papers than they do about private pensions from real life. Now the practitioners are speaking out rather more. And about time. Their practical wisdom is worth more to government than sociological sour grapes from the side-lines.

The State system must be prevented from further expanding out of control, and the Inland Revenue rules must be liberalised to encourage more rapid expansion of private pensions.

If the government persists in its intention to finance higher "flat-rate" pensions by graduated contributions, it would prolong the myth of national insurance (only one-tenth or one-fifth of a pension starting in 1971 is earned by contributions). It would play straight into the hands of, say, Mr. David Ennals, if he is Minister of Social Services in 1974–5 or 1978–9, who would gleefully enlarge them further. It would mortgage money that could, and would, have gone into private pensions. It would in time incite a demand for graduated *pensions;* and the Conservatives would have accomplished nothing distinctive.

It is too late to save National Insurance. The country must be told very soon that the "contribution" raised for pensions is a tax that carries no earmarked insurance claim to benefit. If a face-saving formula must be used, let it be called a social security tax, although even that charade has been dropped by New Zealand. But let it be done openly.

Raising taxes, no doubt, is unpopular. But it would hasten the day when increases in pensions are confined to people in need, a dwindling band. It would accelerate the search for new sources of revenue for other State services—fees for State schools, charges for State doctors and hospitals, and so on. It would hustle the denationalisation of services better run by industry.

The Inland Revenue has become an *imperium in imperio.* What is it doing limiting the allowable pension to two-thirds of final pay merely because this is the Civil Service limit? It took a whole year to pass a scheme for "dynamising" pensions (building in increases after retirement). It has become an arbiter on industrial practices and social policy as well as an examiner of fiscal minutiae. It should not be required to act as judge and jury. Pensions scrutiny should be transferred to an independent office as far removed as possible from the Treasury—or the Department of Social Security.

In Australia the age pension is financed by taxation, means-tested, paid to only *half* of her retired million, *and is half as much again as ours.* In Britain social advance, economic capacity and technical innovation make possible a gradual shift from State to private pensions. The two-car, home-owning, Majorca-holidaymaking plutocrat cannot be treated as the cap-touching worker who peoples *Dr. Finlay's Casebook.*

State pensions, compulsory, universal, and "free" (but paid for, of course, by taxes) are a collectivist anachronism that Conservatives should not conserve. They should say to people of fifty-five or fifty or forty-five—or perhaps forty: "State pensions are not really earned by contributions, and we are winding them up. You are working in times of high earnings. We shall no longer compel you to contribute for a State pension. You may now for the first time save for retirement in any way you wish. And we shall encourage you by adding something for every £ you, or your employer, put into the pension scheme of your choice."

CHAPTER 15

1972

Inflation Is Crueller than Unemployment

> The supporters of big government emphasised the unemployment in competitive industry and minimised the inflation used by government to disguise its failures. The reply was that the unemployment unavoidable in a changing economy competing in world markets was less damaging to the economy than inflation and that the unemployed could be cared for better than the victims of inflation. * In the 1990s the "caring" media are still giving more attention to the "bad news" of firms reconstructing themselves to meet changing markets ("more workers sacked") than to new jobs in growing firms.
>
> (*The Daily Telegraph*, January 1972.)

In 1972 Britain inflation is *more* cruel than unemployment. Why? Because we have learned how to take the sting out of unemployment. But we have not learned how to draw the sting of inflation.

No one who lived through the Great Depression, 1930–3, needs to be reminded that unemployment is cruel. But in 1972 "unemployment" means something very different. The victims of unemployment are now articulate, insistent, even strident. The victims of inflation are the quiet ones; the old, the ill-organised, the savers, the cautious, the uninformed.

No one who has been unemployed, as I was when a new job in July 1950 collapsed with the Korean War, needs to be reminded that unemployment is cruel. It eats into self-respect by excluding its victims from the community of the employed. But the victims of inflation, who made long-term bargains for goods or services in money, who are lenders rather than borrowers, or who expected social benefits from the State, also lose their self-respect. They are excluded from the prosperity that inflation brings to borrowers, traders, the owners of property; and to the tightly-organised in industry, the professions, not least the trade unions. In the politically-dominated, inflation-fed Welfare State it is not the meek but the loud-mouthed who inherit the earth.

A million sounds frightening. But by itself it does not mean very much. A million (or a thousand) rotting on street corners for months and years on end, as I saw in Llanbradach and Bargoed in 1937, would be frightening. A million—or two million—being re-trained from older industries into better-paid newer industries would be the opposite: it would make the whole economy more adaptable and prosperous.

A million out of work means 24 million in work. Four per cent unemployed means ninety-six out of every hundred in regular work, day in, day out. This "unemployment" would not be calamitous for a country like Britain that exports a fifth of its product to import a sixth of its income—*if they were changing jobs.* We have to trade with all five continents. New techniques, and demands, thousands of miles overseas can destroy or create jobs here. We cannot guarantee permanent employment for everyone. Some think they have a right to the job—in shipbuilding, engineering, textiles, say—that they started in thirty years earlier, or in which their fathers worked.

Their grandfathers often came from the farming villages of Berkshire, Bedfordshire or Hertfordshire. If Britain had since 1800 kept ninety-seven or ninety-eight out of a hundred working in the same jobs we should still be an agricultural, sparsely-populated, poor island off the north-west coast of a prosperous, influential, culturally-advanced Europe.

In Britain, since 1946, employers have held on to workers and workers to jobs. Our old industries—coal, rail, farming—have been run down too slowly. Trade unions, anxious to maintain membership, have encouraged men to hang on. Subsidised council housing has made movement expensive—or a gamble. No wonder British employees are not prepared for change.

The State employment exchanges have fallen down on the job of placing people in new jobs. The vacuum has been filled by private agencies, as Christina Fulop recently showed in an IEA Paper. And we should welcome their enterprise even if it has led to over-zealous coaxing of people out of jobs.

Improvement here could reduce the period of unemployment. From 1950 to 1965, when the total unemployed fluctuated in most years between 250,000 and 350,000, about half of them—around 150,000—were out of work for less than eight weeks. Since then, when the total has grown to a million, the number back in work in eight weeks has risen to 350,000. It is with the remaining 650,000 that the failure lies. Some 150,000 or so have been out for over a year. Are they "unemployed" or *unemployable?*

Most of the million are worlds away from the hunger-marching, soup-kitchen unemployed of the 1930s. There are still hard cases to be covered by Supplementary Benefits, but to talk of "the million unemployed" as if they were half-starved skeletons is to make them a political football.

If the unemployed million shocks, the shocked must partly blame the inflation that held back the urge to change industrial methods and attitudes until it came with a rush. That is always the fate of policies that swamp symptoms without touching causes. Sooner or later the British economy had to adapt itself to a changing world. The adaptation has been inhibited by inflation, by reactionary trade union leaders, by the politicians' unthinking endorsement of "full employment." Now we have less than "full employment" and even more inflation.

Few seem to understand the extent of the inflation. If they did, they would be more anxious and angry than they are. From 1949 to 1967 prices rose by between 3 and 4 per cent in most years. In 1968 they rose by 6, in 1969 by 7, in 1970 by over 8, in 1971 by 10 per cent.

If anything in recent British economic policies is shocking, the Great Inflation of 1968 to 1971 should shock. An inflation of 3½ per cent a year halves the real purchasing power of earnings or savings in twenty years. The 1971 inflation, unless it is stopped, will halve real values in seven years. Unless it is reduced very soon it will dawn on more and more people that the best thing to do with money is to spend it quick. And then the fat will be in the fire: for this itself would make the inflation intensify. Once the loss of confidence in currency starts, it is difficult to stop. After futile attempts by government to stop it by shovelling out more money, as in Germany in 1923, the only solution is to scrap the currency and start again from scratch.

In the meantime irremedial injustice will have been done to the weak and the meek, the prudent and the provident.

The victims have been changing. Pension and other cash payments were at the mercy of political expediency until 1970. Then the government announced that they were to be revised every other year; and in December 1971 every year. In the short run this sounds like a victory for humanity. In the long run it would be capitulation to inflation. The government is saying: we cannot control inflation so we shall raise cash payments to keep pace with it. What next? Revision twice a year? Every quarter? Once a month?

If interest rates kept pace with inflation, there need be no loss in saving in the form of money. But they lag behind, because people save for reasons other than to earn interest. They want a nest-egg for an emergency. So they save even though the interest is hardly more, or even less, than the fall in money value.

But they can pay a heavy price for a shrivelled egg. Inflation transfers wealth from people who save in money to those who save in possessions, from the simple to the sophisticated, from the uninformed to the well-connected, from the gullible to the people who know what to expect and how to avoid it.

Inflation impoverishes society as a whole. It distorts relative prices and frustrates effort and enterprise by falsifying the signals that prices give to producers and consumers in a well-run economy.

It is true we are in the hands of the world economy and cannot lose step with other countries. But the internal injustices remain whether the country is in step with other inflating countries or not. And we are not guiltless: for some years we were inflating earlier or faster than others.

In 1972 the chief danger will be not from unemployment but from inflation. In unemployment the task will be to change a stagnant pool of long-term unemployed to a clear-running stream of workers moving or retraining.

And in inflation the task is simple: to stop it. To fulfil that task the government requires strong, persistent, vocal public support in any devices it uses, even if they raise the number shifting from dying to growing industries, further reduce the power of unions to hold the community to ransom, and let lame industrial ducks waddle about in the shallows.

CHAPTER **16**

1977

Police: Compete or Retreat

> Changing market "forces" were making paid private protection against injury to persons and property more flexible than "free" local government police protection. The "public" police should charge for some services in order to improve them. If not, the public would increasingly use private police. And government funds for the "public" police would become less available. * In the 1990s the "public" services, unable to master growing crime, require entrepreneurs more than politicians.
>
> (*Top Security*, December 1977.)

The deficiency of finance for the police forces will not be removed until it is accepted that the police do not supply a wholly public service properly financed by taxation. Police services are partly public and partly private. If the police try to finance themselves wholly from taxation for services that are essentially private they will remain unavoidably short of finance because the citizen will prefer to pay for private security by methods that bring identifiable individual benefits.

No individual citizen increases the protection of his (or his family's) life or property by paying higher taxes. But he can improve the protection for himself, his family or his office, shop or business if he pays for individual, personal services that visibly vary in quantity or quality with his payment. The question is whether they will be provided by the public police or by private security services.

Strictly only that part of police services that cannot be refused to people who refuse to pay are truly "public"; economists call them "public goods." This part may comprise the essence of the police function in preserving "the public peace" and preventing crime which harms the public as a whole. All citizens would gain from this service whether they paid for it or not. Since many individuals would contribute towards its cost even though others also benefited, these others would have nothing to lose by not paying.

They would have a "free ride." Therefore this characteristic police function is a "public good" paid for by all citizens voluntarily agreeing to compel themselves by law to contribute to its cost by paying taxes.

But other police services are not "public goods" because they give direct, exclusive, separable, personal benefits. Four fairly clear examples are attending purely private sports or other events, advising on personal protection against mugging or property (home or business) protection against burglary, transporting cash for payment of wages, and convoying awkward vehicles or valuable contents (pictures, antiques, precious metals, etc.). Even here it is plausible to argue that these private services have a public effect because they benefit other people not directly involved. Directing traffic into a private field for a sports event helps all motorists passing the entrance; convoying an awkward load benefits motorists who want to overtake it or who pass it in the opposite direction. But, by this criterion of indirect benefits, probably every private activity anyone engages in benefits (or harms) third parties. A man who wears a buttonhole (presumably) pleases other passengers on his train; if he sneezes in a theatre he may give his neighbours a cold. But this is not a reason for subsidies to finance universal buttonholes, or for taxing people who may sneeze during the opera.

Some years ago in a pioneering Hobart paper published by the Institute of Economic Affairs Professor R. L. Carter broke new ground by discussing the services for which the police could charge. And in an article in *Police Review* Superintendent John Griffin of the Hertfordshire Constabulary accepted the argument in principle:

> . . . certain specific security functions could be taken under the wing of the Police on a commercial basis and it ought not to be too difficult to draw up guidelines.

The argument can be taken a stage further. Charging may not only be *advantageous* but also *unavoidable* if the police are not to weaken their finances further.

Some police services are "public" goods and others give essentially private benefits that could be paid for by individual charges. The important difference is that people will *prefer* to pay for private benefits by individual charges whether the private benefits are supplied by the "public" police forces or by private security services. The reason is simply that there is a direct link between payment and service received. A man who wants to protect his home more than it is protected by the general patrols provided by the public police—perhaps because he would be emotionally disturbed by a burglary—

cannot receive additional protection by paying higher taxes. He may ask his local police station to keep a special watch on his home; but, if every citizen did the same, no one would receive additional protection because they would not be supplying additional resources—manpower or equipment—from which to provide it. Some may offer to make a special contribution to a police amenity or charity, but such currying favour might finance fringe benefits, not the care of police functions themselves.

So a citizen who wants additional private protection has to use purely personal devices. He may instal expensive locks, safes, an alarm system wired to the police station, double glazing, buy a guard dog. To protect himself or his wife or children from mugging he may equip them with stout sticks, whistles or bleepers. To protect his shop, office or works he may employ Securicor, Group 4 or Security Express. And in all three instances he may take out additional personal or property insurance as a long stop in case the other devices fail to prevent loss, injury or damage.

The citizen will willingly pay for personal, private security services wherever he finds them most effective. Here the public police forces would seem to have the advantage of experience and the prestige of being described as "public." The private security services would seem to be at a relative disadvantage precisely because they are not "public" but independent or "commercial." But the citizen is not concerned with such political distinctions; he is motivated above all to obtain the best protection for his family, his home and his livelihood. And this is the essence of "the policeman's dilemma." For *if the "public" police forces do not supply these personal services, the citizen is driven to obtain them from private suppliers.* Moreover, if he has to spend money on private protection he is all the more reluctant to pay taxes for "public" police services in which he sees no link between the protection he receives and the taxes he pays. If the public police services run short of revenue for their public service of general patrols and crime prevention, the citizen is driven all the more to seek out and pay for private protection. Hence "the policeman's dilemma."

Moreover there is competition not only for "customers" between the "public" police forces and private security services in supplying private security. There is also competition for resources—men, women, vehicles, equipment, etc.—in supplying the characteristic public police service of maintaining "public order" and in providing the personal or private protection against mugging, theft, burglary or trespass. The more police resources—human and material—are employed at political demonstrations, student sit-ins, public protests, Embassy vigils or factory picketing, the less resources are available to protect individuals from mugging, or houses from burglaries and shops or works from trespass. The more the citizen is therefore induced to spend on personal security services.

The vicious circle is thus revealed. The more public police services are financed almost wholly from taxation the less efficient will be their personal services, the more the citizen will have to spend on private security, and more reluctant he will be to pay taxes for the police (or anything else).

So what is the solution? There are three alternatives. First, the "public" police forces can confine themselves to the characteristic "public good" function of public order that only a tax-financed service can supply and leave the personal or private services to the private security organisations. This would seem to be the logical separation of functions. The public police forces would then be smaller, relieved of personal services, but more securely financed because the citizen would more willingly pay taxes for a service he wants but cannot obtain until he shares them with other citizens and pays for them by taxation.

A final problem would remain: money for the police would still have to be obtained from government and its case argued by politicians in the cabinet room in Whitehall and council offices in town halls against other politicians arguing for defence and diplomatic services, education and medical care, nuclear research and overseas aid. The escape for the individual policeman, on the beat or in the operations room, who is not content to have his livelihood settled by politicians concerned not only (say 30 per cent?) with the public welfare but also (70 per cent?) with their own political future, is to move to the private security services where his services are valued more directly by his employer's customers—the individual citizen. Like doctors and teachers, policemen paid out of the public purse are in the party-political maelstrom: their pay is linked to general economic events and General Election tactics. And their claim to be a "special" case is more difficult to demonstrate to twenty politicians in Downing Street preoccupied with other crises than to the millions in the market place with personal safety at stake.

A second alternative is to try to combine public and private police services and hope they will both be adequately financed by taxes so that they can continue to be provided "free" without charging. The national proclivity of the more traditional-minded policeman will be to prefer this course. The chief constable who is offended by the notion of "going into business" by "selling" a "public" service is reflecting the feeling that it is more dignified (and convenient) to be paid regularly by official cheque from government departments than to make out bills to individual citizens, be paid by variable amounts, and give receipts for small cheques or even cash. But he would be wrong. The service he could be supplying would be supplied by a "public" body but it would not be a public service. It would be a private service, and *he would have to sell it in competition with private suppliers.*

In other words, there is no choice open to such a chief constable. He must compete and try to do better than the private supplier. That is the only way for him to finance such services. Taxes to pay for them will be extracted only from an increasingly reluctant public.

And why not compete? I said earlier that he starts with the natural advantage of prestige. And there are also economies in providing, say, private advice on theft prevention based on the "public" good service of theft detection. Moreover competition between public and private security could make both more efficient. The alternative is to see even the private services in which he could compete—convoying, advice, etc.—being supplied increasingly by private firms with no inhibitions about selling their services in the market. In time, also, if he failed to compete, he would see some of his best men transferring to the private organisations.

Two other ways out seem tempting. One is to say that it is the job of government—national and county—to provide the required revenue out of taxes and rates for the public services. But that attitude will not produce the revenue if Whitehall and county hall have other services that seem to politicians even more urgent (public health, etc.) to provide, and if government finds taxes increasingly avoided and evaded—so causing even more work for the police that only they can do: another vicious circle.

The other apparent way out is even more tempting, but even more a mirage. It is to say that the obvious solution is to restrain the private security services so that the citizens will virtually be forced to use the "public" police services. This is the solution favoured by the supporters of wholly government-provided education, medical care, employment exchanges, etc. It is the method of State monopoly. But this is no more of a solution for police security than for these other services. No responsible man will sacrifice the personal safety of his family, the security of his home or the integrity of his livelihood to the notion that he should put them second to his duty to use the "public" service which has not given him the private safety he wants. The citizen who is rebelling against having his child "zoned" into a school where it is unhappy, or seeing his wife wait for an operation for which delay is causing her mental anxiety, will mock the politician who spins him this sort of yarn. There is no way out for the chief constable who conscientiously wants to provide the public with a service and who thinks he can save it (and himself) by calling in the party politician to stop the citizen from doing what he can to prevent his wife from being assaulted, his home burgled and his business ransacked. There is no way out because the police have no monopoly of private security services, and the political effort to construct a monopoly artificially by coercing the citizen would make for low police efficiency, as monopoly always does, and, even worse, the public resentment and rejection of what could be regarded as a new kind of "police state."

The chief constable who sees himself as giving the public a public service is not serving the public if the service is not what they want, or is not available when and where they want it, because it is short of tax revenue. The public is not served by police who rarely patrol the street, who are inadequately equipped to detect crime, who are underpaid, and, because underpaid, understaffed. And taxation will not supply the required revenue, even in normal times without incomes policies.

The third way out now suggests itself. It is for the police to go all out to compete in personal services with the private suppliers. The alternatives are thus competition or contraction. That is the dilemma the police should be investigating. As an outsider it seems to me that an enquiry headed by Sir Robert Mark would be a good way of going about it. The police, the public, even the private suppliers would benefit from the competition.

But the economics of police entrepreneurship is another story. The police have had political advisers, once Mr. James Callaghan, now Mr. Eldon Griffiths. It looks as if they now also require economic and marketing advisers.

CHAPTER 17

1982

The Truth About Unemployment

The total of unemployed was less important than its duration. The longer the movement of labour was obstructed the more convulsive the ultimate social consequences. * The results are seen in the mining, shipbuilding and other industries.

(*The Daily Telegraph*, August 1982.)

MRS. SHIRLEY WILLIAMS (Social Democrat): Has the Prime Minister seen the report of the Institute of Economic Affairs in which it is suggested that there might be as many as five million unemployed at the next election. Will she repudiate that report . . . ?

THE PRIME MINISTER (Conservative): The report is not mine in any way. I have seen only reports of a report of an article written by one person . . .

[Later]

MR. PETER SHORE (Labour): Earlier today attention was drawn to the recent publication by the Institute of Economic Affairs of a new pamphlet in which the central point was the advocacy of five million unemployed as inevitable, necessary and desirable to promote a healthy economy.

(*Hansard*, 27 July, 1982.)

Can there really be a callous ogre who "advocated" five million "unemployed" in a "report" by a reputable economic institute?

First, a few facts: the offending words were not used in a "report" (Mrs. Williams) or "pamphlet" (Mr. Shore) published by the Institute of Economic Affairs, implying some sort of collective agreement by a group of economists. They appeared in the editorial of the July *Journal of Economic Affairs*, which is published by Basil Blackwell of Oxford in association with the Institute. And the editorial was clearly indicated as written by me, as the independent editor, speaking only for myself. It was, like this article, very much a "personal view."

Yes, I said "five million" and I said "inevitable, necessary and desirable." But Mrs. Williams did not check her sources. The word "unemployment" conjures up the long-term worklessness and the hardship of the 1930s. I was careful to define "unemployment" as the redundancy of skill caused by economic change that leads people in a flexible economy with large overseas trade to change their jobs, firms, and homes. Only the free market could reveal how much of such job-changing was necessary or desirable. But in Britain, I said, it could be 5 to 20 per cent of the labour force, or up to five million.

And that points to the fatal obsession with the total of unemployed that has plagued the discussion of unemployment for forty-five years since Keynes and Beveridge, and prevented the discovery of solutions that will elude us until we break down the total into its components. And that is why the CBI or TUC or SDP or Liberal solution of "reflation" (I omit Labour as irrelevant) is too crude.

What is important about unemployment is not its total but its duration or timing. One million out of work for a year or more (roughly what we have now) is a personal tragedy for them and a tragic waste for the country. Five million out of work for a few weeks or months changing jobs from old and decaying to new and growing industries is not a personal tragedy or a national waste, but could be a healthy response to economic change—"inevitable, necessary and desirable."

Since economists are still obsessed with totals, it is not surprising they are echoed by politicians and commentators. The Cambridge Keynesian or Marxist economists talk of five million unemployed in the 1980s. Even the Liverpool market economists talk of unemployment falling from three to 1½ million. Mr. David Young, chairman of the Manpower Commission, says he does not see unemployment falling much below three million. But Mr. Norman Tebbit robustly says he will show it can.

My central argument, for which I will not be pilloried or crucified, is that we should no longer fear a large total provided each man (or woman) is not out of work for long. And if he is for longer than say three months, we should examine the reason and devise the required solution.

1. Some are unemployed because their firms were kept in production by continuing and accelerating inflation, now happily mastered, we must hope for good. These men and women will never return to their artificial jobs. Their only salvation is movement to other industries, possibly in other parts of the country, or, if highly specialised, in retraining.

2. Many of the three million are in dying industries that even inflation could not keep alive because they are being outmoded by changes in the

conditions of supply (technology, etc.) or demand (social habits). It so happens they are mostly in the State sector—chiefly coal and rail—but not by accident because only State monopoly has kept them alive or stopped them running down faster. Some 100,000 or more will leave these industries in the next few years.

3. This evil—the power of monopoly to resist change—applies to all the so-called "public" (in practice often anti-public) services, from education and medicine to refuse collection and fire-protection. A million or more will have to move from this group. The biggest failure of the government is that it does not act on its own advice to prune the labour force. Its record here is very bad.

4. Many—especially the young, the disabled, women and coloured—are kept out of jobs because minimum wages are fixed to suit males of average age and skill. An article in the July *Journal of Economic Affairs* by Dr. David Forrest of the University of Manchester calculates that 40 per cent of youth unemployment in Canada results from this cause. The British figure could be about the same.

5. Trade unions cause unemployment by making labour too dear and resisting new machinery. Professor Patrick Minford of Liverpool has argued, with a wealth of calculation, that the unions have thus destroyed a million jobs. The solution is reform of trade union law. The unions have slowed down the adaptation of British industry to world markets.

6. Many of the six million council house tenants will not move because they will lose their rent subsidies. The solution is higher rents, with rebates in hard cases, or new measures to make rent subsidies "mobile" so that tenants who warrant them take them if they move, as urged some years ago by my friend, the late Professor F. G. Pennance.

7. Some men are better off out of work because social benefits exceed their earnings. The solution is training for higher-paid jobs and lower social benefits.

8. Some, more than we think, have dropped out of the official labour market because they can keep what they earn in the underground free economy to which they have been driven by high taxes. The solution is lower taxes on earnings.

Some of these solutions will be disagreeable. Most require government action. They cannot be put off for much longer by devices like natural wastage, which politicians like because it avoids confrontation with trade unions but which pass on the cost to the whole community and especially to our children in the coming generation.

Unemployment has not increased by 2 million from 1.3 to 3.3 million under Mrs. Thatcher. It was there all the time hidden inside industry and "public" employment. Private industry has shed much of its hidden unemployment. "Public" employment has not.

The final tragedy is that, by deferring these "inevitable, necessary and desirable" movements of labour, past governments have made them more disturbing and convulsive. If there is now friction in the railways, the mines, State education and the National Health Service, it is the fault of Messrs. Callaghan, Wilson and Heath. And the longer the adaptations are deferred, the more disruptive they will have to be.

That is the unpleasant truth no politician can fully tell. It is not for Mrs. Williams or Mr. Shore to suppress it.

CHAPTER **18**

1986

Underground Resistance to Over-Government

> Over-government was driving the law-abiding British into "black" markets, not only to evade taxation. A little-understood reason was that ordinary people lacked the political skills required to cope with government industries and services. The solution was not more repressive laws but less government. * State industry has been partly de-socialised ("privatised"). The latest proposal to regulate car boot sales reveals the instinctive restrictionist tendency in government.
>
> (*The Spectator,* August 1986.)

The British economy is in better—much better—shape than politicians, pundits and preachers (of all denominations) proclaim. And capitalism reasserts its creative powers by spawning new markets to reflect *embourgeoisement* and technological advance at a rate unprecedented since (or before) the Industrial Revolution. Total output is growing faster, industry is prospering more, earnings are higher, unemployment is lower, much lower, and poverty is less common than the professional gloom-mongers assert.

They are deluding themselves and misleading the rest of us because they are still reflecting, at first or more probably third hand, the official government statistics. Whatever the reason—high taxes, rebelliousness against oppressive regulation, natural cupidity—many people are working and earning, buying and selling, saving and investing, even exporting and importing, without reporting to the authorities. They have evidently come to write off the law-makers, regulation-enforcers and tax-gatherers as obstructors, inquisitors (this was an objection to Pitt's original income tax in 1798), officious bureaucrats or impertinent autocrats. Lord (Douglas) Houghton, one-time general secretary of the Inland Revenue Staff Federation (and chairman of the Parliamentary Labour Party) was moved to warn, in 1979, of pushing "the disciplines and fiscal exactions and enforcements" too far. "There now exists a precarious balance between bureaucracy and the public." In 1986 exactions and enforcements are still resented.

Government has, by now, unintentionally created an "underground" that must be included in judging the activity and performance of the economy as a whole. In 1978 the then chairman of the Inland Revenue opined, in evidence to the House of Commons Expenditure Committee: "I think avoidance has become a national habit." A year later his successor ventured an estimate: he thought that tax was evaded on the equivalent of about 7½ per cent of the gross national product.

Since then an estimate by Professor Edgar Feige has arrived at 15 per cent. That seems to me nearer to the real proportion. And, if something is added for barter—transactions without the use of any kind of payment, which are undetectable because it can be regarded as free services between friends as well as evasion of tax—the total could rise to 18 to 20 per cent.

If total economic activity is anywhere near a tenth or a fifth more than the recorded output and incomes, the attempt by government to manage or guide the economy will be in error, certainly in magnitude, possibly in direction. Much of it is inspired by the anxiety to contain and reduce unemployment. But this is the official statistic that is the most misleading of all. The explanation is again the underground.

When Kent Matthews of the University of Liverpool calculated that 1.4 million of the "unemployed" were happily hard at work, full time or part time, and paid in cash, the figure was met with some disbelief. Now it has been virtually vindicated by the ORC (Opinion Research and Communication) Report in May and by Lord Plowden's Committee for Research into Public Attitudes the other week.

We have been mesmerised by the totem pole of "three million" whose regular appearance is met by ritual Pavlovian Labour–Alliance denunciation or Conservative apologia. An economy that exports a fifth of its GNP to pay for imports required for production as well as consumption could do with a fifth of its workforce moving around between home industries in response to uncontrollable overseas markets. That makes five million.

The underground will not evaporate in response to castigation as evil lawbreaking. Some of it is. Most of it is in the direct line of Wat Tyler's rebellion from Kent in 1381, the bloodless Glorious Revolution of 1688 against the divine right of kings to tax (*inter alia*), and the declaration of independence by the British in the American colonies against taxation without representation. The instinct of the British against the arrogance of office thwarted Napoleon and Hitler. It should be cherished, not least because the present British Tax Revolt has been fomented by political misjudgment in overtaxing.

The British do not want to pay higher taxes for more of the same Welfare

State. The opinion polls that find they do are seriously misleading all the political parties. Lord (Joel) Barnett, Chief Secretary to the Treasury under Wilson and Callaghan, has honourably conceded (*Economic Affairs,* forthcoming) that it took Labour a whole year of over-spending in 1975 before it realised that the taxpayers would not foot the bills.

The attitude to the underground will have to change. It may add no more than 10 per cent or 20 per cent to the GNP but it envelopes more than one in ten or five of the populace. Tax rejection has become part of the culture. The British no longer regard what is legal as necessarily moral, nor what has been outlawed as necessarily immoral. How many taxpayers can say they have never understated their income or overstated expenses in earning it?

Legal repression will not suppress the underground: new ways will be found around new proscriptions, and they will be a step or two ahead of the new laws. Unfortunately for government, tinkering with taxes will not evoke much response either: habits (skills? ingenuities?) will not be abandoned except for sizable cuts in taxes.

Until then the solution may have to be an amnesty for all (except the criminally inclined). After all, the underground largely comprises the most adventurous, risk-taking opportunists, whose qualities could invigorate the respectable but too often complacent conformists who are more interested in the old Tory virtues of continuity, custom and tradition, and are generally fearful of change, than they are attracted to what I would call the Whig virtues of scepticism of authority, a preference for liberty over egalitarianism, and a predilection for small government that knows its modest place in the affairs of men.

A final note of cheer for the Prime Minister. Her honest repeated confession of failure to reduce government expenditure could be unnecessary. If the underground has grown appreciably since the 1979 election, the proportion of taxes and government spending to real output may not have risen by much.

The Chancellor, or the chairman of the governing party, might ask the officials to catch up with the economists who have been estimating anything from 5 per cent to 30 per cent for the OECD undergrounds. Better still, since officials may not want to discover too much that has eluded their scrutiny, perhaps un-officials could be better placed to secure the Prime Minister her third term.

PART III

Wither the Welfare State

A: The Growing Disquiet, 1950–1964

CHAPTER **19**

1957

A Private Welfare State?

The *Manchester Guardian* published two sceptical essays when "half-pay pensions" became a tempting offer of politicians. * The State pensions have been made more flexible but they have outlived their day.

(*The Manchester Guardian,* May 1957.)

Plans for half-pay pensions are much in the political air, and they will prompt discussion of many aspects of British social and economic life. One that concerns a growing number of people is the effect of private occupational pensions on the mobility of labour. Occupational pensions are spreading rapidly throughout industry. In 1951 about 6.3 million people were covered, 2.4 million in the public services (including half a million in mining), and nearly 4 million in private industry. By early 1957 the total had risen to over 8 million. If the number in the public services is much the same, the coverage in industry has risen to about 5½ million. Since the labour force of 22 million contains 7 million women, only a minority of whom are in pension schemes, getting on for one in two of all men employed are now covered.

Occupational pensions have spread for various reasons: increasing company taxation, the inadequacy of the national retirement pension, the greater ease with which workers can be retired without ill-feeling or hardship. But the need to find some method of retaining workers in a sellers' market for labour has been prominent in recent years. Overfull employment has played havoc with the stimuli that normally make for the optimum distribution of labour. Employers hog their men, even if not fully employed; employees flit from firm to firm in search of higher pay. The resulting disruption of production schedules, waste of training, and increase in costs of recruitment have been common diseases in post-war British industry. How far pension schemes have kept turnover down is debatable. Job-flitting is most common among the younger wage-earners, who put a distant pension a poor second to an immediate wage increase.

The mobility of labour is impeded by the loss of pension rights on a change of employment, and, in this respect, private industry compares unfavourably with the public and quasi-public services. The preservation of pension rights in public employment is common, but in private industry it is still exceptional. Preservation is not general in the privately administered schemes of large firms. In insurance company schemes employees leaving jobs voluntarily normally surrender their policies for cash, which can be much less than the money they have paid in.

In a few industries or professions pension rights are preserved on a change of employment within the industry or profession; there are such schemes in the Merchant Navy and in the flour-milling industry, and several groups of associated companies have combined to establish a single-pension scheme, within which employees' pension rights are preserved on a change of employment. A recent scheme is that for engineers established by the Engineers' Guild, and applicable to the profession as a whole.

But there is a long way to go. The question now for industry and the insurance companies is not whether to permit employees to take pension rights with them when they change jobs, but how.

There are two methods of preserving pension rights—"transfer value," by which a sum of money representing the value of the accrued interest in the old pension scheme is used to buy similar rights in the new scheme, and "cold-storage" benefits, by which deferred or paid-up benefits are given to the employee to carry with him until he retires. Each has merits, and drawbacks. Transfer values are in some ways simpler, because records do not need to be kept of former employees' pensions, and employees eventually draw one pension instead of several from different sources, and possibly calculated on different principles. "Cold-storage" would make for greater mobility, because a new employment need not have a similar pension scheme as the old, and, indeed, need not be pensionable at all.

But two questions of principle come to the fore. First, will it still be possible to use pensions to stabilise staffs? Secondly, will transferability come voluntarily or (as some have advocated) will it be stimulated by a denial of tax concessions, or be made compulsory by law?

There is a fundamental conflict between labour stability and mobility, and to the extent that pension rights tie employees, they impair mobility. But these things are not absolute. Since the largest labour turnover occurs among short-period employees, it is impracticable to give pension rights before a minimum period of service. Some actuaries have suggested that pension rights might begin after five years, and reach full-size after fifteen.

These periods seem too long to permit the mobility desirable in a flexible economy. But high labour turnover is essentially a product of overfull employment: if we can reduce the overload on the economy, job-flitting should fall away. But if pension rights are given after short periods of service, they will be less effective in stabilising staffs.

For private industry, which needs labour mobility even more than the public and quasi-public services, all this means four things. First, occupational pension schemes are coming to be regarded less as the reward for loyalty and more as deferred pay that should accompany employees when they change jobs. Second, pension rights should, where possible, be preserved. Third, systems of transfer payments and cold-storage benefits should aim to discourage job-flitting, but not the job-switching provoked by changes in supply and demand unavoidable in a flexible economy. Fourth, since pensions will lose their value as ties, new "fringe benefits" to hold particularly valued employees—help with buying a house, school fees, doctors' bills, and so on—may have to be devised. We may, in fact, see a private Welfare State grow within industry not to avoid taxation but to reproduce the differentials which high taxation has tended to wipe out.

CHAPTER **20**

1958

Why State Pensions?

> Labour's proposed new graduated State pensions were not required to prevent the "two nations" in old age. * Warnings of the adverse long-term effects were ignored by all "pensioneering" parties in the 1960s and 1970s. The high tax costs of price-indexed pensions for more pensioners have at last been seen as weakening the national finances in government borrowing.
>
> (*The Manchester Guardian,* June 1958.)

The State pension, which is intended to provide basic needs for everybody (even, ironically, those who do not need it), is being financed less and less by insurance and more and more by taxpayers' subsidy. A new pensioner in 1958, with a wife five years younger, will have paid, in his own and his employer's contributions, less than a thirteenth of the capital fund required to yield the pension. Mainly because the cost of State pensions would rise from £480 million in 1957–8 to £980 million in 1979–80, the National Insurance Fund will go from a small surplus last year to a deficit of £480 million in 1979–80. This assumes unchanged basic rates, and credits the £120 million annual Exchequer contribution.

Partly to find new money for rising pension costs, partly because of the new idea in Britain that the pension should vary with income, the case for replacing equal by graduated contributions and benefits is being increasingly discussed. The Labour Party started the discussion with its proposals for pensions equal to half pay. The life assurance offices are now continuing it with their perhaps reluctant acceptance of the view that a pension designed to supply basic needs could properly vary with income, although they add that the benefit should "mature quickly" so that the cost to the contributor is made clear and that the graduation should be "strictly limited." A third impetus to the movement comes from those who favour graduated contributions (to yield more money) but not graduated benefits.

The argument that the State system must be extended to save it from breaking down is hardly adequate unless the extension can be justified on its own merits, because it is based on a wholly new principle that could have far-reaching and hardly realised consequences. Labour's case was supported by the "two-nation" argument that a third of the people will retire to relative affluence on an occupational pension plus the State pension and the other two-thirds to relative penury on the State pension alone. The Government Actuary has estimated that 7 million men, out of 16 million employed, are now covered, or nearly a half. Even women, who are not so interested in pensions, are covered to the extent of nearly one in four, or 1¾ million out of 8 million. Occupational pensions, both insured and self-administered, have been covering several hundred thousand more people each year. The rate of increase would have been even higher were it not for unfavourable circumstances, some of which are passing and others of which could be removed by government.

The "two-nation" argument rests on the view that occupational schemes are impracticable for small firms, for manual workers generally, or for particular industries. The Government Actuary's survey found over 28,000 schemes with under fifty members.

The Labour Party suggested that occupational pensions would be beyond most employees in agriculture, distribution, engineering, and building. A draft scheme for agriculture has now been drawn up by the National Farmers' Union. In distribution there are various schemes suited to small firms, for whom special techniques, such as a master policy needing only minor revision for each case, have been devised. In engineering there are plenty of schemes in operation and being planned. In building the scheme operated by the National Federation of Building Trades Employers is being used by many medium-sized and smaller firms; and the life offices and pension consultants have devised schemes for others. A scheme for part of the fishing industry is also under discussion. The difficulty of casual employees and of small firms could be overcome in various ways: individual policies, group schemes, possibly a private pooled arrangement embodying a clearing house for "cold-storage" claims.

The argument that a graduated scheme must be introduced because basic needs vary with income is questionable. There is no public demand to pay additional contributions (and taxes) for still higher State pensions. A man earning £12 a week does not require more calories or warmth to keep alive than one with £10 a week. Even "strictly limited" graduation would establish a precedent. It is true that if the graduation were widened by some future government more money would have to be raised in contributions, and public opposition might furnish a control. But it is not clear that a new national pension fund would be operated with pensions rigorously tied to contributions. The probability is that the vested interest in graduated pensions would induce contributors to pay in as much as rising prices or more ambitious notions of basic needs seemed to justify.

If a new system of graduated contributions and/or pensions cannot be justified on its own merits, how else can the rising cost of pensions be financed? One method would be to postpone the pensionable ages, as recommended by the Phillips Committee, or at least to bring women into line with men. Biologically and economically the case is unanswerable, especially if the advance in ages is confined to employments involving no heavy physical strain. A second method is to find some way of confining the existing pension to those who need it. The political objections to a means test are obvious; but so are the economic dangers of indiscriminate expenditure. No one has earned the State pension, not even the voluntary contributors, and it is taking nothing away to deny it to those whose incomes enable them to dispense with it.

If these methods of easing the financing of State pensions are politically difficult, then some such arrangement as the following ought to commend itself to those who wish to combine practicability with principles. First, the basic rates should be frozen and increases in benefits granted on evidence of need. Secondly, obstacles to the spread of private pensions should be removed; the practice of individual Inland Revenue examination could be replaced by standardised rules, compliance with which would bring automatic approval; and the tax treatment of pensions arranged by persons in non-pensionable employment or by the self-employed could be equalised with those of persons in pensionable employment. Thirdly, occupational schemes should be controlled by encouraging the preservation of pension rights (and perhaps flexibility in retirement ages) by tax advantages, discouraging excessive ploughing back in internally administered funds, requiring such funds to make returns of income and outgo, and, possibly, treating life office and internally administered funds as investment trusts for the purpose of government supervision.

Pension planning should not be determined by the need to raise a few hundred million pounds; it goes to the roots of our economic and political institutions. Before undertaking a further extension of State pensions we should remind ourselves of first principles: why State pensions were introduced; whether they are still necessary; for whom; and for how long. Living standards have changed beyond recognition since State pensions were introduced fifty years ago. Private saving for retirement is now possible for most people through personal or group insurance schemes. The tendency of social policy to be determined by the immediately practicable or expedient is inducing many to reconsider the future of the Welfare State. State pensions are a part of it that could gradually be wound up as the conditions that gave them birth pass away.

CHAPTER **21**

1960

Contract In or Out?

> Two articles advised contracting out of the Conservatives' new scheme graduating pensions with income. But the Government went ahead. * Their 1990s' mood on pensions has become more realistic.
> (*The Times*, January 1960.)

The brewing industry has long been known for its good relations with its employees. Lately it has also been showing increasing enterprise in its trading and commercial activities. Both these characteristics are reflected in the decision by Ind Coope to contract out of the government's new graduated pension scheme in which contributions and pension benefits vary with earnings; the basic scheme, requiring equal contributions and paying equal benefits, remains compulsory.

Ever since the National Insurance Act establishing the graduated scheme was passed in July 1959, there have been discussion and cogitation in the life offices and among the pension consultants and consulting actuaries on whether to advise employers to contract out or not. The problem has been one of the most complex that has faced the experts since occupational pensions came to Britain thirty years ago. Not surprisingly, there have been differences of opinion.

It is easy to see why. The decision to contract out or not cannot be made solely by reference to established facts. Certainly, the first step is to assess the cost to the employer (who must make the decision after giving notice to employees) of contracting out or going into the State scheme by comparing the contribution rates required.

So much is certain. But it is not very much. Broadly, it will be a few pence or shillings a week a head cheaper for an employer to put his lower-paid and older employees into the State scheme and to contract out his higher-paid and younger employees. This points to three key elements that may, and probably will, vary in the next few years. First, the general level of earnings: as these rise it will be better to contract out given groups of employees; secondly, the contributions and pension benefits in the State scheme: if these rise it will be better to put given groups of employees into the State scheme; thirdly, the pensions that can be bought on the open market through life assurance offices or directly: if these deteriorate it will be better to put employees into the State scheme, but if they improve it will be better to contract out.

Since employers will not wish to contract in and out every year or two when the balance of advantage changes in favour of State or private pensions, some judgment on the probable trend of developments must be attempted. And this is where there is room for difference of view and intuitive feel about the likely course of events.

In the meantime, the employer can start with a figure of the saving from contracting in and the cost of contracting out. The decision will not be based entirely on them alone. For against the cost of contracting out he will set the possible, probable, or hoped-for gains. These relate essentially to his relations with employees. Better—or continuing good—relations may be thought worth paying for.

It could be argued that since the employee is going to draw the "basic" £4 per week for a man and wife from the State, he is not likely to fall out with his employer if the additional graduated element also comes from the State. The reply could be that while the employer has no alternative but to put all his employees into the State for the basic pension, he is free to keep them out of the State and put them into his own scheme for the additional benefits. Moreover, the general expectation is that the basic pension benefit will remain little changed while the additional benefits, both in State and occupational schemes, will grow with rising prices and/or living standards.

The administrative problems under the various possible arrangements are themselves an additional aspect of costs. Here again opinion is divided. It would be "unnecessarily complex" to contract employees into the State scheme and provide through a private scheme the additional benefits firms may wish to give them. These benefits would also allow for past service, which the State scheme does not cover.

Time is not on industry's side. The Government Actuary estimated in 1958 that a year or two earlier there were some 37,500 occupational pension schemes, of which nearly 10,000 covered fifty or more employees. The total schemes now probably number about 40,000. If many employers take no action until, say, the autumn, the Registrar of Non-Participating Employments may not be able to give his decision before April 1961, when the government scheme is due to begin. If so, employers who wish to contract out will find themselves in the State scheme; the contributions they paid will not be recoverable, and they may find getting out of the scheme even more difficult than staying out in the first place. Early action is therefore advisable.

Several wider issues for which there may not have been enough time in the discussions on the National Insurance Bill can now be considered more fully.

One is the great importance of pensions in the growth of "fringe benefits," and in employer-employee relations generally. One pension scheme will cost £100,000 a year for some 3,500 employees, or about 12*s.* a head a week; and the pension will be £2 15*s.* 3*d.* a week, compared with the State's £2 1*s.* 6*d.* after forty-seven years' service. Not every firm can be as generous as this, particularly those with a large proportion of lower-paid or short-term employees.

Yet too little is known of how much is spent by industry on fringe benefits, and how large pensions loom in them. The *Survey of Large Companies* published recently by the Institute of Economic Affairs, and based on 151 firms, showed that many spend well over £1 a head a week on welfare benefits as a whole (pensions, canteens, education, *ex gratia* payments, sports facilities, etc.), and that pensions comprise 53 per cent of the total expenditure. Firms thinking of contracting in lower-paid or older workers and so saving 2*s.* or so a week a head will have to consider whether this saving is worth making if they are prepared to spend much larger sums to build a contented and loyal team of employees.

The attitude of employees themselves might also be given more thought. Those in an occupational scheme could feel secure in the knowledge that the contributions paid by them and/or their employer would eventually go to pay their pension (since a fund would be created), while in the State scheme the contributions would be paid out almost at once to other people who had already retired, so that employees who retired in the future would in turn have to depend on other contributors for their pensions. It is understandable if employees are sensitive to the distinction; and it is significant that the trade unions have in general been in favour of the contributory principle in National Insurance precisely because it established, at least on paper, "rights" to the pension.

A further reason why other firms may wish to contract out is that occupational pensions bind a firm and its employees together—and not only during working life. Those who value personal relationships in industry will know what that means. A retired State pensioner would hardly be welcomed for a cosy chat in Whitehall.

No doubt contracting out schemes will be studied by other firms to see how far they might reap the advantages of good employee relations and flexibility. For the rapid growth in occupational pensions since the end of the war has been based not only on their tax advantages and their value in reducing labour turnover, but also on the need in a free labour market to offer similar benefits as other employers. If the importance of good relations with employees is rated so highly that many employers with schemes are prepared to bear the additional cost of contracting out rather than abandon or mutilate their schemes, and other employers establish private schemes rather than go into the State scheme, what may follow?

The government (and the opposition) have often declared that they wish pension schemes in industry to thrive and spread. Many employers may decide that they cannot both contract into the State scheme and maintain or introduce private pensions. Contracting out may therefore take place on a larger scale than allowed for in the government calculations. The finances of the State scheme would then be weakened, and more money might have to be found out of taxation than already provided for in the proposed annual £170 million Exchequer subsidy. Alternatively, money might be taken from the part of the National Insurance Fund held against possible claims for unemployment benefit; and so long as unemployment remained low this would be a fortuitous nest-egg. Other alternatives—such as altering the conditions to make contracting out more difficult or costly—would presumably be avoided in view of the government's promise or pledge on private pensions.

In these circumstances, a possible way out would be to postpone the State scheme in order to give industry and the pension specialists time to cover more people beyond the 7½ million men and 2 million women already covered. Money to pay existing and prospective pensioners would then be found from general taxation, which could be reduced as the pensioners passed away.

In either event, whether the State scheme begins in April 1961 or not, there would seem to be a case for a new measure, which might be called the Private Pensions Easement Bill, to remove the administrative and legal obstacles to a faster growth of occupational pensions and to provide further fiscal or other encouragements. If the State scheme does begin in April 1961, such a Bill would be an earnest of the government's intentions towards pensions in industry; and if the scheme is postponed, the Bill would enable private pensions to spread more rapidly.

CHAPTER 22

1960

Pensions and Property

A surprise invitation from G. R. E. (later Lord) Howe to write for the Conservative Bow Group journal when his party was in office produced a critique of its new pension scheme for raising revenue to help the National Insurance Fund. The political cost would be to bring the State into private lives for the next fifty years. * The basic pension will linger into the twenty-first century.

(*Crossbow,* Spring 1960.)

One who is neither a Bow Grouper nor a (political) Conservative of any sort should explain his presence in these hospitable columns. The free society requires us to be conservative about the principles that underlie freedom—personal responsibility, diffusion of initiative, dispersal of property-ownership as the source of power—but radical about the legal and institutional framework required to preserve them in a changing world. The conservative radical (or radical conservative, or plain liberal) is radical in a different sense from that attributed to Labour but more conservative than some Conservatives. He finds no easy home in Labour because a political party based on a protest against injustice is liable to become reactionary when the wrong is righted. And he finds no easy home in the Conservative Party because it has harboured too many who failed to see the need for changing the framework and who seemed to think it permissible to infringe the principles so long as it was Conservatives who infringed them.

These faults were most evident in the 1930s, when trade depression seemed to unnerve the Conservative Party and propelled it into policies—in coal, transport, agriculture, international trade—that violated the basic tenets of private property and the free economic order. In recent years one has come to expect better things, and they have come in the post-war policies on food subsidies, restrictive practices, produce markets, rents (until the General Election undertaking), on fiscal control and monetary management. But, whatever the good intentions, the mitigating circumstances, the needs of the hour, the 1959 National Insurance Act and its system of graduated pensions must be regarded as an example of the weaknesses that Conservatives have not, it seems, after all left behind.

The issues are seen clearly from a consideration of the reasons given for the measure. One is that it was necessary to put the National Insurance system "on a sound financial footing." The need for a larger inflow into the National Insurance Fund has been increasingly apparent for some years, not least from the statistics of population. The shortfall in funds in the next few years is likely to be a couple of hundred million pounds a year. We are already committed to compulsory saving through the State for the "basic" pension. Are Conservatives really satisfied that to raise £200 million or £300 million a year is a good enough reason for bringing the State into our private lives for the next fifty years or more for a *second* pension? Was it really beyond our wits to have devised a method of raising the money without saddling ourselves with another slab of Statism? It could have been raised as a straightforward tax if its purpose had been adequately explained to the electorate. Such a levy could then have been diminished as the need for it to pay the National Insurance "pension" and the equally misnamed National Assistance (between which there is little difference) fell away with the passing of the generation of needy retired people.

Instead the new scheme would commit us to build up a structure of "rights" to State pensions far into the twenty-first century. For there is a difference between the financing of the basic "pension" and the financing of the graduated pension. The basic "pension" is, by now, largely a State benefit; nine-tenths of the capital for it is provided by the taxpayer. It is no longer a pension accumulated by contributions. And, provided the benefit is paid to those with need, there is no reason why it should not be accepted with honour. But the graduated pension is, and in the absence of inflation will remain, a true pension built up gradually on contributions paid by the potential pensioner and for him (as a form of deferred pay) by his employer. Since no fund is accumulated, the pensioner's expectations must be based on political promises and unforeseeable economic contingencies. But the rights to the pension are being accumulated by virtue of contributions. Their failing is that they are paper rights. That the contributions are paid out almost at once is not the contributor's concern; that is the headache of the contributor and taxpayer of 2008, who will have to pay the pension. And the subsidy from the Exchequer—of £170 million or more a year—is increasingly provided by the beneficiaries themselves; if Mr. Colin Clark's calculations are anywhere near the mark, the wage-earner is taking in most of his own washing.

Hence, while it would produce neither injustice nor hardship to wind up the "basic" National Insurance "pension," perhaps by reducing the benefit to the actuarial value of the contributions, or raising the contributions or both, and relating the resultant amount to needs, it would be much more difficult financially, and perhaps savour of political sharp practice, to wind up the graduated pension.

The second excuse, that it was necessary to have a counter-weight to Labour's national superannuation, is now seen in the event to be problematic and unconvincing. Labour may really have thought that it had, by design or accident, devised an election winner. It is not clear that the Conservatives would have suffered electorally without a counter-weight. We cannot tell how many votes were won by the Labour and Conservative pension schemes. But neither can the electoral strategists on both sides show that no votes were *lost* because of them. There is in fact evidence which suggests that the electorally decisive uncommitted or thinking margin of the population was bored with bribes.

But this is to put the argument at its most cynical. There is, after all, something to be said for not touching pitch. Representative democracy reached a new low ebb on the evening before polling day when the sovereign electors of Parliament were treated like bidders at an auction. It is to the credit of the Conservatives that they did not join in the competitive offers of higher "basic" pensions.

The third pretext for the graduated State pension is that it was necessary because private pensions are not spreading fast enough. Certainly, "only" eight million employed men out of sixteen million and "only" two million women out of eight million are covered in private occupational pension schemes. Certainly, the schemes vary from generous to meagre, the latter being mostly schemes installed before the war and not brought up to date. Certainly, "only" about 100,000 people have been covered by new schemes each year. But in the circumstances influencing or determining the rate of advance, this is no mean achievement. Some employers have been short-sighted. Some trade union leaders have been suspicious or obstructionist. Younger employees have—understandably—been more interested in immediate pay than in distant retirement. The Inland Revenue has not been as helpful as it could have been by appearing to examine each scheme as though it was primarily a device for tax avoidance. Changes in the tax treatment of pension schemes in the 1956 Finance Act have consumed actuarial and other scarce energies in revision of schemes that would otherwise have been used to instal new ones. And the life offices themselves have not always shown the energy or the competitiveness that could have gone into the pensions business.

But none of this was or is inevitable. Employers are being forced by competition to add pensions to their fringe benefits. The trade unions are waking up—encouraged by the end of the sellers' market in labour. Employees are becoming more pension-conscious. The Inland Revenue has become more helpful. And the life offices are becoming more efficient through automation and more competitive, not least through the increasing activities of brokers and consultants. If Conservatives really wished above all to see pension schemes cover as many people as possible as soon as possible, their path was clear; they should have removed all the obstacles and provided all feasible encouragements. Until they had done that, the complaint that private pensions were not spreading fast enough was inadmissible, and they had no business thinking of a new State system.

It is true that not everyone can be covered in an occupational scheme. Casual workers, the self-employed, the fee-earners and the free-lances, women who work for only a few years before marriage: to cover these people in occupational schemes may be administratively difficult or costly. But those of them who so wished could be encouraged to save for retirement personally by suitable tax arrangements; the 1956 annuity scheme, for example, is not a big success so far, and could be taken further. Then there are the small firms—in agriculture, building, and elsewhere; it may be costly to devise schemes to cover five, ten or twenty employees. But there are ways of reducing the cost by grouping. And, if not, the small firm must pay more per employee in administrative charges: this is one of the diseconomies of small size. The view, held surprisingly by some pension specialists, that small firms cannot be serviced, is a fallacy. There is no inherent difficulty here: the fault lies in the charging system, which is too rigid; insurance and pension scheme costing needs to be brought up to date.

In any event, why must we *all* save for retirement through pension schemes? There are other ways that may suit our circumstances, temperaments or whims better: the Post Office, house purchase, unit trusts, the old sock or the Old Master. Even if we suppose that employers and trade unions were too slow, employees too foolish, and the pension industry too hidebound to cover quickly everyone who wanted to be covered, why on earth should the State step in and provide the pension machinery itself? There is a confusion here that has bedeviled thinking on economic and social policy for too long. It seems to be argued that because people are not wise enough to do things for themselves, they must be forced to do the wise thing *through the State*. This is a *non sequitur*. If it is desirable for the State to lay down standards for, say, the contents of jam or pickles, it does not have to establish a Ministry of Jams and Pickles with nationalised jam and pickle factories. Even if, which may still be true of a small but dwindling minority, it is necessary to force people to set aside part of their earnings for their retirement, the State need only require that a minimum amount or proportion of earnings be put by in defined forms. And, as elsewhere, we should find that private arrangements often surpassed the State standard.

CHAPTER **23**

1961

Social Services in the Late Twentieth Century

> The test of a humane society was whether it helped most the people in most need who could not help themselves. Social benefits generally did not pass the test. Thinking in all parties was at fault. * Near the end of the century the to-ing and fro-ing of taxes to government and back in benefits still increases. No government has found the solution of cancelling them against each other.
>
> (*Swinton College Journal,* March 1961.)

We have had the free society (Beveridge), the responsible society (the Conservative "One-Nation" group), the irresponsible society (Professor R. M. Titmuss), the welfare society (the Liberal Unservile State Group) and the affluent society (Professor J. K. Galbraith). But the *humanity* of our social arrangements is not the least criterion by which they should be judged.

The simple and stark issue is this: is the community helping most those who need most help? Apart from capital outlay, we are spending about £800 million a year on State education, £750 million on the National Health Service, £650 million on State retirement and over-sixty widows' pensions, £160 million on National Assistance grants, £150 million on State sickness benefits, about £140 million on family allowances, £120 million on State housing, nearly £100 million on nutrition services, £100 million on war and other disablement pensions. And there are smaller sums: £50 million each on unemployment and industrial injury benefits, £25 million on child care, £13 million on non-contributory old age pensions, £4 million on industrial rehabilitation and the training and employment of the disabled. The administration of National Insurance benefits alone is costing nearly £50 million. In all, these "social services" are costing £3,300 million a year.

How much good is it doing? The National Assistance payments are not as generous as a wealthy nation can afford. The war pensions also are not overgenerous. More could be spent on child care and on the training and employment of disabled people. But is all the money spent on education going on those who cannot afford to pay? Even after Mr. Enoch Powell's increase in contributions, is the money spent on the National Health Service helping those who most need it? How much of the retirement pensions go to people who have not paid for them and do not need them? Are the family allowances going to the purposes for which they were intended? How much of the housing subsidies are subsidising people who can afford to pay full rents? Is it proper to supply free libraries for people who are paying for less "essential" services? And what is the point of paying money or supplying services to people whose incomes are enough for them to do without it or pay their cost?

Further, in so far as people are paying for these services by charges, insurance contributions or taxes, what sense—and how much waste—is there in forcing them to buy the services from the State? And how much more generous could we be to those in need if we cut out all this to-ing and fro-ing of money from consumers, contributors and taxpayers to the State and back again?

We have been so long looking closely at the alternative methods of building the road that we have lost sight of where we want it to lead us. Those who founded the Welfare State were concerned with ensuring minimum standards in health, education, and housing and minimum income in unemployment and retirement for people whose incomes were too low to provide for themselves. The social services—whether provided by transfer payments, by aid in kind, or by taxpayer-assisted social insurance—were substitutes for personal income. They were temporary until income rose sufficiently to dispense with them. In the perspective of history, some of the social services we have known would seem to have a life of fifty to seventy-five years.

Unfortunately, thinking on the social services has turned up a blind alley. There was, first, the collectivist notion that they were a means of socialising income that made all men brothers. Its latest formulation is in Professor Titmuss's "badge of citizenship" that is worn by all who participate in the free, equal and permanent social benefits. Regrettably, Lord Beveridge lent the notion some non-socialist support by his advocacy of minimum social benefits to which all would have a right irrespective of payments or income. This notion was also socialist in essence; it was never well based in political philosophy, human psychology, or fiscal practicability. For those who value human dignity, personal liberty and common humanity, universalism is unacceptable.

The second source of confusion is the failure to distinguish between social standards, social financing, and social provision. Inadequacy of private money incomes, "primary" poverty, was and remains the essential reason for the social services. It can be extended to include the "secondary" poverty of people with enough income but not sense to put first things first (parents who buy frills rather than food for their children, or who spend and leave nothing for their retirement, etc.). Yet these two are not enough to make the case for *State*-provided services. A third condition is required: that people cannot obtain them except from the State, or that State services are inherently superior to private services. Primary poverty is met by transfer payments; secondary poverty by gifts in kind (e.g. milk—which need not be free) or statutory requirements (e.g. insurance against ill-health). Neither necessarily requires services conceived, organised and administered by the State.

The neglect of the distinction between social standards, financing and provision has distorted the British social structure, so that people in need are given less than we can afford and others are discouraged from ever thinking seriously about education, health, or housing, which they look to "the government" to provide.

It has caused an unnecessarily high proportion of income and spending to be channelled through the State. It has raised taxation to levels at which incentives are impaired. It has weakened the personal sense of responsibility on which a free society must rest. It has loosened the bonds of family, the unit of our social structure. It has threatened the integrity of our public life. This error has led us into State pre-natal and post-natal services, State child care services, State hospitals, State doctors, nurses and medicines, State schools, State unemployment insurance, State (or county) libraries, museums and galleries, State homes, State pensions and State death grants. Eighty, fifty, or even thirty years ago, there may have been no practicable alternative to State provision of at least some of these services. It could be argued that people in primary poverty would have spent State grants on drink, or that people suffering from secondary poverty could be better guided by providing public services than by requiring them to buy on the open market. But now?

It is true that nearly two million people receive National Assistance, and that they have another half-million dependents. Further, there may be another half a million or a million people who qualify for assistance but do not claim it for various reasons. But for the remaining 90 or 95 per cent of us primary poverty is happily no more; and it must be difficult to say of people who are trusted to vote for statesmen empowered with decisions over their very lives that they cannot be left to put first things first in the ordinary business of everyday affairs. There may still be thousands, or even hundreds of thousands, who do not look after their children or their aged parents. But that is no reason for treating *everyone* as though he were still suffering from primary or secondary poverty.

Yet this is what we do. We assume that *every* man may neglect his wife in childbirth; that *every* man may fail in educating his children; that *every* man may neglect his family—and himself—in ill-health; that *every* man may squander his earnings and starve in unemployment or in old age. And so we compel *every* man to pre-pay for health, education, unemployment, and retirement services or income.

Not only that; we compel him to buy all these services *through the State.* But why should we? If education is desirable to the age of fifteen, why should not people who can afford it be required to buy it in the open market? If standards are too low, the State can specify them and ensure that they are observed by inspection. As the demand for private education increases—as it is doing even now—the number of suppliers will increase, and competition will help to ensure the required standards. And a regime of diversified private educational services would be more adventurous, less satisfied with the mediocre and the conformist, and less susceptible to political influence than general State education.

Compulsory buying of State services is no longer suited to a free, affluent, responsible Britain in the 1960s. Rising incomes and growing personal responsibility make it possible and desirable to transfer decisions on elemental *personal* matters from public officials to individuals and from State to private provision. Which services are ripe for such transfer, and at what rate the transfer should take place, require lengthy investigation and research to determine. But the principle is clear enough: in the next ten or twenty years we should be able to pass from the stage at which we assume that all need assistance or guidance except those who show they do not to the stage at which we assume that none need assistance or guidance except those who show that they do.

The government of such a society would be advised by a Permanent Commission on the Social Services investigating services that could be transferred from public to private decision and from public to private provision.

On what lines would it work? First, it would devise methods of finding people in need. How many there are in all we do not know. But we must see how much there is in the estimates of the "submerged tenth" or even "fifth" of the population (i.e. five or ten million people) made by Professor Titmuss and his associates and repeated by Mr. Gaitskell.

Secondly, the commission would gradually reduce the weight of abortive and wasteful public expenditure by devising methods of withdrawing transfer payments from those who do not need them or who had not paid for them. In the health, education, housing, libraries and other services, the method would be probably that of raising the charges gradually until they covered costs. Mr. Powell has recently made a good start. In national pensions there would be the difficulty of removing the nine-tenths that represents the transfer payments because older people will have arranged their private saving on the expectation of receiving the State pension. The solution is to freeze the basic pension rate; there is no good reason for giving increases to 5½ million pensioners who have not earned them and who include 4 million or more who do not need them. Whether the method used is that of raising charges or reducing benefits, the purpose would be to move the taxpayer's subsidy away from people who do not need it to those who do.

In this process some means must be found of exempting people still in primary or secondary poverty. Primary poverty can be identified only by assessing means either by personal enquiry (the means test) or by a written record of income as an automatic indicator of entitlement to assistance or exemption from increased charges. The opposition to the personal enquiry into means is overstated by well-meaning social workers and by prejudiced politicians. In any event personal enquiry looks like being unavoidable for many now receiving National Assistance. Three hundred thousand are aged eighty and over and a further 660,000 are in the seventies; experience during the war when visiting was difficult suggests that many old people would have difficulty in supplying written information sufficient to dispense with personal visits. A further reason for retaining, for some time, the visits of the National Assistance Board's ten thousand staff is that they are often virtually welfare officers as well as income assessors. But means could be found to assist old people to make written records, and if welfare visits are desirable they could be arranged in other ways. In the future the use of income returns that would yield codes as indicators of entitlement to assistance seems to have many advantages. It would remove the objections to the personal visits and to the need to initiate a claim. In so far as the objection is to receiving assistance as such, there seems no way out except recognising that there is no indignity in accepting assistance where there is real need—and that there is no difference in principle between accepting National Assistance and accepting nine-tenths of the National Insurance pension benefit or any other benefits that have not been paid for.

Income codes would also make possible a systematic programme of annual increments of charges over, say, five or ten years until the costs of the services were covered and the unwanted and unwarranted subsidy removed. Thus parents of children at State schools might pay five shillings weekly per child in the first year, rising by small amounts each year. And there is no reason why people who use public libraries, galleries and other sources of culture should not be required to pay for them—unless they can show that they cannot.

Thirdly, and concurrently, the Permanent Commission would devise a system of contracting out of the social services. If the 1959 National Insurance Act, which established the new graduated pension scheme, teaches us the practical possibilities of large-scale contracting out, it may yet do more good than harm. By next April it is expected that 3½ million out of some 10 million employees covered by occupational pension schemes in public and private employment will be contracted out, and the number may rise after April. If contracting out of State pensions is permissible for people who can provide retirement income privately, it is no less proper in principle for people who are prepared to buy, in the open market, health, education, housing, library or any other social service. Various methods could be adopted: excusing the relevant social insurance contribution, returning the notional cost of the social services not used, allowing the cost of private services against tax, and so on. None of these methods is perfect, but any of them would be better than the present practice of *discouraging* personal responsibility and private provision by requiring the contractor out to go on paying for services he does not use. On the contrary, we should encourage contracting out by making it as easy as possible. Those who remain dependent on social services would have them provided by the taxpayer without charge, or would pay according to their means as indicated by their income codes.

We have become so accustomed to thinking of the State as the necessary, or desirable, or sole provider that we shall have to build a new set of institutions if private provision is to grow. Three things seem necessary. *First*, information. If people are to buy private rather than State education they should know what they are buying. It is of interest to note how well the market works. The organisers of *Which?* are now publishing *Where?*, an information service on education that should guide parents away from the less satisfactory private schools and so in time build up confidence in private education. *Secondly,* until demand for private services develops on a large enough scale, there will be pockets of poor service. Nursing homes are a frequently quoted example. For such services, minimum standards, reinforced by periodic inspection, are a proper province of the State (or of local authorities). *Thirdly,* there should be plenty of lively competition between private suppliers. Given information and minimum standards, competition will not debase but will improve quality in time. Here the State might step in as a competitor in order to keep the market open and free—provided it does not subsidise its service and stay in the market when its purpose has been served.

It has been said that the universal system is administratively simple and matches assistance to needs to some extent since recipients with large incomes repay part of the assistance in tax. This was a better argument in the 1930s than it is in the 1960s, and than it will be in the 1970s. It presupposes a continuance of high taxation (how much of the £1,500 million of transfer payments will be returned in tax and how much will remain with the recipients?) and a mounting waste in administration through first paying and then recovering assistance from more and more people; and it is a confession that universalism is wrong in principle.

An approach to the humanist principle of matching assistance with needs should have three results. *First,* it will enable us to be more generous to the most needy. By far the biggest payment out of the National Insurance funds is to the retirement pensioners. Much of the £650 million must, even after tax, remain with former highly paid working people, with salaried men, businessmen, ex-service officers and others, who have not earned it. *Secondly,* the gradual reduction in abortive social expenditure should enable us to reduce taxes. Some cut is imperative, even if it is not possible to produce cast-iron evidence of the impairment of incentives. The view of the Royal Commission on Taxation is of little relevance here. Quite apart from the case for a reduction in order to limit the province of the State, we must take steps to break the vicious circle which causes even better-off people to use State services (for which they and others pay in taxation) because they "cannot afford" to pay for the services privately "owing to high taxation." This dirtying of one another's washing is a built-in inflator in the structure of the social services. *Thirdly,* a change from universalism to humanitarianism would make it easier to increase spending on desirable social services that cannot be provided through the market.

Ought total spending to go down? Or should the abortive expenditure be redirected elsewhere, so that the total remains unchanged, and there is no room for tax reduction? While it is possible to see social services that should be expanded—not least child welfare—one need not share the fashionable enthusiasm for new forms of collectivist culture, youth services, organised sport, and the rest. Nor should one accept the curious argument that runs: as national incomes rise, we can afford to spend more on the social services. This myopic inversion fails to see that as private incomes rise we *need* to spend *less.* Unless some new and unexpected social need arises that people cannot be left to pay for, or that the market cannot supply, the weight of social service expenditure should fall in the next ten years relatively to total national income and absolutely.

Those who see logic, good sense and humanity in this approach may yet have a remaining doubt: is it practical politics?

For people who have faith in the human spirit the answer must be yes. Affluence means nothing if it does not bring a man the opportunity to do more for his family as well as help the underdog. Men of modest means are throwing off the burden of dependence on their neighbours. They are buying their homes, taking out life assurance, putting savings in unit trusts, insuring privately for medical services, paying for schools, for doctors . . . We should place no obstacles in their way; we should rather nourish, nurture and fertilise the natural urge to independence that self-respecting men feel as by their efforts and good fortune they earn enough to pay their way, stand on their own feet, and look their neighbours in the eye. They are losing interest in "welfare" that means the rule of the bureaucrat, high taxation, inflation. They want to get on, and their revolt in 1959 is a foretaste of what is to come. Of course, re-arranging the social services will have to be done gradually, consistently, humanely. But none need suffer, and all stand to gain. It should not be hard to "sell" lower taxation, wider choice of public and private services, a better chance to get on, more generosity for the needy. Nothing need stand in the way if there is the will to refashion the social services to fit the second half of the twentieth century.

CHAPTER 24

1962

Social Services for the Future, Not the Past

The first of over fifty articles for the Telegraph newspapers, Daily and Sunday, 1962–1992, directed at the "Conservative" public. Although incomes might double from 1962 to 1996, government was allowing choice in consumer goods but not in welfare. * Recent reforms to allow choice by decision of suppliers in education and medical care retain ultimate power by politicians: consumers—parents and patients—have no decisive individual power to opt out.

(*The Daily Telegraph*, June 1962.)

If Britain's national income rises at the rate of some recent years—2 per cent—it will double in thirty-six years. It will have to rise at 3 per cent to double in Mr. Butler's twenty-five years. And if it rises at 4 per cent, the National Economic Development Council's figure, it will double in eighteen years.

But whether incomes double by 1980 or 1996 we should all, as a nation, be quite a bit better off in the next ten or fifteen years.

In the 1960s and 1970s, also, you might suppose that in all social income groups we would increasingly have a good idea of what we want to buy with our earnings, and how to get good value. And if our native wit is not enough we can have laws to defend us and consumer organisations to advise us. But in order to learn we must be allowed to choose.

Yet the future our political leaders are building for us is one in which we shall be free to please ourselves in buying some of the less urgent things in life like entertainment, holidays, motoring, sports, hobbies, drinking, smoking, betting and so on, but not so free over education, housing, health services and saving for retirement.

This curious division cannot be explained on the ground that education, housing, health and pensions are "basic" while the other services are not. For what is more "basic" than food?

I suggest the real reasons are habit, muddle and ignorance. People of all political parties have come to regard State education, council housing, State health services and State pensions as inevitable for all time. Yet they are necessary only as long as we are unable to provide or judge for ourselves. Where is the sense in having vast, political organisation for schools, homes, hospitals, pensions, once we can afford to buy them out of income and enjoy the advantages of choice and control by paying direct rather than through taxes or rates?

Secondly, muddle about the purpose of the so-called "social services" has gradually spread into all parties. We have lost sight of the fundamental aim—that these services were to be provided "free" by the State to help people in need. Nowadays they are discussed as if they were intended to distribute free gifts to all and sundry.

This has some ludicrous results. People who are really in need—probably well over 2½ million old people, widows with children, the chronically sick or incapacitated, and so on—cannot be helped as much as we can afford. As more people pay taxes we are handing out free gifts to ourselves at our own expense. The politicians can solicit support by promising us benefits for which we ourselves pay. And we have to maintain scores of thousands of officials to collect and return our own money.

Thirdly, ignorance. Some pooh-pooh the idea that people may like to provide for themselves. But half a million children are at private schools, 6 million own their own homes, 1.5 million are covered by insurance for health services, and over ten million are saving for retirement through private pensions schemes. These numbers could have grown much faster. We simply do not know how many million more would want to do all these things for themselves instead of paying taxes and having officials to do them, *because there is no free choice.*

If you pay income tax you are helped in buying a house by the allowance on the mortgage interest, or in contributing to a pensions scheme, or to life insurance, by the allowance on the premiums. And the House of Commons recently debated arguments for allowing £75 a year against income tax for school fees and £15 a year for health insurance.

Such allowances would make the choice less biased in favour of the State. But we must go much further. For they do not reach the millions who pay little or no income tax but who pay tax indirectly through their purchases of furniture, clothing, tobacco, drinks, and so on.

Many, direct and indirect taxpayers alike, understandably feel that so long as they are forced to pay for State schools and health services they intend to use them rather than pay twice. And the more they have to pay for State services the less they can afford to spend on private services.

But even now many more people could afford to pay school fees by spreading them over the years before or after school through insurance or "hire purchase" (one company offers a scheme in which a father aged forty-five can provide fees of £200 a year for four years by paying under £11 a month over eight years, with life cover). Recent mortgages arranged by two building societies show that people earning £600 a year can buy a home. Insurance for private medical treatment costs only £15 to £25 a year. And about £60 a year at thirty, well within the means of many young men, buys a pension of at least £500 a year at sixty-five, with a lump sum of about £2,000 rising to £5,000 for his family if he dies before.

If people really prefer to spend their money as they do now, that is their business; they are responsible enough to know what they are doing. But their range of choice is narrow and could be much wider.

The government does not say "You may either pay taxes and have the State service or keep your money and buy it where you like." It says "If you don't want the State service you must still pay for it." Nor is there much persuasive advertising for private education, health services or pensions, compared with the £300 million-worth for consumer goods and services for which there is free choice. And the State, of course, finds compulsory buying of its services a cheap substitute for advertising.

Politicians will not be more energetic in freeing choice, especially over education and health, until there is more evidence of growing demand for private services. The private services or the institutions that supply the means to pay for them would make faster progress if the politicians removed the obstacles.

In housing and pensions, buying, selling and legal procedure could be made simpler and cheaper; and, as in the United States Federal Housing Administration, we might insure mortgages up to thirty and thirty-five years to reduce deposits and repayments. Particularly in education and health, the big obstacle is the payment for the State service by people who do not use it. "Contracting out" is now allowed for the graduated (but not the basic) State pension because ten million people have an interest in private pensions. It will have more political support in education and health as private provision spreads.

An alternative that would preserve the redistributive effect of "free" State service is to give people who want to buy private services drafts representing the real cost of the State services they would have used. Thus for private health insurance a man with a wife and two children would have available not the £8 13*s.* 4*d.* that he (and his employer) pay to the National Health Service, but perhaps £30 to £50.

Services that only public authorities can provide would, of course, continue to be financed out of taxes. And services such as child care and retraining of the handicapped would require more State financing (though not necessarily State organisation). But out of expenditure on State "welfare" approaching £4,000 million a year—nearly half the total public expenditure of £8,000 million, including defence—taxes could be reduced by £1,000 million or more a year in the not too distant future.

But if the politicians wait for the suppliers, and the private suppliers for the politicians, who will move first? The solution is for both to move at the same time. The politician needs to raise his sights and to have a little more faith in his countrymen. The insurance companies, building societies and "mutual" organisations need more competition to stimulate increased initiative, experiment and drive, and more liberal legal controls.

More than that: we could encourage both politicians and suppliers by more knowledge about what people would want if they had a free choice. Since there is no free market, we must find out by research, and there is little doubt that, whatever some politicians and sociologists say or hope, people will want to be free to spend their incomes on "welfare" as well as non-essentials. We should rejoice that they want to stand on their own feet, not force them to wear crutches.

Is it necessary to recount the advantages? We should have more flexible, more experimental, more personal services. We should be able to give much more generously to the remaining people in need; in our wanderings up the blind alley of equality we have neglected the real if dwindling problem of poverty. We should be able to reduce taxation. We should go a long way towards taking education, housing, health and pensions (and therefore the pay of teachers, doctors and nurses) out of politics. And we could, and probably would, spend *more* on private and State education, health, housing and pensions as a whole than we do now.

The mature society would be free, responsible, humane. Nothing need stand in the way except habit, muddled thinking and ignorance.

CHAPTER **25**

1962

Universities Out of Politics

Government financing of higher education in a political democracy implied control by the State. Academic independence required dispersed private financing: student fees, grants, research fees. * The Robbins Committee in 1964 proposed 10 per cent of university income from students. (Committee members varied from 0 per cent to 40 per cent; 10 per cent was the compromise.) The solution, originating in the Institute of Economic Affairs, had to wait for the private University of Buckingham in 1972. Students of state universities are paying more in fees but government is reluctant to renounce political influence.

(*The Statist,* December 1962.)

How to prevent political misuse of higher education: this—and not the debate among politicians, educationists and sociologists about curricula, the (alleged) autocracy of professors, teaching systems, the size and shape of buildings, equality between "Oxbridge" and "Redbrick," or even the rate of expansion—is the crucial problem to be solved in the years ahead. It would be a Pyrrhic victory if the 110,000 university students and 100,000 students at technical colleges, polytechnics, institutes of higher education and teacher training colleges were to become intellectual cannon-fodder for purposes laid down increasingly by politicians or political doctrinaires.

This is the danger in the tendency of higher education to be financed increasingly through the State. In England academic freedom has until recent years seemed safe because the universities and colleges were largely endowed by private benefactors. Parliament supplied only a third of the income of the universities (excluding Oxford and Cambridge colleges) forty years ago, but today nearly three-quarters. Most of this money—about £74 million in 1961–2—is channelled through the University Grants Committee which is financed and staffed by the Treasury. The use of an intermediary is supposed to ensure independence for the universities. Does it?

No doubt the universities could say a good deal if they were bold or incautious enough to think aloud in answering the question. Professor Stephen Toulmin of Oxford has described "people in the academic world" as "State pensioners"; "the old spirit of independent self-government has been largely destroyed by fifteen years of growing dependence on the Treasury." This dependence was demonstrated starkly when the Treasury overrode the UGC earlier this year and university salaries became entangled with pay pauses and party politics.

To the pleas that we take health and pensions out of politics we now have to add education. This is a *cri de coeur* that should make the politician blush. But as long as British universities are heavily financed by the State, they must expect it, sooner or later, to call the tune.

Evidence of government influence is clear though often indirect. Governments are supposed to be able to take a long and a wide view of national needs and resources, and they are urged to expand the universities to produce specialists in this or that or the other to keep up with the Russians or the Martians. Accordingly they expect the universities to train specialists of stated types. They indicate more or less unambiguously the kind of research that should be conducted. They are a major employer of graduates in government research establishments and in some fields virtually the sole employer. They are sometimes the only or the main source of information on which research is based. They are the largest patron, the only employer of experts on official committees of enquiry, the sole source of honours. Is academic freedom assured when it may be tactless to reach unfashionable conclusions or inconvenient to attempt unorthodox experiments?

The relations between governments and universities in Africa and Asia show lessons we cannot ignore. In America President Eisenhower warned in his farewell speech of the danger of making scientific research the tool of the defence programme. In Britain some see the dangers of political influence. Bristol University is hoping to raise £10 million from public funds in the next ten years. The Chairman of the Appeal Committee, Lord Sinclair of Cleeve, said the aim was to meet the need for the university to retain "a proper measure of autonomy and independence." The vice-chancellor, Sir Philip Morris, was more explicit: "learning and the advancement of knowledge [should not be] contaminated by the exercise of undue influence from any quarter . . . [the government of the day] must not be in a position to interfere in the educational mission of the university."

But if the government of the day supplies three-quarters of the money, it *is* "in a position to interfere in the educational mission of the university." The only certain way of removing such temptation is to increase the universities' income from other sources. The two that suggest themselves, business endowment and students' fees, have shrunk in the last forty years, endowments from a third of the universities' income to less than a twentieth, fees from a third to barely a tenth. How can these sources be strengthened?

Evidence submitted by Professor A. T. Peacock and Mr. Jack Wiseman of the University of York to the Robbins Committee on Higher Education emphasised "the threat to the independence of the universities and their growing reliance on funds from the central government." They argue that if the State continues as the largest financier of higher education parliamentary control should *increase,* but that the personal economic benefits of higher education should be paid for by the beneficiaries through fees (vocational training seems a clear example) and that the indirect "social" benefits should be paid for by the community at large, not merely through grants but through tax reliefs to encourage donations by individuals or firms. Since universities differ in endowment and voluntary support, government should compensate for low endowment incomes with once-for-all capital grants.

It has been suggested by Professor Toulmin that government grants go not to the university but to the student to enable him (or her) to pay the full cost of higher education. This change would create a market in which the universities could compete for students. Messrs. Peacock and Wiseman go further and elaborate the case, widely analysed in the USA and applied in Europe, for fees paid out of government loans.

They argue that the private capital market cannot supply such loans because the borrowers have no security, so that private loans would have to carry "prohibitive" rates of interest and/or be repayable over a short period. Does not this argument leave the family out of account as the borrowing unit? If secondary school fees can be financed by life insurance before and during the school years, there seems nothing in the nature of the parent-child relationship that makes these methods impracticable for university fees. Special terms for State loans would nevertheless be justified if they were related to income.

Messrs. Peacock and Wiseman argue that the fees system would have two advantages: it would discourage students from wasting their time at university by emphasising the moral responsibility to the community to use their opportunities conscientiously; and it would prevent graduates who emigrate from avoiding paying for the next generation's education by taxation. The third and more fundamental advantage would be the lessening direct dependence of the universities on the State. In other countries many students work during term and are able to pay fees for evening university teaching; this is a further argument against indiscriminate State grants or subsidised loans.

An objection to financing fees by State loans rather than by grants is that parents with higher incomes would invest more in their children. Peacock and Wiseman would therefore give exceptionally gifted children State bursaries awarded on the GCE or university entrance examinations, and less bright children worthy of "social investment" grants-cum-loans, the proportions varying with family means. But many people with little capital have incomes high enough to pay fees in full or in part, if not by cash then by borrowing; education is no less worthy of buying than furniture, cars or holidays abroad. Moreover, State help is apt to dry up the springs of self-help. These issues have been fogged because the State has used education to give equal opportunities to all, irrespective of, and not in proportion to, their capacity to benefit from them. This is the source of the confusion in much recent literature on the social services. It illustrates the conflict between equality and progress that sociologists have failed to resolve in calling for the abolition of poverty on one page and demanding uniformity in treatment on the next. In education it implies that no more shall be given to any promising child than can be given to every child. This politicalisation of learning constitutes as potent a reason as any for keeping the State as far away as possible from higher education.

The other source of independence is endowment by business organisations and individuals. We must welcome support by industry for the new universities. It is no less true of a businessman than of a politician that if he gives money he is tempted to influence its use; and it might be just as damaging and debilitating for a university to be dependent for three-quarters of its money on a businessman as on a government. But it is healthy, for example, for the Chairman of the Council of the University of Sussex to be a southern counties businessman, Mr. S. M. Caffyn, for the University of York to be supported by the Rowntrees' money, and for Lord Rootes to be a moving spirit in the University of Warwick. The State is one; businessmen are many. Whatever the buffer-effect of the UGC, the views of the government of the day on the conduct and direction of university education cannot be ignored for long, even if only because they are supposedly based on the best available information about future "national needs" and because they appear sanctified as being "in the public interest." But the views of businessmen can be resisted because they cannot be urged with the authority or cachet of government, because they probably differ from the views of other businessmen, and because if they are ignored and their support is withdrawn the consequence is not catastrophic.

In time rising income could provide the universities and other institutions of higher education with income from fees to cover costs. Until then we can encourage individuals and industry to support them, and we can develop means of enabling fees to be paid through life assurance and perhaps "hire purchase," or by State loans or loans-cum-grants to students. There is no other way to take "higher education out of politics."

CHAPTER **26**

1963

Beveridge Came Too Late

The sceptical New Society readership of State officials and students was told the 1942 Beveridge "plan" was the outdated dream of a liberal mind set in the inter-war years or before the First World War when Beveridge studied unemployment. He had not allowed for post-war social advance. He later repented, but too late. He had given the politicians a dangerous toy that brought them votes. * The question now is not whether to privatise welfare but how and how soon.

(*New Society*, February 1963.)

In British history "Beveridge" will be known as the name of a philosophy of social policy as well as of a brilliant public servant. Like his great contemporary, Keynes, Beveridge the man will be variously interpreted according to the prejudices of the interpreter. But, more even than Keynes, his influence came too late; his advice was applied in 1948—partially and distortedly—when time would soon make it increasingly out of tune with the opportunities and urges of a new age.

Social Insurance and Allied Services was published in December 1942 and debated in the House of Commons in February 1943. Post-war Beveridge is fourteen years old. Beveridge the philosophy goes back to 1909 when social security in embryo was in part conceived by Beveridge and introduced by Lloyd George. The philosophy took more definite form in 1924 when Beveridge published a booklet whose title indicated the scope of his thinking: *Insurance For All and Everything*. It was advance notice—or fair warning—to Churchill's war-time government of what to expect if they commissioned him to report on social insurance.

They were not disappointed. Beveridge's scheme for all-embracing social insurance expressed the feeling, familiar to Christian and communist teaching alike, that the members of society should care for one another in times of trouble—sickness, accident, unemployment, old age. Its grand design was of an enormous Friendly Society. It embodied the spirit, and was the creation, of its times. But for that very reason its relevance was at risk when war gave way to better times.

Beveridge could not be expected to foresee full employment and the unprecedented high employment of married women. And he did not allow for their consequences. The report looks back rather than forward. Beveridge had concluded after the great depression of 1930–2 not only that chronic unemployment must be ended once and for all but also that poverty must be abolished by social insurance benefits for everybody as a right, earned by contributions and paid without a means test, in incapacity, unemployment and old age. This structure was to be buttressed, first, by children's allowances, to ensure that provision for a child should not depend on the size of its family, second, by a free health service for everyone, and, third, by full employment.

On paper the structure seems to stand. Indeed, some people in the three political parties talk of building on Beveridge's foundations. Yet look closer and you see that some of the foundations were never laid, others are crumbling, and the remainder hold up a structure that appears increasingly out of place in its new social and economic surroundings.

The central arch itself has finally collapsed. After fourteen years, social security no longer rests on social insurance but on social subsidy. The contribution is less an insurance premium than a tax. This system is described jocularly as "pay as you go" and dignified with the actuarial term "assessmentism." The contributor has to depend for his benefits not on his (and his employer's) contributions but on the politicians' ability to persuade the taxpayer to pay them.

The largest part of the system is the retirement pension; in 1961 it took nearly £800 million out of total payments of £1,200 million. Yet a new pensioner in 1961 with a wife five years younger had, since 1926, contributed (directly or through his employers) only a tenth of the capital fund required to yield the pension; the rest came from the taxpayer and was in essence no different from National Assistance, except that it was received by millions who did not need it. The total capital fund required to pay all benefits is now probably around £25,000 million (that is, more than a year's gross national income and almost as much as the National Debt) and there is no chance of creating it. The fund stands at a puny £1,100 million; only the new graduated pension contributions have saved even that amount from shrinking. National Insurance is a political pretence for which businessmen would have been howled down by present-day moralists.

National Insurance has been destroyed because the main pillar that was to support it was simply omitted. Beveridge had recommended that the retirement pension be built up over twenty years as contributions accumulated. The advice was brushed aside by the post-war Labour government which began to pay almost at once a pension much larger than could be justified by the contributions. Mr. Gaitskell subsequently tried to explain away this fatal flaw by claiming that twenty years was a long time to wait and that the general public would not have accepted this "discrimination against pensioners" because unemployment, sickness and other National Insurance benefits were being raised. But there is no parallel between funding pensions and other National Insurance benefits.

The old people were not being asked to wait twenty years for an increase in their income; those in need would have had the difference made up by taxation through National Assistance—a method which had the advantage of concentrating the increase on people who needed it most instead of dispersing it among retired dukes and dustmen alike. If it was endangering the structure of National Insurance to pay universal pensions before the accumulation of contributions, it was perilously near playing politics to pass the buck to "public opinion." Not least, if the objection, or pretext, was the National Assistance "stigma," it is at last being recognised to have been misunderstood.

The frustration of Beveridge's state pension policy illustrates a weakness neglected by social scientists. Social security places concentrated power in the hands of politicians who, able, upright or well-intentioned as some may be, cannot be expected to run it as intended by economists, sociologists, or actuaries, because they are fallible humans subjected to relentless pressures. Why were State pensions and National Assistance scales raised in 1951, 1955 and 1958 shortly before elections—and again now?

Beveridge advocated equal benefits in return for equal contributions (in each category of contributor). This principle was based on assessment of the amounts of money required to provide "subsistence" as suggested, *inter alia,* by the Ministry of Labour enquiry in 1937–8 into working-class household budgets. The minimum requirements of food, clothing and shelter necessary to sustain life vary by age, sex, occupation and region. A single standard of subsistence assessed by averaging will give some people more than their needs and others less, although some local variation and discretion are possible. Apart from differences for single and married and for working and retired people, Beveridge's principle of equal benefits was generally accepted and applied in 1948. Later some sociologists discovered a new reason for differentiation, especially in retirement: that needs varied with customary living standards so that pension benefits should vary with income. Hence Labour's *National Superannuation* in 1957 which promised graduated pensions in return for graduated contributions, and the Conservatives' reply with the graduated pension scheme of 1961; and hence the new arguments for graduated unemployment and other national benefits.

The argument for varying benefits with income is unconvincing. A man who earned £16 a week does not need more coal and calories to sustain him and his wife in retirement than one who earned £14. If he wants a higher standard of living in retirement he will save for it. If he prefers to spend his earnings while working he is free to do so. There is no clear case for forcing people to postpone income in order to ensure a living standard varying with their earnings from work.

There is no stronger case for graduating unemployment or sickness than pension benefits. The Labour Party argument for graduation cannot be based on the hardship of a small minority of families accompanying the small increase in unemployment. It is more difficult to insure privately against loss of income due to unemployment than to sickness or accident, which can be objectively defined and testified, although if it is desired to ensure income in unemployment additional to the National Insurance benefit it could be based on the criterion of unemployment used by the State. But people with higher incomes can by definition provide against unemployment by saving or borrowing against future earning. That a minority have not provided adequately for unemployment is no reason for requiring the rest of the population to provide more for basic requirements through the State. Nor is there now enough reason for raising the whole structure of National Insurance benefits for everybody and for all time because some have lost employment in industries facing declining markets. The right course is to offer additional income according to needs.

The use of social insurance benefits to counter unemployment is also misguided as long as the pretence of insurance continues. The proper method is through National Assistance.

The debate on equal graduated benefits is further confused by the larger sociological disputation on the nature of poverty and its relationship to equality. Poverty defined as insufficiency of income to provide the means of subsistence—Seebohm Rowntree's "primary poverty"—has all but vanished, and with improving education so could the "secondary poverty" caused by ignorance in spending otherwise adequate income. This is poverty in absolute terms.

Of course we may say that poverty is relative, and that a man who is well-fed, well-shod and well-housed may feel "poor" if many of his fellow-men are better-fed, better-shod or better-housed; but in these terms "poverty" is, by definition, universal and ineradicable except in a new Erewhon where incomes and wealth are equal. In this sense "poverty" has lost its implications of deprivation. Its meaning has been strained beyond common sense to what has been called the Theory of Perpetual Poverty. We must ignore such intellectual blind alleys and concentrate on removing poverty defined as inadequacy of income or knowledge of how to use it.

It is argued below that, as society becomes wealthier, we should be more generous to people with low incomes. The number who qualify for assistance would then rise. But it would be a curious use of language to describe this situation as an increase in "poverty." The sociologists have spoken of the submerged "fifth" (later reduced to "tenth"). Nearly two million people now draw National Assistance for themselves and some half a million dependents. These are the "submerged" twentieth. If we raise the assistance scales we might increase the number qualifying to, say, three million with perhaps three-quarters of a million dependents. These would be the new "submerged" fifteenth, but we should be supporting them at a level well above "poverty."

The real problem would be the damping effect on personal provision through saving. The higher the minimum standard of living regarded as tolerable, and the nearer it is to the average living standard, the less some people will be inclined to provide for themselves. This was Beveridge's objection to a means test. The risk must be run. But as incomes rise fewer will spend up to the hilt in their working lives in order to get more out of their neighbours in retirement. Recent history shows that although assistance scales have risen in real value people are saving more, and more people are saving.

Beveridge devised the earnings rule as a compromise between compulsory retirement as a condition for receiving the retirement pension and unconditional payment of the pension at sixty/sixty-five. It was an attempt to reconcile humanity, by permitting pensioners to earn up to a limit without penalty, with economy, by reducing the pension for pensioners who worked part time. Private pensions are paid at retirement but they have been earned by contributions. State pensions are not fully earned, and it is not easy to argue that they should be paid in full to pensioners who are willing and able to supplement them.

Beveridge hoped that in time National Insurance would make National Assistance and a means test unnecessary. He was defeated not least by inflation, and the number helped by National Assistance has grown from 0.85 million in 1948 to 1.94 million in October 1962. But it has been the political and philosophic objection to a means test that has made it difficult to give more generous help to people on National Assistance. For if increases in the pension benefit must be universal, millions of pounds must be paid to millions of people who do not need it (and have not paid for it). More generosity for the submerged requires a means test to ensure that it does not go to those who are not submerged.

Curiously, most of those who have had the opportunity to study the needy, such as Mrs. Dorothy Cole-Wedderburn and Messrs. Utting, Lynes and Townsend, have invariably tended to urge that social benefits must be universal, even though more than half of the retirement pensioners are not in need. The confusion of the problem of poverty with that of equality makes it more difficult to be generous to the submerged twentieth (or fifteenth), and others such as war pensioners. Professor R. M. Titmuss recently put the error on record:

> Many of us must . . . now admit that we put too much faith in the 1940s in the concept of universality as applied to social security. Mistakenly, it was linked with economic egalitarianism. Those who have benefited most are those who have needed it least.

The tragedy is that the obstacle has rested on political misjudgment and intellectual fallacy. Social scientists and politicians have long misunderstood the objection to the means test. It was not to the declaration of income, which is made by most citizens in the income tax return, but to the onus to initiate a claim and to withstand personal investigation by a public official. At long last there are signs of clearer thinking. Some Conservatives have been arguing that social assistance should be matched to needs. In September 1962 some Young Fabians told their elders that "it would be utterly naive" to suppose that State pensions could be raised to a level that would take most recipients off National Assistance; "there is really no other solution . . . [than] some kind of income test." More recently, in November, Labour's spokesmen on pensions indicated that, although it intends to raise the basic pension, it proposes to introduce an income coding in National Assistance—RAYN (receive as you need).

Beveridge was concerned to treat poverty by establishing a minimum level of National Insurance benefits. But he was sufficiently a liberal to argue that people should be able to provide more for themselves if they wished. The Beveridge report said:

> The state in organising security should not stifle incentive, opportunity, responsibility; in establishing a national minimum it should leave room and encouragement for voluntary action by each individual to provide more than that minimum for himself and his family.

In 1948 Beveridge wrote *Voluntary Action* to show how it might be done. But apart from accepting the principle of contracting out from the graduated State pension, which it would have been politically impossible to refuse, neither Conservative policy nor Labour proposals have shown much concern for voluntary action in social welfare. Beveridge's family allowances were designed to deal with a lingering deficiency in primary poverty. It must be supposed that the additional income is resulting in more being spent on children than would otherwise have been the case. Perhaps an attempt might be made to find out.

The National Health Service, the second of Beveridge's supporting "assumptions," is now being examined more dispassionately than in its early years. It was (and is still) credited with medical advance that would have come without it; its failures were explained away by reference to avoidable administrative shortcomings; its achievements were magnified by disparagement of the voluntary medical services before 1948. The sociological appraisal of the NHS by Professor Titmuss and Dr. Brian Abel-Smith largely ignored the economic criteria of cost and efficiency. The PEP report *Family Needs and Social Services* conveyed an impression of general public satisfaction but threw little light on performance. But in the last year or two the more critical examinations by Professor John and Mrs. Sylvia Jewkes, Dr. Dennis Lees and Dr. John Seale have indicated disturbing weaknesses. There has been little success in relating payment to value of service—the annual awards for "distinguished" general practice indicate a groping towards market pricing that recognises the inefficiency of the capitation system; preventive medicine has been neglected; British doctors have been replaced by others who are often inferior; no new hospitals have been built. General practitioners have also tended to become clerks and classifiers; and time is wasted on superficial maladies at the expense of the seriously sick.

Beveridge has claimed he was defeated *inter alia* by inflation. But inflation was in large part the outcome of State welfare and of the full employment he wanted to underpin it. No party comes well out of the post-war scene. Labour and Conservative politicians have used the welfare services to win votes; Liberal politicians have promised increases to all and sundry. And when it seemed difficult to raise revenue to pay for welfare by taxation, Labour hit on—and the Conservatives applied—the idea of graduated contributions as a source of income.

The link between full employment and inflation is no less evident. Between 1921 and 1938 unemployment among persons insured against it varied between 10 and 22 per cent, with an average of 14 per cent. The Beveridge Report assumed that unemployment would average about 8½ per cent. In 1944 he elaborated in *Full Employment in a Free Society* his argument that social security required "always more vacant jobs than unemployed men." But he thought it would not be possible to reduce unemployment below 3 per cent to cover change of jobs, seasonal slackness and fluctuations in international trade. Unemployment has never in any year since 1948 been as high as 3 per cent and both Labour and Conservatives see almost certain political death if they allow it to exceed 2 or 2½ per cent. In an economy that has had to make large-scale structural changes to rid itself of out-dated industries, absorb rapid technological innovation, and adapt itself to large changes in international markets, the efforts to maintain unemployment at or below 2 per cent were almost certain to produce inflation. In the anxiety to expand the social services indiscriminately there has been neglect of the need to adapt them to ease the changing employment required in a dynamic economy dependent on imported food and raw materials. The evil of chronic long-term unemployment is its moral corrosion. There is no moral corrosion in unemployment of even 4 per cent—a million—provided it is of men and women who are leaving decaying industries to join prosperous ones and who are well looked after in the process.

Beveridge was defeated by more than the politicians, inflation and the cult of equality. He is being defeated by the urge of the very people whom he wished to give security to make their own lives outside the State when rising incomes enable them to do so, even in spite of its power to compel them to pay for State services they reject.

The State offers "free" education, but the waiting list for nursery schools, prep. schools and public schools lengthen; half a million children are educated outside the State and the number grows steadily. The State offers a "free" health service but the number insured for private medical attention has increased from 100,000 in 1948 to 1½ million in 1962 and it continues to rise. Public authorities offer housing at subsidised rents but the number who own their homes had increased from 3.7 million in 1948 to probably 6¼ million in 1963 and is growing by about 200,000 a year. The State offers a pension graduated according to income "backed" by the taxpayer but 4½ million out of 10 million people are contracted out in occupational pension schemes "backed" by themselves and their employers.

These figures do not indicate the full extent of the public's preference for private welfare because it is not presented with a clear choice. The State gives tax encouragement to people who save by life insurance or pension schemes or who buy their homes. But it penalises those who buy education or health services privately; as recently as June 1962 a Conservative minister and Labour M.P.'s rejected arguments for tax allowances for school fees and private health insurance. It allows contracting out for graduated but not for the basic State pension.

And while it compels people to subscribe to its services, the suppliers of private services—schools, doctors, insurance offices, actuaries, private health insurance organisations, building societies—do not bring themselves vigorously to the notice of the public, often thinking it wrong to do so.

Many people do not exercise a choice, or are not even aware of its existence. How many *would* prefer private to State services if they had a free choice? To find the answer we must create either a free market in reality by allowing full contracting out (or get as near as possible to it by allowing tax refunds on the cost of private services) or a synthetic market by calculating the amounts that could be repaid to people who bought private services (or that would not be taken in taxation or social insurance contributions in the first place) so that potential buyers could indicate their choices.

As an approach to a full scale national survey the Institute of Economic Affairs recently commissioned a pilot survey based on a sample of four hundred in order to discover the probable orders of magnitude. The questions were cast in general terms and the findings are necessarily provisional. Between a quarter and a third would prefer private to public services. The fuller survey would be necessary to check and elaborate these proportions. But it seems almost certain that periodic surveys at three- or five-yearly intervals over the next few decades would show a growing preference for private services as incomes rose, the quality of services supplied by State monopolies was more critically appraised, and the advantages of a competitive choice in free markets were experienced by families in widening social and economic groups.

Beveridge could not foresee that with rising incomes and inflation social welfare would increasingly require the collection and dispersal of growing sums of money from and to the same people. In 1961, £4,250 million out of public expenditure of some £9,000 million went on welfare services and transfer payments. In 1954 private enterprise in the shape of Mr. Colin Clark showed that many people of even modest income were paying in taxes almost as much as they were receiving in benefits. We have had to wait seven years for the official survey of the Central Statistical Office into the impact in 1959 of taxes and social service benefits on households of given size and income. Although limited and qualified it suggests that the income of a wide range of households after tax and allowing for social service benefits was little different from their original income. It should be possible to effect a given degree of redistribution of income by a smaller weight of taxation and social service administration.

What remains of Beveridge in future welfare policy? Social insurance is no longer insurance as normally understood and practised; the benefits do not rest on the creation of a fund but on the taxpayers' willingness to provide them. Even in this sense social insurance has become a vast engine for raising taxation and paying it back. Universality is out of date; humanity and efficiency require discrimination.

The purposes of welfare policies should now be (a) more aid for the declining minority in need, (b) more freedom of choice for those who can be independent, (c) less party politics in social welfare.

What needs to be done?

- The primary requirement is more generous aid above subsistence level for the needy. In an affluent society such a level could add a degree of comfort without approaching average earnings or appreciably discouraging saving. This requires a new government service to seek out people in need and to end once and for all the dispute between the sociologists, who claim far more are in need than are helped by National Assistance, and the National Assistance Board which rejects the sociologists. In the meantime the broadcasting services should be required to advertise National Assistance.
- We should work towards fusion of National Insurance and National Assistance and their ultimate replacement by taxation as the source of sound benefits. Except where earned by contributions, "insurance" benefits and assistance payments should be merged and paid according to need.
- For this purpose, and to avoid the two central objections to a means test, we should use an automatic indicator of entitlement to assistance, a code based on a written statement of income. If this is what Labour now has in mind, we should welcome its abandonment of universal-

ism. And if the Conservatives are returned in the general election they should at long last adopt an idea that has lost its political risk by Labour's belated approval.

- The graduated State pension scheme should be wound up.
- The National Insurance Fund should be run down, and in the meantime invested to earn the highest return outside the nationalised transport, electricity and gas undertakings where it has lost heavily in capital value.
- Charges, beginning at a nominal rate and approaching the full cost, should be paid for State services by people who can pay as determined by the income codes. To RAYN we should add PAYC.
- The purpose of public services should be to provide *minimum* requirements, difficult as they are to define, not *optima,* which are politically and economically impossible. Minimum requirements are the same for all; there is no reason for graduating social benefits with previous income. But social assistance should be varied according to needs.
- Minimum standards in education, health services, etc., regarded as desirable should be laid down by the State, but people should have the choice of providing them privately.
- There is no way of taking welfare out of politics except by taking it as far as possible out of the State. The supply of private services by commercial firms, mutual non-profit-making organisations, friendly societies, trade unions, clubs, churches, and other voluntary and local organisations should be encouraged by a legal and institutional framework designed to ensure (a) *information,* until the private suppliers provide it themselves, (b) *standards,* enforced where necessary by frequent inspection, and (c) *competition,* which would in time make standards unnecessary.
- People should be permitted and encouraged to provide more than the minimum for themselves by tax allowances on school fees, health insurance premiums and savings to provide income in sickness and unemployment or by contracting out.
- Since the social unit is the family it should be strengthened and encouraged to provide for its needy members by larger allowance for dependents.
- To facilitate economic growth and help avoid the inflation that would corrode welfare payments, the manoeuvrability required in a dynamic economy should be eased by government-assisted mobility of labour.

- A Permanent Commission on the Social Services should advise on (a) the public services that can be run down as people indicate a preference for private services; (b) public services that should be expanded, for example, child care, or introduced.

Education, homes, health, income in unemployment and retirement . . . these are too important to leave to the electoral processes of party politics. (So, too, is defence, but defence must be provided collectively: many welfare services need not.) Socialist and liberal economists, sociologists and politicians may debate the case for and against expanding the public sector or returning it from the State to the market, but in a world in which rising incomes will make the 1960s and '70s a very different place from the 1920s and '30s, and in which the urge to independence and the demand for a choice will grow, welfare policy will be decided increasingly not by politicians, or by social scientists whose ideas they absorb, but by the people themselves. It looks like being concerned not with deciding *whether* to transfer much of welfare as we have known it from State provision to private choice in markets, but *how.*

CHAPTER 27

1963

Homes: Clear the Obstacles

> More people had the means to own their homes, but there was no free market. The obstacles were political rent restrictions, the anti-commercial mentality in the building societies, the sociological antagonism to private "landlords." * The political obstacle remains into the 1990s. Five million families live in government-owned homes.
>
> (*The Building Societies Gazette*, February 1963.)

Stripped of its verbiage and jargon, the central problem of housing the people is that there are millions who want better homes and can pay for them but who are being stopped from getting them.

The central reason is that there is no smoothly working market in which people who want homes and people who would supply them can get together easily, simply and cheaply. What stops the creation of a market? Four kinds of people, or ideas, can be identified as the culprits: political, anti-commercial, sociological and philosophic.

The market for rented homes was first damaged in 1915 wartime when rents were frozen at the August 1914 level. Since then, apart from partial thaws, the market for houses to let has remained largely frozen and paralysed. Every first-year student of economics knows that if you fix a price below the free market level you inflate demand and kill off supply. This, moreover, is the fundamental reason why millions of houses have turned into slums, neglected by owners and tenants alike: the four million decaying homes in Mr. Lewis Cohen's language, although surprisingly his pamphlet does not mention rent restriction in explaining the decay. And this is the reason for the unnecessary incursion of local councils in home building, a task for which they are not fitted.

The history of rent restriction shows once more the emptiness of the notion that politicians are dominated by concern for the public good. Homes have become a football of local politics and national politics, dominated by vote-catching, from local hanky-panky and fiddling to the Conservatives' 1959 General Election pledge to leave rents frozen for the duration of this Parliament, a pledge that will hardly be remembered as the second most unsordid act in history.

The first need in letting people who want homes get together with people who can supply them is to remove the politician who stands in their way. "Take homes out of Politics" should be the battle-cry.

The second obstacle is the anti-commercial complex. If people are to supply houses to buyers or tenants, they must expect to earn as much on their investment as they think they can earn elsewhere. Their investment must be *profitable.* Mr. Cohen's pamphlet points to the difficulties: "the ownership of tenanted properties [has been made] extremely unattractive to the vast majority of investors." He quotes from Mr. J. B. Cullingworth's article in the *Guardian* last year which reported that the typical landlord in Lancaster was an old-age pensioner (usually a widow) burdened with a house inherited from a father or husband, and adds that only 100,000 tenanted homes have been provided with modern amenities financed by improvement grants and that the 1961 increases in the additional rents allowed for houses improved with a grant will not be enough to induce owners to use the improvement grants because they are not "professional property investors concerned with efficient housing management and *maximising profits*" (my italics).

There you have it. Surprisingly, Mr. Cohen's pamphlet does not draw the logical conclusion. Instead of urging a free market in which it would again be possible to invest profitably in improvement to homes, he asks for subsidised mortgages from the taxpayer (including the old-age pensioners burdened by owning an unprofitable house).

But more than that building societies—including Mr. Cohen's—like to emphasise that they are non-profit-making institutions. And that is a large part of the problem. *If maximising profits is a good thing in building, selling or letting homes, it is no less of a good thing in financing them.* What induces building societies to be efficient? In a commercial enterprise you make a profit or go out of business. "Non-profit-making" is a high-sounding description that can not only indicate a lack of rapacity but also conceal complacency and lack of drive. In any event, the term "non-profit-making institution" itself begs the question. Do building societies set out to make losses?

No less than "profit-making" institutions they must cover their costs, which means make a profit, whatever you call it. It would make for clearer thinking all round if we cut out this verbal shadow-boxing.

But even more important, it would do the building societies good to get more competition from outside the "movement." There are pace-setters in mortgage interest rates not only among the more independent building societies but also among the insurance companies. On a long-run view the institutions that finance house ownership may have to offer lenders and investors among the higher rates in the market, and it will be profitable to do so: the demand for homes will continue high and new building could exceed 300,000 units a year, when the millions who can afford to buy homes realise, or are shown by advertising, that they can do so by changing their conservative habits, by spending less on (say) smoking, drinking and betting, and more on homes, health, education and pensions. But in the short run, and in particular areas, there is no reason why mortgage rates should not fall. The offer of house loans at 6 per cent by the London and Manchester Assurance Company (profit-making) is a welcome sign of vitality in the market for house loans.

The homes market needs the spur of profit. There is a vast hunger for houses. Mr. Cohen's pamphlet recognises it and wants to "harness the care and pride of home-ownership" to save old houses from decaying. But the number of families that live in houses they own has risen only from 3.7 million in 1948 (out of 13 million homes) to 6.4 million in 1960 (out of 16 million), or an average of only 200,000 a year. A vigorous house-financing industry could have done better than that. And if it had made profits in the process the new home owners would not have cared a tinker's cuss.

The third obstacle is that discussion on housing policy has been influenced far too much by sentiment and not enough by sense. This is largely the fault of sociologists who have covered acres of paper with arid description of poor homes and their miserable inhabitants and followed it with advice on policy based on failure to analyse or understand causes or, even worse, political prejudices in favour of State action. They have provided buckets of sympathy, but hardly a drop of understanding. They have looked at symptoms but ignored their origins.

One more obstacle remains to be removed: the notion that social assistance must be equal. This means that subsidies must be available to all council house tenants. And this means that less help is given to people who may need it most, such as slum dwellers.

Some Conservatives with their ear to the ground have already cottoned on to this confusion. The Political Council of the Junior Carlton Club has looked at its party's housing policy and found it wanting. Of its two proposals the first, for higher improvement grants, is, like that for subsidised State loans to building societies, a palliative that may patch the successive administrative expedients and make them tolerable for a little while longer. The second—which goes to the root of the problem, the reconstruction of the market—is that the housing subsidies should be related to need, so that more expenditure is devoted to slum clearance.

The details of the proposals—that the subsidy take the form of a Rent Assistance Fund administered by councils that run rebate schemes, or by the National Assistance Board—are less significant than the recognition by politicians that it is becoming politically possible ("practical politics") to confine the housing subsidies to people in need. Until recently Conservatives would not touch the idea with a barge-pole. Now it has reached down from a few liberal economists to practical politicians. It is encouraging to find Conservatives adjuring their ministers to show courage and determination in dealing realistically with a problem that is "bedeviling national and local finance and creating unjustified inequalities."

As in competition elsewhere, new ideas soon catch on. It is not clear which side came first, but there are significant hints at this new thinking among Labour as well as Conservative politicians. Sooner or later there was bound to be a halt to the process of distributing subsidies to all and sundry when more and more people did not need them and those who did saw that they were being sacrificed on the altar of the political dogma of equality. But it seems that the Labour politicians were waiting for their intellectuals to provide some reputable arguments.

At last they have appeared on the horizon. In discussing the future of National Assistance a group of Young Fabians has bluntly told its elder that "it would be utterly naive" to raise the basic pension for all pensioners and that assistance must be related to a test of means. Once this idea is accepted on the Left, it cannot stop at pensions but must extend to other forms of assistance out of taxation, including housing subsidies. And once it is accepted by one party it becomes "practical politics." It is this fundamental change in the purpose of the Welfare State—from a vast machine for shovelling out equal benefits to an instrument for helping people in need—that is ignored by those who make large assumptions about the necessity for State subsidies for housing in the next twenty years.

The political "wall" between the would-be home owner and the house supplier will crumble as incomes rise, the urge to home ownership spreads and the doctrine of equality collapses in increasing conflict with justice and humanity. The anti-commercial wall may stand up longer, but people who want houses and those who can supply them will find ways round it. The sociological and the egalitarian walls will disintegrate in the next ten years. Increasingly, a new market for homes in which demanders will freely meet suppliers will be created.

How? This is where public authority comes in, not to replace the market but to provide the legal and administrative framework for it.

First, it will provide the broad physical framework of town planning.

Second, it will set minimum standards until competition among suppliers and knowledge among buyers make them unnecessary.

Third, it will supply money to people with low incomes—the aged, incapacitated, with large families, and others. Thus we can create a market for homes that will work efficiently, that will clear the slums much more quickly than now seems likely, that will offer the widest possible choice of homes to the people and honest incentives to builders and lenders to provide them, that will remove the immorality of mixing housing with politics, and that will humanely give most help to those who need it most.

CHAPTER **28**

1964

Wanted—Home Entrepreneurs

> The building societies were advised to move with the times by modernising their image from a non-profit trustee "movement" to profitable commercial businesses with efficient financing methods and marketing. *
> This change took almost twenty years until the 1980s as the freedom of competition attracted insurance offices and banks into the open market.
>
> (*The Building Societies Gazette*, August 1964.)

In the spread of home ownership from nearly seven million to perhaps ten or twelve million in the next ten years, the building societies can play a leading part. But to do so they will have to change their methods and attitudes.

First, they should replace the high-minded, starchy, patronising image of a "social service" by the image of a business run by fallible men who are trying to do a good job not because they love their investors or mortgagors but because borrowing and lending are profitable. I really don't know what good is done by trying to wear a halo, talking down to the man in the street as if he were being done a favour, and generally regarding him as a bit of a simpleton, as much building society publicity seems to do.

As a former borrower, I am prepared to accept that the people who run the building societies are moved by a spirit of public service and a sense of mission to help people to own their homes. But a desire to serve the public, like patriotism, is not enough; and paradoxically it is not necessary. I am not much comforted to know that the directors and executives *want* to serve me unless they demonstrate also that they *can* serve me. And even if the existing men *do* serve me well, how can I be sure that their successors will also be men of public spirit?

But why should I be concerned about their *motives?* I don't ask my butcher or my hairdresser whether he wants to serve me. I judge him by *results.* If his service is better than I get elsewhere, I will go back to him. If not, I will go elsewhere.

Why do the building societies work so hard to create the image of "social service"? Do they really want to get themselves associated in the public mind with, say, the nationalised railways or post office or municipal buses, often more accurately described as surly services? What is wrong with claiming the patronage of the public because of honest-to-goodness value for money?

To say that the aim of the building societies is to be of service to the public is in economic principle a truism or a fallacy. They offer a service no more and no less than commercial enterprises, since if they did not sell something that people were prepared to pay for they would have to shut up shop. Unless they are in a perpetual sellers' market and have a monopoly, they "need" their borrowers no less than the borrowers need them. And their borrowers are doing them just as much a "service" in borrowing as the building societies do their borrowers in lending.

Second, but how can we as mortgagors feel that the service of the building societies is good? Because of competition with other lenders of money for house purchase. Much more comforting to me than the feeling that the men who run building societies are upright, public-spirited, "do-gooders" is the knowledge that they must strive to give me good service because if they do not I shall go to an insurance company, a bank, or my local council.

Mr. S. W. G. Morton may be right in saying in his recent address to the International School that "the logical aim" of the building society movement must be "to secure a monopoly in home-ownership finance," but only in the sense that every man, firm or method seeks to excel and to better other men, firms or methods. It would be a sad day for the building societies if they ever achieved the monopoly. For if history is any guide they would then become unspeakably pompous, sadly sanctimonious—and intolerably inefficient.

Of course, competition within the building society movement would remain. But the removal of competition from outside would strengthen the centrifugal pressures and make the movement even more centrally inspired than it is now. Instead of "recommending" interest rates it would "indicate" and then fix them. And there would be no Halifax or scores of little societies to go their own way to suit individual policies and local conditions. It would be too much like a nationalised industry or a medieval corporation.

Third, why this anxiety to escape from the commercial competitive image? Don't the building societies pay competitive market rates for the capital they borrow, the offices they buy or rent, the stationery, typewriters, electric light, furniture they buy, the labour they hire? Then they can't afford to give away anything for nothing. They can't subsidise anybody. They can't afford charity. And they can't afford inefficiency. They must therefore act commercially. It follows either that the building societies do not offer a "social service" or that a "social service" is not incompatible with commercial conduct.

As it is the building societies present the impression of a monolithic movement, which cannot be good for its public "image" in these days of suspicion of monopoly. Mr. Andrew Breach speaks of "the requirements of the movement as a whole." But I cannot see why one rate of interest should suit 375 building societies, small and large, local and national, centralised and decentralised, any more than one price should suit several hundred insurance companies, local authorities or builders. It could be regarded as, in some respects, an agreement to restrict competition. And it is a strait-jacket that unnecessarily strains the cohesion of the movement in which co-operation in matters other than the price of money could be fruitful.

In any event, growth as measured by assets is not necessarily a better incentive or indicator of efficiency than the capacity to avoid losses and earn the surplus over costs that we call profits. Commercial enterprise has demonstrated that increasing size does not necessarily bring increased efficiency or better service to the public. As Mr. Morton shrewdly observes, a growth in assets may satisfy personal ambition. I would add only that growth may also remove the check to inflating costs that is exerted by competition.

Fourth, high-mindedness prevents the building societies from coming down to earth and talking to the common man in the language he understands. It is fashionable for literary and political critics to deride commerce and all that; but at least firms that sell consumer goods take pains to find out what the consumer wants. They have learned the common touch. The building society is still aloof and superior.

Fifth, for all the soothing invitations to "come and talk over your personal position with the manager of your local branch," how much *personal* service does the movement give? I don't have in mind merely the impersonal treatment that the intending borrower receives from junior staff in the branches of the larger societies. (In this respect the smaller societies are usually much better: for fifteen years I was a mortgagor with a small society and throughout I knew I could telephone and talk to the secretary.)

I mean rather the use of impersonal and therefore *inhuman* general rules such as the mischievous one that a borrower shall not repay more than a quarter of his earnings. This rule could make sense only if all men distributed their income in much the same way—if they smoked, drank, gambled, motored, etc., etc., the same proportion of their income. For if not—*and they do not*—why should there be any rule for the proportion they should spend on their homes? Why should the non-drinker, or non-smoker, or non-motorist not spend *more* than the others? *Any* rule is bound to exclude some men from home ownership who should be welcomed, and include others who should be excluded. And since the proportion will tend to be put conservatively on the low side to minimise the bad risks, it follows that many people are being unnecessarily stopped from buying their homes.

When I argued two years ago in the *Statist* that as incomes rose people might want to spend a higher proportion of it on housing and that we should not object if the proportion rose from a quarter to a third, Mr. George Brown commented in the House of Commons (2 May 1962):

> If we start encouraging people to spend that percentage [33⅓] of their income on rents they will be in arrears with their rents and mortgages very soon.

To talk like this is to think of the working man as though he still wore a cloth cap and muffler and still needed shepherding. And the building societies also still have much the same paternalistic "We know what is good for you. We'll look after you" attitude. Yet these men and their families increasingly wear good clothes, eat well, own cars, spend a lot on smoking and drinking, go abroad for their holidays and are accumulating savings and investments in the post office and in industry through life assurance and pension schemes.

The only way in which many still live as they or their fathers did between the wars is in shabby housing. And that is largely because rent restriction, perpetuated by party politics, has discouraged the entry into house-building of labour and capital that by now could have raised the annual production well beyond 300,000 or 350,000 to 500,000 or even 750,000. The only part of the housing sector in which the ordinary man is enjoying as high a standard as he does in food, clothing, furniture, etc., is where there is a free market—in house purchase.

State provision of housing through local authorities raises housing standards at first but after a few years council housing becomes neglected and shabby, tolerated but unloved by their occupants. And it will not be before the market for housing is freed from politics that the remainder of the slums will be abandoned. But it is a tragedy to frustrate the man who is able and willing to spend more on a better home.

Sixth, the professional, "non-profit-making," non-commercial atmosphere of the building societies is preventing them from recognising themselves for what they are: money-lenders who try to earn an honest living borrowing money at one rate of interest and lending it at a higher rate. They should be not afraid to say as much and act as such. They should make their "shop fronts" less forbidding and more inviting. They should let their hair down in their advertising. They should cut out the pompous language in their public pronouncements and use plain English. After all, it is a reflection on the whole "movement" ("movement"? why not "business"?) for the Co-operative Permanent to tell the people in large letters that they are a FRIENDLY building society. Aren't the others? Then it is high time they were.

And it's time the building societies made much more use of the methods of advertising, marketing and selling that commercial undertakings have pioneered and used successfully to attract attention to new foods, clothes, labour-saving devices and amenities of all kinds that have made life immeasurably pleasanter for people of middling and lower incomes. Sometimes they have offended against standards of taste and manners. There is no danger the building societies will do that. But the opposite excess of reticence and timidity can be even more prejudicial to the welfare of the common man. They must begin to think about adapting the techniques of modern marketing—market research, motivational research, test marketing, direct mail, personal selling, television. There is a long way to go.

Seventh, high-mindedness is no excuse for high-handedness or the appearance of high-handedness. The intending mortgagor is not told why he will not be allowed to see the survey for which *he* pays. Among the whole series of bills he has to foot is that of the *building society's* solicitor. The interest on his debt is usually calculated on the outstanding balance at the beginning of each *year.* If he wants enterprising design or unusual materials he will be frowned on and turned away, even if he is able and willing to pay for it. (The risks of wood are irrelevant; what is fire insurance for?) His personal prospects of higher earnings in later life are rarely allowed for by adjusting the repayments through the mortgage years.

All these are failures to consider the individual mortgagor's feelings or circumstances. They are evidence of the lack of competition among building societies. And they are symptoms of the follow-my-leader mentality in which only a few societies or men dare to be non-conformist and pioneer new ideas and methods.

Eighth, the building societies are using money lent to them for house purchase to invest in government securities or local authority mortgages. This seems a bold assertion: it is based on two premises—first, the law requires liquid reserves of only 7½ per cent of assets; second, bad debts are less than $1/20$ per cent. I do not see how this can justify holding 12½ to 15 per cent in cash or investments with public authorities—not all of which in any case are highly liquid so that they can be encashed to meet a demand for withdrawals.

I can see more reason in market fluctuations for holding 5 per cent in free reserves when the law required only 2½ per cent. *The Services of a Building Society,* which I take to reflect the view of the Building Societies Association, says "Admittedly, the possibility of loss is remote, because of the careful way in which the societies judge the risks of lending money to a particular person on a particular house, but the fact has to be faced that the unexpected may occur."

But this is not how the economy is conducted. If we all immobilised reserves necessary to cover every possibility, the economy would grind to a halt. The real test is whether the societies would lock up as much as this if there were more competition for shares and deposits so that they had to earn higher yields or charge more for mortgages in order to outbid competing institutions.

Now that the 1963 Trustee Investments Act has extended trustee status to some industrial investments it is silly to limit building societies' investments to public authorities. When I suggested in the *Gazette* (September 1962) that it is unjustifiable to hold 15 per cent of the assets in liquid form, there was sceptical eyebrow raising. Mr. Lewis Cohen has several times made a related proposal. In the meantime perhaps several hundred million pounds are being denied to would-be home owners.

Ninth, for its status as a non-profit-making organisation, the building society has to suffer the indignity of special control by legislation and detailed control by the Chief Registrar of Friendly Societies. What a paradox that is! The building society wants itself thought of presumably as something better than an ordinary commercial undertaking yet the law lays down the proportion of special advances, the Registrar is empowered to control the contents of advertisements and even to prohibit advertising *in toto,* etc., etc.

I know no other industry that is treated like a nest of potential thugs—not even the detergent industry which is reviled and derided by the critics of commerce.

The power of the Registrar to stop the flow of savings to a building society is likewise incompatible with an organisation that must inspire public confidence to the point at which it can represent itself as a social service concerned only with the public good.

Tenth, the status of trustee is bought at too high a price. The 7½ per cent liquidity ratio, the 2½ per cent reserve ratio, the 10 per cent special deposit limit and the £7,000 limit to personal loans inhibit the ability of the building societies to compete with other lenders and reduce the earnings on the investment of liquid reserves. If more savings were attracted by better publicity and more energetic salesmanship the savings-attraction of trustee status could be dispensed with. Other financial institutions do not need trustee status to attract savings: they do it by building up public confidence, offering higher yields or the prospect of capital appreciation. If the building societies do not offer these advantages, others will.

And this indeed, is the essence of the argument. If the building societies want to continue to provide the mass of the finance for house purchase the methods they use will not be theirs to choose. The choice will be determined by the consumer, by competition, by the market. The building societies have no legal monopoly: their business is not protected by law from competition. If other methods suit the would-be house purchaser better because they are more flexible, more informal, more persuasive, he will use them. It does no service to the building societies to suggest that the methods that suited them in the past will necessarily serve them and the community best in the future.

Building societies should:

1. replace the image of "social service" with that of *efficiency;*
2. replace the urge to monopoly with the readiness to meet competition;
3. stop banging the "non-profit-making" drum;
4. acquire the common touch in their relations with borrowers—and investors;
5. emphasise *personal* service—and in particular abandon the 25 per cent rule;
6. use modern marketing methods to arouse the interest of millions of tenants in house ownership;
7. root out all forms of high-handedness;
8. increase to a maximum the money lent to house owners;
9. agitate for more freedom of manoeuvre under the law;
10. exchange trustee status for more effective means of attracting savings.

PART IV

Wither the Welfare State

B: The Mounting Attack, 1965–1970

CHAPTER **29**

1965

Shop with Welfare Vouchers

> The argument had made enough headway for a mass circulation newspaper which sensed that embourgeoisement would provoke impatience with the patronising State. Vouchers with choice would replace "free" State, tax-paid services without choice. "Massive effort" should be made by private competing suppliers "to persuade us to spend more on schools, hospitals, homes, pensions." The suppliers were then not always entrepreneurs but professionals. * In the 1990s Norwich Union in health insurance and Marks and Spencer in pensions are galvanising the market; but a long way to go.
>
> (*The Sun*, May 1965.)

Isn't it time we stopped thinking of the social services—schools, health, pensions—as something that should necessarily be provided by the State, through taxes and yet more taxes?

Millions of people in Britain have never had much choice of a home to live in, a school for their children, a doctor or a method of saving for retirement. Most of us must take what the State provides.

These services are not free. We pay, through taxes, for almost all the education and health services, and for a large part of pensions and housing. The country spends about £5,500 million a year on State welfare.

Yet we still lack smaller classes, more teachers, better school equipment. We need less-crowded surgeries and hospitals, more *personal* service from doctors and nurses. We need faster demolition of slums and a comfortable home for everyone. And larger pensions tailored to *individual* needs.

We could have all these in ten, perhaps even in five, years. But not if we wait for overworked politicians and public officials. We must adopt new attitudes, use new methods, enlist new men.

If a government manages to squeeze another £100 million or £200 million for welfare out of a tight budget of £10,000 million, they feel pleased with themselves. But to do all we want would take ten times as much—more like £2,000 million.

We shall never pay enough taxes to do it. Few individuals will work harder to pay more taxes for anything. Even now we grumble about paying too much, and most of us avoid taxes where we can.

Whatever new taxes are devised, on companies, capital gains or anything else, no government will find it easy to take much more than 40–45 per cent of all incomes.

Some people say: slash defence costs. Well, I remember walking in a student procession behind a banner which proclaimed: "Scholarships, Not Battleships." That was before the war. Twenty years after VE Day we are still spending £2,000 million a year on defence.

Maybe the costs will come down—some time. But must our children, slum-dwellers and aged go on waiting for disarmament?

If higher taxes are self-defeating, and we cannot wait for ever on defence economies, the alternative is to give us, as individuals, the chance to go shopping for welfare—just as we can go shopping for food, clothing, furniture, holidays.

There is no shortage of these consumer services. And if, by their individual efforts and without waiting for everyone else to pay higher taxes, parents could choose to give their children a better start in smaller classes, if they could live in more pleasant homes, have more personal attention when sick, and more ease in retirement, many would work harder to get these benefits.

Then, I predict, the shortages would melt. The trouble now is that far too few of us have the choice.

But who will show us what we *could* get? We shall never know until men of enterprise offer us a choice in welfare as we now have in ordinary consumer goods.

There is plenty of competition for our custom in the shops.

Why not in welfare?

Of course, you can already pay fees (or insure) for a private school, doctor or dentist, or a pension. But you have to pay twice. You have to pay for the State service whether you want it or not.

This is all very well for the relatively few wealthy, but not for the millions who *cannot* pay.

The State should therefore refund the relevant taxes if we prefer to buy private services.

Or, better still, since many pay little or no income tax, the State should give everybody welfare vouchers (rather like luncheon vouchers) so that we can all buy the State or private service of our choice.

We should then find far more private suppliers of welfare offering their services in the market.

We must in such ways harness the inventiveness and energy, the prospect of personal profit and the discipline of loss that put life into other parts of the economy.

We should encourage those who have good ideas for improving welfare; and we should not mind rewarding them generously.

Let us channel scientific inventiveness and commercial drive into welfare. Who knows what new or better schools they could produce? Or hospitals and methods of treatment? Or ways of paying for housing? Or pensions that go on growing up to and *after* retirement?

We shall never know until these things can reach us in a free market.

There are already some enterprising suppliers, but not enough of them. Many building societies are slow to lend money on houses in new designs or built with new materials (wood or stone); and slow to lend to people with small incomes.

Life assurance firms have good ideas on pensions, but are slow to get them going.

The health insurance organisations are timid or lack the common touch.

Enterprising private educationists could set the pace more briskly than most education authorities.

There is not enough vigorous competition between private suppliers, or between them and the State.

To get things moving, three things are needed:

- We must accept that if we want more welfare we must spend much more on it *voluntarily.*
- There must be a massive effort by the suppliers, in the press, on television, on posters, to persuade us to spend more on schools, hospitals, homes and pensions.

And let them use the skills of the advertising man—without the inanities he puts into selling soap, soup and cereals.

- We must remove the commercial stigma from welfare. Many people in all parties have got into the habit of thinking that education should

> be "free," that health services should not be "sold for profit," housing should be "a public service," and pensions run by the State because commerce and industry have not provided pensions for everyone.

Instead, we should be glad if anyone earns a profit so long as he provides a better welfare service that benefits the whole community.

CHAPTER 30

1965

A Free Market—or Political Mortgages

> The building societies were beginning to see they must compete for new consumers in housing or accept continuing political supervision. They had been changing mortgage interest to ingratiate themselves with government. They were not advertising effectively. Their future lay with the market. * The late 1980s and early 1990s saw the dawning truth. They could now do still more by campaigning for reduced legal/surveying costs and faster documentation.
>
> (*The Building Societies Gazette,* June 1965.)

In the last few weeks the building societies have stared truth squarely in the face: the truth that they are borrowers in a competitive capital market who cannot or will not use competitive interest rates. Their dilemma now is that they must either abandon their non-commercial pretensions and recognise that they must play the market or weaken public confidence in them as the main providers of finance for house purchase, risk losing their independence from political influence and endanger their whole future as substantial financial institutions.

The reluctance to follow the movements in interest rates closely turns on four reasons, one plausible, the second debateable, the third fallacious, the fourth dangerous. The first is the general desire to avoid the administrative and accounting costs of frequent revisions of interest rates. But these economies must be balanced against the losses of revenue on the capital withdrawn by investors who are not philanthropists, to whom the building societies' posture of "non-profit-making" public service means nothing and who, not unnaturally, put their families before the building societies and invest their savings where it can earn most.

If, in the past, the building societies have not lost investors despite higher interest rates elsewhere, they may have to reckon with more sophisticated investors in the future. The taxation of short-term capital gains, extended from Mr. Selwyn Lloyd's six months to Mr. Callaghan's twelve months, will make the market less flexible by discouraging short-term switching. Nevertheless if other investment institutions can change their interest rates frequently with changes in the conditions of supply of savings, the building societies cannot remain austerely aloof. If other savings institutions can use computers, so must the building societies. There are more competitors for savings than there have been in the past. And they may all have to contend with a world in which Bank rate, in accordance with the recommendation of the Radcliffe Committee, is changed more frequently than in the 1950s.

The second reason is that it was thought that Bank rate would not remain at 7 per cent for long. No one can be sure, but there seems to have been here more than a dash of wishful thinking. Whatever one's political opinions, it is difficult to suppose that the intention to tax profits and enterprise more heavily, to continue restrictions on rents, to nationalise steel, the apparent hostility to industry, and the emphasis on redistributing wealth rather than increasing it will increase confidence in other countries that the pound sterling is a strong currency. And if they think otherwise, Bank rate will not come down soon.

The third reason is the desire to avoid "penalising" or "burdening" existing mortgagors who came in at a lower rate of interest. "Why should existing borrowers pay more because we have to pay higher interest rates on new money to lend to new borrowers?" is the rhetorical question asked by some building society men. It sounds humane and plausible; it is muddled and superficial.

If building society share or deposit rates change less frequently than Bank rate, then over a long period—the ten or twelve years of most mortgages—the mortgagor will not pay more. It is only because we have lived through twelve years of generally rising interest rates to reflect the growing demand for money and capital that borrowers seem to be burdened with gradually rising rates; but without rising rates there would be less money for mortgages.

The choice is between cheaper and more mortgage money. Any building society administrator who feels for his existing borrowers should ask himself "Why should new borrowers suffer by having no mortgages at all because existing mortgagors who have been favoured with out-dated low rates refuse to pay a little more?"

And it is only a *little* more. Why has this not been made known to the general public? Why has there been no real information in pounds, shillings and pence in the advertising by the Building Societies Association or by individual societies? A rise in interest rates from 6½ to 6¾ per cent would require an increase in repayments per year of 3*s.* 6*d.* for each £100 over twenty years. A £2,000 borrower would have to pay about 6*s.* more per month (or extend the repayment period). If the rate had been raised to 7 per cent—enough to slow down or stop the outflow of investments—the borrower would have had to pay 12*s.* 6*d.* more a month or about 10*s.* after tax. Is it really argued that 2*s.* 6*d.* a week would have crippled households that spend ten or twenty times as much a week on smoking or drinking or other consumption goods—especially since, in any case, they don't have to pay it at all?

The fourth reason for failing to offer competitive market rates of interest is the wish to avoid criticism from the press or the politicians. No less than businessmen who work openly for profit and are not ashamed to say so, building society administrators do not like newspaper criticism. But if it is founded on error—for example, the notion that building society costs are too high and that a reduction would release large funds for mortgages—it is the societies' fault for letting journalists misrepresent them. They should do something about it—employ people who will explain building society policy, not explain it away. They should certainly not let their sins of omission be witnessed on the young couples who want a mortgage and would be prepared to pay a few more shillings a week to get it.

But more than this lies behind the self-paralysis of the building societies in recent times—long before the Labour Party came into office in October 1964. It would appear to have been the wish to avoid offending politicians, or the desire to placate them. This is a dangerous game for the building societies. Politicians of any party who are offended or frustrated have power to do harm: the Building Societies Acts could be made more restrictive; or other difficulties might have been created. But other institutions have tried appeasement and have burned themselves badly.

Playing politics may be expedient if it is played from strength; it is sheer folly if it depends on the good will of politicians. They may make promises in good faith; but they can invariably plead a change in circumstances to justify breaking them, they cannot bind their successors and they are not immortal.

The *impasse* is now of the building societies' own making. They kept interest rates down to please the Government; now the Government can say with some logic and justice: "You are failing to provide the people with house mortgages; we must now do what you have failed to do; we must give the local authorities funds to lend to would-be house purchasers." And what is the building societies' reply? Nothing. They have gambled on political patronage and lost.

None of the expedients and palliatives which they have produced goes to the heart of the problem. The proposal of Mr. C. J. Dunham of the Co-operative Building Society to raise the limit for individual investments beyond £5,000 is sensible and might draw in more money; but it is hardly fundamental. In any event a man with £20,000 can invest it in four building societies.

Access to the banks for funds, as suggested by Mr. Roy Matthews and Sir Herbert Butcher, of Abbey National, might help but only as temporary first-aid: British banks are still essentially providers of working capital for industry.

Lord Cohen has proposed that the government should make funds available to the building societies for lending on house mortgages. There is a case for government funds to be used as building society mortgages for people who cannot repay mortgages, as in the 1959 House Purchase and Housing Act. *But it is very damaging to ask for government funds to replace savings that the building societies have failed to attract in the normal course of their business. Why should the government lender or the taxpayer provide funds which the building societies cannot or will not attract by using the machinery of the capital market?*

If it is considered necessary to use the proceeds of government borrowing or taxation to finance house purchase, why should the building societies who are not doing their job be chosen as the vehicle? *And if they are provided with public funds why should they remain free from direct political control?* As a taxpayer I should expect Parliament to keep a close watch on anyone to whom it lent my money. If the building societies want to stay "out of politics" they must refuse public money; if they accept it they must expect sooner or later to become instruments of the government and party politicians.

The proposal of Mr. Roy Matthews for Housing Certificates to be issued by the government to building societies to offset the funds they hold with local authorities as part of their liquid funds is no better. It reflects the excessive liquidity that most building societies indulge in because the pressure to use their funds most profitably in house mortgages is not strong enough.

I do not for a moment accept the view of Mr. Ian Maclean of the Halifax that "a satisfactory margin above the minimum [required for trustee status] is essential if the confidence of the public is to be maintained." How much is "satisfactory"? The margin varies in different building societies. Is it argued that investors invest more where the margin is higher?—or that they have any idea what the margin is at any moment of time? If money is locked up in local authorities the solution is to unlock it. It is not the business of building societies to act as investment trusts for local government.

The proposal of Professor A. J. Merrett and Mr. Allen Sykes that the full income tax rebate on the standard rate of tax be allowed to all mortgagors whatever their marginal rate of tax is a sensible extension of the rebate to people with lower incomes. It seems to have attracted the notice of a prominent Conservative politician. Yet in a sense it parades under false colours, since tax cannot be rebated to people who have not paid it in the first place.

A more straightforward way to assist wage-earners and lower-salary earners would be to issue a housing "voucher" to be used, on the principle of a luncheon voucher, for repaying a mortgage. The voucher could be the same amount for every house purchaser; or, to encourage people to spend more on housing, it could be a proportion of the purchase price, with an upper limit.

Unfortunately, Professor Merrett and Mr. Sykes, like Mr. Lionel Needleman, have uncritically accepted the gratuitous assumption that house purchasers should not spend more than 25 per cent of their income on housing. Since household expenditure budgets vary widely between and within income groups, such an arbitrary, standard ratio has little substance or reality. Unfortunately it is used to bolster the argument that many millions will never be able to afford the housing they "need" and that therefore housing subsidies must continue till kingdom come. When we are anticipating a doubling of private incomes in twenty years, such a proposition seems incredible.

There is no lasting alternative to variations in the interest rates on shares and deposits to raise money from investors for house mortgages. The markets for money and capital are highly competitive and have become more so in recent years. It may be that some building society administrators find this adjustment of interest rates too competitive, and commercial pressures in general uncongenial. Their susceptibilities should be respected, but the consequences cannot be ignored.

It is futile for the building societies to claim that they are borrowing and lending more than ever before. In a generally expanding economy, it would be surprising if they were not. What matters is whether they are borrowing and lending enough to remain economically prosperous and politically invulnerable. In recent months most of them, with significant exceptions, have failed to do this. Basically the reason is that they have had an exaggerated respect for politicians and have failed to see that their ultimate strength—political as well as economic—is in the house owner. If the number of home owners were not seven million but twelve million, no political party would dare do anything to cripple them.

But they have forgotten the Psalmist's injunction ". . . put not your trust in princes." Let them not reflect the awe in which many stand of politicians to whom we surrender more than two-fifths of our income and stand mutely by while they spend it in ways we should not approve in our homes, our places of work, our clubs, our churches.

It is time the building societies put their trust in the people they claim to serve.

CHAPTER 31

1965

Privatise Welfare

A New Strategy

> The argument was extended in the "quality" newspapers: a sustained argument for using the profit motive in social policy. People would work to earn and spend more on better-than-State welfare if they could see a connection between their payment by prices and the services they received: the argument later accepted by Labour ministers Houghton and Crossman. Lloyd George's strategy was to see the goal and not the obstacles. A new such leader was required to undo the legacy of Lloyd George. * 1994: the new leadership is awaited.
>
> (*The Times*, July 1965.)

A new approach to social policy is overdue. So far we have relied on the State and the machinery of politics to provide the mass of the people with education, health services, pensions and (for several million) housing. Social and economic advance makes it possible to accelerate the pace at which we give the needy more help, allow the relatively affluent more choice, and enlarge the resources employed in welfare as a whole. To do so we must reinforce the political process by the profit motive and galvanise both by persistent pressure from the populace.

Public policy on social welfare in Britain should long have been passing from preoccupation with the 5 or 10 per cent relatively needy or irresponsible to the desires of the 90 or 95 per cent who are neither. But political conservatism in all parties and administrative inertia have tended to apply to both groups the same principles of equal State benefits paid for by compulsory insurance or taxation.

Politicians are usually and necessarily slow to change their minds. After years of opposition to a means test Labour proposes to use it in its minimum income guarantee. Conservatives have thought on comparable lines. Experience has emboldened both parties. The partial removal of rent controls did not bring the Conservatives electoral catastrophe in 1957; nor do early reactions suggest that a means test would bring Labour down in 1966. But both parties still move warily. Conservative and Labour M.P.'s opposed, as a source of privilege to the wealthy, an amendment to a recent Finance Bill to give tax rebates on school fees up to £75 a year and private health insurance premiums up to £15. Rebates of income tax would by definition be confined largely to people with middling and higher incomes.

To reach the lower-salaried and wage-paid man who pays his taxes indirectly on his beer, wine, tobacco, motoring or other purchases we should have to give him a voucher to pay for the welfare services of his choice.

It is difficult to think of any simpler yet more powerful method of giving the man of middling or lower income a choice in welfare now open only to the man of means who can both pay his taxes and find the fees for private education, health and other services. And nothing less than pressure from millions of customers able to go elsewhere if dissatisfied would galvanise the suppliers—State or private—into life.

A wider choice by tax rebates or vouchers would enlarge the resources of manpower and capital invested in education, health services, housing and pensions. As long as welfare services are financed largely by taxes and social "insurance" it will not be easy for a government of any party to spend much more on them in the next few years.

The essential requirement is a massive but voluntary increase in purchasing power spent on welfare. The £200 million or so that politicians can find in a year in a tight budget is a tithe of the amount required—much more like £2,000 million. Only industry and commerce, using the methods of persuasion with which it sells consumer goods and services, could do it. The entrepreneurs who have transformed the lives of ordinary people since the war—in their homes, their diets, their clothes, their amusements, their holidays—could do the same in education, health, housing and pensions.

It has been said that businessmen and advertising men have been insensitive, alienated the finer tastes of the cultured, overworked the repetitive reminders of the "adman" and the vulgar methods of the market place. They might similarly go to excess in producing and selling welfare. But they would get the results that elude the politicians. They have abolished "shortages" in consumer goods; they could abolish "shortages" in welfare.

Crowded classrooms, overworked teachers, poor equipment; sweated and underpaid doctors and nurses; overcrowding in slums, under-occupation of homes; mean, standardised, politically precarious pensions: these inadequacies could melt if we used the profit motive and the consumer orientation of competitive industry. We could reach Newsom's, Crowther's and Robbins's target in half the time, build hospitals as rapidly as houses, double the output of homes to 750,000 a year, raise pensions much faster than if we depend on the political process.

We should also put more resources into welfare if we paid for individual services by fees or insurance than if we continued to buy standardised services from the State and paid for them by taxation. Few people will work harder to pay more taxes. The common reaction is rather resistance. Taxation is not regarded as payment for benefits; it is a loss, a deduction from pay, an imposition tolerated grudgingly where unavoidable, but avoided where it can be.

It may be possible to raise taxes on compassionate grounds to give more to pensioners; but whatever new taxes on companies or capital are devised, no government will find it easy to take in total much more than 40 to 45 per cent of national income except in wartime or with severe penalties unacceptable in Britain in peacetime.

The attitude of millions of salaried and wage-paid people could be very different if better education, improved health services, more comfortable homes, larger pensions were freely available for purchase by individuals in the open market. The prospect of giving children a better start in life, the family earlier and more personal attention in sickness, living in a home that could express individual tastes and idiosyncrasies, and accumulating a retirement income that brought peace of mind and a sense of financial independence—these opportunities could spur many people to more effort. Welfare expenditure as a percentage of national income could rise substantially and quickly without fuss, without inflation, without enmeshing welfare in party politics, national finances or balance of payments crises.

The requirements for the new approach are four. First, a strong injection of commercial drive—and the prospect of profit. Private welfare services are run by two kinds of people—the professional and the commercial. The professionals—teachers, doctors, building society administrators, actuaries—provide the technical expertise but they are normally not entrepreneurs by nature, temperament or training, and they are inhibited in selling and advertising. It is from the more commercially minded that initiative and enterprise chiefly originate.

Second, we must abandon the anti-commercial mentality which decrees that education shall be "free," health services shall not be "run for profit," housing shall be "a social service," and pensions the domain of the State.

Third, welfare needs to be advertised no less than consumption, or rather much more, because consumption has had a long start and the potential customer is largely unaccustomed to buying welfare in the market. Never in all their lives have millions of working people now adept at shopping for consumption exercised much of a choice in schools, doctors, hospitals, housing or pensions. They will need persistent persuasion on television, in the press, on posters to spend more on welfare and to wean them from their consumption habits.

Fourth, however virile the welfare services, they might find it difficult to sell in competition with "free" or subsidised State services to people who must "pay twice." There is a Gordian knot to be cut. The politicians will not easily offer an unbiased market choice by removing the double payment unless the private suppliers reveal a large unsatisfied desire for it. The suppliers cannot easily expand until the politicians create an unbiased choice.

The knot can be cut by creating a hypothetical market. The nearest solution is a cross between public opinion polling and market research such as attempted by Mass Observation and in the University of Virginia.

Lady Violet Bonham Carter has said of Lloyd George fifty years ago: "He was a great initiator and it was his strength that he saw the goal and not the obstacles." The statesman who will now show the way to more choice in welfare will leave little administrative, actuarial, and political difficulties behind in marching towards the goal.

CHAPTER 32

1966

Politics Looms Too Large

> The Russians were demanding economic choices their leaders would have to yield. The British could not be far behind. A House of Commons debate showed little awareness of the potential for reform. * By the 1990s the politicians still make tempting offers of "free" goods and services in return for votes. The economy is still debilitated by political short-termism. But when the people can escape, the "politically impossible" excuse is wearing thin.
>
> (*The Spectator*, March 1966.)

Is it time the politician was deflated and put in his place? He should re-read Shakespeare. In war we can stand—we desperately need—a warrior-leader Churchill. In peace the politician who pretends to:

> . . . imitate the action of the tiger;
> Stiffen the sinews, summon up the blood,
> . . . lend the eye a terrible aspect

is an embarrassing clown.

> In peace, there's nothing so becomes a politician
> As modest stillness and humility.

His job is then to construct the rules (on property, contract, etc.) within which the rest of us can get on with the business of earning a living and enriching ourselves by coming together in markets to exchange the products of our skills and services.

The politician in the Soviet Union has come to see that in the second half of the twentieth century the children of even a predominantly peasant population with little experience of freedom can no longer be kept in paternalistic subjection. They will not be denied cultural expression. They are demanding economic choice. In time they will expect political freedom.

The politician in Britain harbours illusions of omnicompetence. He thinks he can decide the rate at which the well-off children of the depressed middle and working classes of the 1930s shall be allowed freedom in education, health services, housing, pensions. But is he not sitting on a volcano he has suppressed for twenty years since the end of the war and which now shows signs of erupting? Few MPs who contributed to the debate on the Welfare State in the Commons in 23 February seemed to have much idea of the stirrings below the surface. They are emotionally tied to a world in which welfare policy is decided by the small minorities of people in exceptional need. But even the question-begging discovery of seven million "poor" by Professors Abel-Smith and Townsend will not help them.

The future of the Welfare State, State welfare, the social services will not be decided in Parliament. It will be decided by the people. They will decide it not as voters in the ballot box, but as consumers in the market place. For twenty years they have had increasing freedom of choice for their food and drinks, their clothes, their furniture and household equipment, their entertainment, amusement and holidays. The common man and his wife from Leeds and Preston and Leicester and Cardiff are treated like lords and ladies at the grocer's, the hair-dresser's and on the plane to their fortnight in Spain. They are accustomed to "Sir" this and "Madam" that. Will they tolerate much longer being treated as servile, cap-in-hand supplicants in the local State school, the doctor's surgery, the hospital, the council housing manager's office, the Ministry of Pensions counter?

Average household incomes, now £24 a week, will probably rise (in *real* terms) to £45 by 1980 and to £65 by 1990. The White Paper on Public Expenditure blithely anticipates an increase in spending (in real terms) on State education from £1,600 million to £1,900 million by 1969–70, on health from £1,300 million to £1,500 million, on housing subsidies from £160 million to £260 million and on pensions, assistance, allowances etc., from £2,400 million to £2,900 million.

What sort of world does this conjure up? One in which parents send their children to State schools in which they have almost no choice but spend freely on extra-mural education in books and holidays? In which people spend freely on food and clothing that keep them in good health but submit to being marshalled by doctors and nurses when they are ill? In which millions show off their latest cookers and stereophonic record players to neighbours but submit to front-door colour schemes specified by a butcher on the council? In which most salaried and wage-paid people are accumulating a personal or occupational pension but have to pay £2 or £3 a week towards a compulsory State pension? Disraeli gave us the Two Nations, Lord Snow the Two Cultures. Our slow-moving politician envisages the Two Standards. Professor Galbraith beat him to it with his "public squalor, private affluence." But they both misread the lesson: the market works—there is no shortage of consumer goods; the ballot box does not—the shortage of schools, doctors, houses, is all around us.

The contrast is obtruding itself everywhere. It will become even more stark as incomes go on rising. Its full extent is not known. It is latent, buried, undiscovered for two reasons.

First, because there is no freedom to choose. The man who would spend something on his son's or daughter's education is discouraged: if he wants something better than the secondary modern or comprehensive school, he cannot pay fees because he must pay taxes for the State schools he does not use. And the same with health and other State services.

Second, the politician does not know the full extent of the coming conflict between freedom in consumption and unfreedom in welfare, because he does not ask his people what they would like or tell them what they could have. The politician gets his information on public opinion on welfare from party workers, fragmentary snatches of conversation with people, exchanges with journalists who tell him their own opinions or the views of articulate readers who write to the editor. None of these sources represents the people as a whole. None of them reflects the underlying state or currents of public opinion.

And when efforts are made to find out, they are met with scepticism, cynicism, stubborn incredulity or obfuscation. In 1963 a national sample of married men of all social groups between the ages of twenty-one and sixty-five was asked if it would either pay more in taxes or contributions for better State education, health services or pensions or pay less in taxes or contributions to provide for people in need but themselves pay privately for the schools, doctors, hospitals and pensions of their choice or be allowed individually to contract out and again pay privately. It split roughly half and half on education, but rather less than half were in favour of paying more taxes for better State health services and pensions.

Now this result may have been a fluke. And many hoped it was. But much the same result came up in 1965. Still possible, but much less likely. Yet again the findings were discounted: the questions were too complex, said the *Statist,* and too simple, said *Socialist Commentary.* Possibly one of them was right. But only this week a survey for Noble Lowndes, the pension specialists, has shown that 70 per cent of a national sample of employees thought that pensions should be arranged privately (by individuals or employers) and only 28 per cent by the State. Perhaps the doubters will find new criticisms.

There is mounting evidence that rising incomes and social standards will intensify dissatisfaction with compulsory State welfare for captive customers and the demand for a choice. If there is still doubt, let the political parties set up their own inquiries. Let the government put its Social Survey (in the Central Office of Information) on to discovering whether people want a choice. *Best of all, let the people contract out of State services they do not want, and see what happens.* That would settle the argument once and for all.

This is not a difference in party politics. It is a matter of common observation and common sense. In the Welfare State debate Mr. William Hamilton concluded from some temperate sentences in an article of mine that I was a Conservative. His surmise was miles wide of the mark. I have never voted Conservative. It is Mr. Hamilton's party that should show its respect for the people by taking a lead in allowing them as much freedom in choosing education, hospitals and pensions as they now have in buying entertainment, holidays and do-it-yourself paint.

But, of course, we must be "practical," "hard-headed," "realistic." Politics is "the art of the possible." A new policy on welfare must be "politically possible." How long do politicians think they will be popular on the Two Standards? It will be a great day in British social history when the political parties stop buying votes by State benefits and compete in options between State and private welfare. The Conservatives, late in the day, have begun saying the right thing. Does it not occur to Labour that there might be votes in it?

CHAPTER **33**

1966

Tax State Benefits

> A new argument anticipated political thinking in the early 1990s: income tax on social benefits in cash and kind. Universal State pensions could be run down before the 1980s. The proposal shocked a future Conservative minister: "Yes, but we could not tax our own people!" * In the mid-1990s a Conservative minister announced the State pension would begin to be run down in the second decade of the twenty-first century.
>
> (*The Daily Telegraph,* October 1966.)

What are we trying to do with the elephantine machine we have created for collecting nearly a quarter of our incomes in taxes and paying it back in "welfare"?

If you think "elephantine" too strong, consider the figures. In 1966 we shall be taking £7,000 million in taxes, rates and social insurance contributions out of total incomes of about £31,000 million.

Are we trying to play Robin Hood? If so, we are hardly succeeding. Robin Hood did not waylay all the travellers through Sherwood Forest; he used a rough-and-ready means test of personal appearance and apparel. And he did not chase after his victims to return their possessions.

The latest calculations of taxes and social benefits by the Central Statistical Office, recently published, are for 1964. They confirm that, except for households with exceptionally high incomes of over £2,000 a year and those with exceptionally low incomes of less than about £450 a year, the end result of this elephantine activity is to leave most families with about 20 per cent of where they were to begin with. In a word, 80 per cent of all the financial coming and going is about as sensible as carrying coals to Newcastle. There must be a simpler, less costly way of switching income from the better-off to the worse-off.

One reason for this bizarre result is that there is simply not much hope of squeezing more tax out of the "rich." That is why most tax revenue has to come from people with middling and lower incomes.

We have gone about as far as we can in taxing the higher incomes from work, enterprise and saving. But we can do something about the second reason why the to-ing and fro-ing of taxes and benefits has relatively little effect on switching incomes.

The reason itself is clear enough. It is simply that very little of the £7,000 million is distributed on the principle of giving most to the people with least. Some of it is: most obviously National Assistance allowances (but they account for only about £250 million) and education grants (but they are only about £80 million).

A second group of payments is regarded as having been bought: the so-called "national insurance" benefits from maternity through sickness and unemployment to retirement pensions and death grants. They account for about £1,800 million. But that term "national insurance" is very much a politician's misnomer; especially in pensions it is very different from the system of insurance by which people build up superannuation rights from invested funds.

A third group of State benefits is taxed, so that at least part of it is recovered from people who need it least: mainly retirement pensions and family allowances (around £160 million). But all this still leaves about half of the £7,000 million distributed as free or subsidised goods or services in kind on which no tax is levied at all.

On at least the £50 million spent on child care, this is of course right; indeed much more should go to children who need it, and, if the proposals outlined below were adopted, much more money would be available for them. The remainder comprises four items: free State education and subsidised adult education take about £1,500 million; school meals, milk and welfare foods around £150 million, the National Health Service and local welfare services about £1,350 million and housing about £850 million.

How far do these services in kind go where there is most need? Everyone may use State education and, for ludicrously small fees adult education (courses on the Etruscans and the birth of Roman power, Kemsing through the Ages, the Impact of European and Asian culture on Africa are running in Sevenoaks now at £2 for twenty-four lectures). Over 90 per cent of families send their children to free State schools and may receive free milk and subsidised meals. Probably fifty-one million out of a population of fifty-three million use nothing but the NHS. A lucky four million out of seventeen million families occupy council houses or flats, mostly subsidised.

But how many need free or subsidised State benefits in kind—or the cash benefits, allowances, grants, pensions?

Only in the past few weeks we have learned from a Ministry of Pensions survey into a sample of eleven thousand pensioner households that rather more than half of the pensioner couples have a private income of £10 or more a week and a sixth £15 or more a week. We should rejoice that a large and growing proportion of them are drawing pensions from their former employments, or are fit enough to go on working, or are receiving interest on investments, but can this growing income be entirely ignored in allocating tax revenue to pensions in the next ten to twenty years?

How many people *must* have free medicines, doctors, hospitals? We don't really know. In justifying his abolition of the prescription charges last year, Mr. Kenneth Robinson, the Minister of Health, was quoted as reporting a survey which found that 14 per cent of the sample said they could not pay for medicines. Even if this were so, what about the 86 per cent?

How many people *must* have subsidised council housing? No government has really found out; or, if it has, it has kept the information very much to itself. A private survey in June this year found that 4 per cent of households with higher incomes and 15 per cent of those with middling incomes occupied council houses. What were they doing there?

How many families *must* have family allowances? We don't really know. We do know that four million families take them; and that some families could do with larger allowances and many should not be taking any at all.

What can we do about all this? Some people don't want to do anything. They rather like to see the State take such a large slice of personal income and dish it out again, either because they want to see incomes socialised, or because they think equality of treatment avoids envy and is "socially cohesive," or because they have contempt for the ordinary family and its capacity to spend its money as it thinks best.

The socialisers do not care about personal liberty. The egalitarians cannot see that equal treatment of people in unequal circumstances is inequality. And the paternalists do not see that people will never learn to spend wisely if they are given "free" State services that deprive them of choice.

If we reject these solutions, the alternative is, ultimately, to reduce taxation and social insurance and let people decide for themselves whether they want to buy welfare from the State or privately. But there are three things we can consider in the next few months.

First, we might tax cash benefits at rates high enough to leave little or nothing in households that do not need them. Family allowances are the obvious first candidate for such treatment. But we must also reconsider the tax status of retirement pensions. They are taxed as earned income, although they are earned neither by work nor by National Insurance contributions; they are largely financed out of current taxation and are in this sense heavily subsidised.

It would entail hardship for people with low incomes aged forty-five or more to run down the retirement pension by taxation; but it can hardly continue indefinitely as a universal benefit into the 1980s. Certainly for younger people the retirement pension could be run down in the next five or ten years.

Secondly, cash benefits not now taxed should be considered for taxation. The largest category here is the range of National Insurance benefits. Low-income households need larger benefits but high-income households can manage on smaller benefits.

The notion that these benefits are bought by contributions is a political fiction; the contributions are a form of taxation, and are so treated in official government records. Taxes are not earmarked for specified benefits. Since the benefits come out of taxation, they can be treated as discretionary disbursements of public revenue and made subject to taxation in conformity with public policy.

It follows that the move to graduated benefits is wrong-headed. If people with higher incomes are to pay higher contributions for higher benefits they can, by definition, be allowed to provide for sickness and unemployment in ways which they themselves prefer by private saving or insurance. Here again there is a sorry tale of Conservatives thoughtlessly following Labour thinking without seeing where it would lead.

Thirdly, we should consider whether State benefits in kind available to everyone should remain untaxed. State education virtually puts perhaps £140 a year into the pocket of a man with a boy or girl at a grammar school (£280 if in the sixth form), probably over £100 if at a technical, secondary modern or comprehensive school, £80 if at a primary school; and it matters not whether the father's income is £500 or £5,000 a year.

The National Health Service adds some £100 a year to the income of a man with a wife and two children, no matter his income; and it adds more the higher the income because it is untaxed. Except in areas with rent rebate schemes, a council house will give its occupant a tax-free subsidy of about £60 a year whether the household has an income of £800 or £3,000.

In all, about £3,500 million goes into households of all types as notional additions to income that are wholly untaxed.

The taxation of benefits in kind would have three highly desirable results. First, it would yield revenue to provide more generous aid to people in need among large families, pensioners, the mentally sick, neglected children, widows. Second, it would make possible a reduction in taxation on earnings from work, enterprise and saving and thus increase national income. Third, it would encourage a shift out of overcrowded State services and enable their standards to be raised by reducing the size of classes, the length of hospital waiting lists and of council house queues.

It is time to doubt whether there is logic, economy or humanity in continuing the vast structure of indiscriminate benefits in kind.

CHAPTER 34

1967

Make Social Services Selective

> The battle of ideas against universal benefits was won in the 1960s. But it took thirty years for reasoned argument to reach the politicians. * In the 1990s even "social democratic" academics have accepted the principle and humanity of selectivity. The Labour leader is still attached to universalism and his Commission on Social Justice may echo him—in conflict with the Labour-inclined Institute of Public Policy Research which had shown early conversion to market solutions. That tension might galvanise the market-inclined Conservatives.
>
> (*The Times*, September 1967.)

> "Would . . . a general increase in family allowances . . . be the best way of using scarce resources when so much needs to be done over the whole field of social services, not only in cash payments but also in health, housing, and education . . . ?"

> "Whatever system is adopted for family endowment, it will be selective."

Miss Margaret Herbison, who was then Minister of Social Security, was announcing more than government policy on family allowances in the April Commons debate on family poverty. She was heralding a change in the principles underlying government social policy. A question the TUC will be examining this week is not whether there will be a change from universal to selective social benefits but first, how soon it will come and in which services, secondly, by what mechanism, and, thirdly, how it will affect the organisation and financing of welfare.

No doubt the debate will continue as an intellectual rearguard action by the universalists. It will be argued that discrimination according to need entails inequality, that it will create social divisiveness, that other countries spend more on social benefits than we do, that some benefits are earned by insurance contributions, that incentives will be blunted, that in any event taxes make universal benefits selective. But these objections do nothing to make it easier for the Government to raise the tax revenue required to remove the remaining pockets of poverty and to provide social benefits at the rising standards made possible by technical advance and expected by citizens accustomed to them in everyday consumption.

Nor does the solution lie in economic growth. Even if the annual rate rose to 3 per cent it has still to be established that taxpayers will voluntarily yield enough of their rising incomes to finance social benefits. Recent work in the economics of public finance by Professor J. M. Buchanan and his associates at the University of Virginia suggests that individuals will not voluntarily contribute enough to the financing of "public goods." Mr. Douglas Houghton has also developed the argument that people will not readily pay more in taxation or social insurance which bears no relation to the services they receive.

The latest universal increase in the basic State retirement pension must be nearly the last. The tax on it (as earned income) will reduce the amount left with the better off; but many pensions will be left with tidy sums they do not need. Part of the pension will have been earned by contributions; but mostly less than one tenth. Many pensions could do with much more help; but a universal increase will give them less than the nation can afford.

None of the objections justifies a universal increase. It will add a further £130 million a year to the public sector even if it is financed by higher insurance contributions. The earner does not distinguish rigidly between the National Insurance contribution as a premium paid for a benefit and income tax as a compulsory levy: both are deductions from income imposed by the State; both may raise costs; both blunt incentives (with the recent increases a man will pay 15*s.* 8*d.* and his employer £2 1*s.*, including SET); both are in part passed on to the consumer arbitrarily according to the conditions of supply of and demand for products and producers in each industry or firm.

Not least, the Ministry of Pensions inquiry into the financial and other circumstances of retirement pensioners in June 1966 reported that one in six retired couples said their total income was £15 or more a week, and we may assume that they did not overstate it. Many more will have growing incomes from earnings, occupational pensions and interest on savings in the next five and ten years. Although it has happened in Sweden, no British government would find it easy to reduce the State pension. Unless further increases are confined to people with lowest incomes, a growing proportion of social benefits will be abortive. The Government have claimed that the Supplementary Benefits Commission has humanised National Assistance;

it cannot therefore continue to imply that a stigma adheres to supplementary pensions. If the Government persist with their universal increase in pensions in the name of insurance, equality, incentive or administrative convenience, will they at least tell us how much of the £130 million will be abortive?

If the pension increases were selective, the children could have had more than 5*s.* a week in family allowance before the end of October and more than 7*s.* before April.

And what of other National Insurance benefits? The insurance principle is again debatable. But the proposal, approved in principle by both Labour and Conservatives, that sickness and unemployment benefits should vary with earnings, runs directly counter to the trend towards selectivity. Graduating sickness and unemployment benefits with previous earnings in return for graduated contributions may make sense as an interim measure to avoid a marked drop in earnings. But it makes no sense as part of a social policy based on selectivity to compel people with higher earnings to insure through the State when they can, by definition, provide in ways they prefer by saving or private insurance. The case for compulsory insurance, and even then not necessarily with the State, is limited to providing a minimum unrelated to earnings.

One day the anomaly of taxing only some cash benefits—and of not taxing benefits in kind at all: council house subsidies of anything from less than £20 to over £100 a year, education of £140 a child at secondary schools and £280 in a sixth form, £30 in medical insurance—will also have to be faced.

In the United States Professor Milton Friedman of Chicago has suggested that some two-thirds of the £15,000 million of social benefits in 1963 supplemented incomes above the £1,000 a year defined by the President's Council of Economic Advisers as the American poverty line. A similar proportion in Britain would imply that £4,500 million of the current £7,000 million social benefits are abortive. The scope for humane reform of British social benefits on selective lines is humbling. Replies to Commons questions asked by Mr. John Biffen showed that only some £175 million of the £1,350 million spent on education, almost none of the £1,250 million on medical care, an unknown proportion of the £750 million on housing, and only £300 million of the £2,450 million on social insurance benefits in a recent year makes any distinction between people who do or do not need the cash, or who could or could not pay for the service. The pockets of poverty are an act of government.

Further increases in social benefits could be related to means in a period no longer than it need take politicians to explain the change to a populace more ready for it than they commonly suppose. Of a national sample of men and women aged sixteen to sixty-five, 65 per cent told Mass Observation in April that they would be more prepared to pay taxes if their money was spent on social benefits and services "for people who need them most." Only 35 per cent favoured their taxes being spent on benefits regardless of earnings.

The instrument of selectivity will not be the conventional means test that requires the claimant to initiate a claim and to withstand personal interrogation into means. The solution favoured by Mr. Patrick Gordon Walker, the reverse income tax, goes back in principle to the American economist, Henry C. Simons; it has been advocated in Great Britain for at least ten years; it has been vigorously introduced by Professor Friedman into recent American discussions on poverty and social policy; and it is appraised by Mr. Houghton in his Institute of Economic Affairs Paper *Paying for the Social Services.* The device is an *automatic* indicator of entitlement that avoids the objections to conventional means tests and replaces most of them. An income return would indicate who was to pay taxes and charges for hitherto "free" State services and who was to receive money grants, "reverse taxes." Mr. Houghton has dismissed Inland Revenue objections by the reminder that it rejected PAYE as impracticable during the war two years before it was introduced. But there are three difficulties.

First, a disincentive effect has been alleged by Miss Herbison. It is a risk that must be run. A disincentive is inevitable in any form of social benefit; it is human nature for a man who is given help to help himself less. But the reverse income tax is not a rigid minimum income guarantee which a man would receive whether he helped himself or not. If the current "neutral" income at which there is neither tax nor reverse tax is £750, a man earning £850 who pays, say, 15 per cent tax on the "surplus" £100 would be left with £835 and a man earning £650 might receive 60 per cent of his "deficit," leaving him with £710. The incentive to earn would remain.

Secondly, it is said that workers would be demoralised by seeing the less conscientious collect larger supplements. This fear hardly squares with the view that pride would stop the wage-earner from asking for help he could dispense with by working.

Thirdly, earnings may fluctuate weekly; income codings could not be changed weekly. But earnings tend to be received monthly; bills can be stretched over several earnings periods; local Supplementary Benefits Commission offices could make interim advance payments on pay slips; more frequent code numbering will become possible when, as Mr. Houghton pertinently observes, twenty million PAYE assessments are processed in eight Inland Revenue computer centres. Not least, the costs of administering a reverse income tax must be contrasted with that of distributing hundreds of millions of weekly penny packets and collecting taxes on several million, an effort that smacks not only of carrying coals to Newcastle, but also of carting much of it back to Whitehall.

Charges could raise additional sums out of which to improve State services. This is the case for charges for prescriptions and hospital treatment made by Mr. Houghton, and eloquently argued by Mr. Brian Walden and Mr. Desmond Donnelly. But the effect could differ from the intention.

If the charges were low, say a nominal half a crown for a visit to a doctor, or £5 for a week of hospital treatment, they would not bring in much additional money. But if they were nearer to the cost, say 10*s.* for a visit to a doctor and £25 for a week of hospital treatment, they might draw in more funds to the NHS, but they might also have two further effects. First, having to pay a near-market price on a State service would increase the demand for private service that offered choice of a surgeon, a range of timing, convenience and comfort, for which millions more than the small numbers that now insure privately could pay without financial strain. Secondly, the creation of the new risk that a man might have to find, say, £50 or more for hospital treatment would induce him to cover it by private insurance.

The outcome would depend on the attitudes to paying charges as well as taxes and social insurance for State services, to the comparative advantages of State and private services, and to the apportionment of rising incomes between welfare and other forms of expenditure. But it may have to be accepted by people adhering to a wide range of social philosophy who have seen, at last, that taxation and social insurance are not enough.

CHAPTER 35

1969

Workers Reject State Welfare

> Lloyd George, Churchill, Beveridge, Attlee could not have foreseen that the common people would in time reject "free" minimum benefits in favour of the maximum benefits they could pay for. * Government has increasingly had to compete with private services. But the rising taxation required is displeasing the voters whose support it had hoped to win.
>
> (*The Sunday Telegraph*, March 1969.)

Once again, on Thursday, Parliament debated social welfare. Once again detail threatened to drown principle, and party politics to obscure people's preferences.

Lloyd George, Churchill, Beveridge, Attlee—the founders of the Welfare State—would not have believed that their work sixty, forty and twenty years ago could become outdated so soon. The sons and grandsons of the men to whom they gave pensions, National Insurance and Social Security in 1908, 1925 and 1948 are no longer satisfied with "basic benefits" and *minimum* standards: they want the *best possible* services and *maximum* standards.

Rising incomes have given them improving quality and personal service in the everyday purchases they make from private, competing suppliers; yet in medical care, education, housing and saving for retirement they are confronted by a State supplier that imposes queuing and rationing, waiting and form-filling, regulation and control by a benevolent bureaucracy. In everyday consumption they are the master/consumers in a buyers' market; in "welfare" they are beneficiary/supplicants in a sellers' market.

The contrast becomes starker as government fails to raise sufficient tax revenue to provide State welfare at rising standards. The wage-earner who experiences "middle-class" quality and service in consumption cannot see why he should not have it for his family in his home, for his wife or children when they are sick, for his children at school. He will question and reject

State welfare all the more as he realises that it is not a gift from "the State," or a transfer from the rich, but that he is paying for it in taxes.

The middle-class politicians who run the political parties cannot easily discern these aspirations because they provide no sympathetic machinery accessible to the wage-earner by which he can express them in his day-to-day purchases. Politicians and their academic advisers who have never known a day of want cannot understand the contrast in the horizons of the low-wage worker of the 1930s and the relatively opulent earner of the 1960s. Until recently they were content to suppose that the wage-earner should be—and was—grateful for the welfare the State gave him. Now that Labour intellectuals are discovering he is not, they are puzzled, angry and abusive.

Socialist Commentary, the monthly of the moderate Labour intellectual, puts (in its March issue) a brave face on the results of a sample survey of opinion in November/December. The commentary by Dr. Mark Abrams is a scholarly attempt to analyse the results that leaves Labour with some consolation. The editorial comment (the editor is Dr. Rita Hinden) employs euphemisms and manages to end with almost a flavour of euphoria. The Labour Party has not always been well served by its intellectuals; its working-class leaders should interpret the results for themselves.

The comments create the impression that the government is thought to have handled "social welfare" best: 26 per cent of constant Labour supporters and 14 per cent of former Labour supporters said so; "housing" scored 8 per cent and 1 per cent. The astonishing omission from the survey was the effort to discover opinion on whether State welfare should go where it could do most good, that is, to people in most need, or whether it should go to all and sundry. Yet for five years or more this has been the increasingly dominant focus of discussion in social policy. "Social welfare" for whom? Should benefits continue to be largely universal, requiring £8,000 million to be raised in taxation and paid out partly (or largely) to people who do not need them? Or should they be "selective," so that the 10 or 15 per cent of people in need receive more—much more—help?

Until recently Labour's social policy advisers have been "universalists." They are now in disarray: Professor Peter Townsend of Essex University remains an unrepentant and embittered "universalist," busily discovering pockets of poverty and eloquently urging policies that would deny the poor the help they could have; Professor Brian Abel-Smith, adviser to the Minister of Social Security, has been seeing the sense in selectivity, although he takes the usual civil servant's refuge in "administrative difficulty"; and Professor R. M. Titmuss of the London School of Economics, the most mystical of the triumvirate, is now bravely advocating both, thus cleverly combining the incompatible with the unattainable.

But Labour's politicians know better than to continue philosophical schizophrenia about "social equality," "social divisiveness," or "social cohesion" that has no place in the life or hopes of the working man, that leaves the needy shockingly neglected, that blithely assumes governments can tax more than taxpayers are prepared to yield. Mr. Roy Jenkins is proposing to make social benefits selective by taxing them. This is a half-way house that shirks the opportunity of remaking welfare policy; but at least it recognises the waste and inhumanity of universal benefits.

Socialist Commentary knows that for several years social researches have revealed a wide difference of public opinion on universal versus selective social benefits. The most systematic have been those conducted by Mass Observation for the Institute of Economic Affairs in 1963, 1965, 1966, 1967 and 1968. The 1967 survey showed that 65 per cent preferred to pay taxes for selective benefits and 35 per cent for universal benefits. Higher-paid wage-earners divided in roughly the same two-to-one proportion, but the lower-paid were even more emphatic: 71 per cent in favour of selective benefits. And this is not surprising, since the lower-paid would gain more from selective than from universal benefits.

A field study in 1962 by Research Services for the Institute of Community Studies had found the deep division of opinion, although the results were not published for four years till 1966. Forty-six per cent of the manual workers said subsidised housing should be subject to a means test and a further 27 per cent that housing should not be subsidised at all; 48 per cent thought that university education should be means-tested and 45 per cent that it should be universal. In 1967 a report by F. G. Pennance and Hamish Gray for the IEA found that 65–75 per cent of the lower earners favoured concentrating housing aid, if necessary by means tests.

These diverse surveys based on varying methods and samples make *Socialist Commentary*'s conclusions practically meaningless and misleading. It should indeed have known this from its own results, for when its sample was asked which policies the government had handled "particularly badly," *the second most common complaint was that social benefits were not provided more selectively.* (The most common was rising living costs.)

The failure to distinguish between universal and selective benefits made useless the replies to what could have been an important question: whether people preferred more State welfare ("hospitals, schools, pensions and so on") for higher taxes or fewer State services without more taxes. *Socialist*

Commentary rejoices that 48 per cent of the sample as a whole preferred the first and only 32 per cent the second. But a further 5 per cent again introduced its opposition to paying people not in need, even though the question was not asked. And 47 per cent of the "working class" (*Socialist Commentary's* term?) were for more State welfare, less than half, *and so were less than 54 per cent of the "middle class."* This is no universal welcome for higher taxes and more State services.

But even the 48 per cent who favoured "more social services" cannot be said to support the government's universal welfare. If they had been asked to decide between universal and selective State welfare the evidence of social studies suggests that the vote would have fallen to about half. And among the "working class" it would probably have been even lower.

Little wonder that people have been spending more on a choice in welfare despite the additional cost imposed upon them of paying for State services that they do not use. More people in all income groups are insuring privately for medical care, paying school fees for smaller classes, buying homes in which they are their own masters, and saving through pension schemes suited to their circumstances. And more would do so if the providers were less timid and tepid, more aware that they were providing services that more and more people will want. The hope is that in a liberal, opulent society all will have the services they prefer.

Only middle-class leaders and intellectuals can be surprised—or dismayed—by these developments. Labour leaders and thinkers who are of working-class origin or sensitive to wage-earners' aspirations understand better what is happening.

Mr. Brian Walden, Labour MP for Birmingham All Saints, the brilliant son of a miner who became a teacher of economics at Oxford University, has sensed the mood: he argues that people would pay more for welfare but they are stopped by the State. Mr. Raymond Fletcher, Labour MP for Ilkeston, has also sensed it: he believes there is little enthusiasm among wage-earners for more "social wages" paid for by higher taxes deducted from wage packets. A Left-wing Labour writer says there has been a glacial shift in working-class attitudes since 1948. Most courageous of all, Mr. Desmond Donnelly has rejected the government that he believes has lost touch with the wage-earners he represents and whose hopes it does not reflect.

Whenever the people, not least the wage-earners, are asked unambiguously which they prefer, vast numbers, often overwhelming, prefer private to State welfare. In 1965, 70 per cent of a sample of employees surveyed by Mass Observation for Noble Lowndes said they preferred occupational or personal to State pensions. In an IEA survey in 1965, 55 per cent of lower-paid wage-earners said they would prefer to pay lower taxes and pay for medical care privately; 43 per cent said the same of education and 57 per cent of pensions. In 1966 a survey by the British Market Research Bureau for BUPA, the health insurance organisation, found large support for a choice of private health services. In five and ten years' time these figures will be even larger (as a 1968 IEA pilot survey indicates).

The emerging wage-earner will in time fulfil his aspirations for himself, his family and the causes he values despite obstruction by government. *Socialist Commentary* condemns "defectors" from Labour for being "concerned with their own pockets." This is a caricature.

A man who wants to keep more of his earnings rather than see them spent by politicians and civil servants (who, after all, are hardly likely to know his wants better than he does himself) is not therefore selfish or callous. He probably "cares" about the sick and the old and the needy even more than the man who has to be taxed to support them. But after he has helped people in need he wants to be able to decide for himself how he spends his money on his family—for medical care and education and housing and saving for retirement as well as for food and finery and smoking and drinking and motoring. He could be allowed a choice, and encouraged to spend more on welfare, by tax rebates, grants or vouchers. But the politicians will not let him, from Sir Edward Boyle and others among the Conservatives to Mr. Anthony Crosland and Mrs. Shirley Williams in the Government.

Mr. Crossman has seen, at least, that the wage-earner wants to own his home and that he values a stake in a private pension that is safe from government depredation. Mr. Crossman still seems to think that private medical care and education is a minority rich man's privilege. Mr. Crossman must be wondering whether in the sophisticated 'sixties and 'seventies his pensions plan—or any more State welfare—will win votes. He has yet to see he is sitting on a bonfire of government benevolence that is being ignited by rising incomes, growing aspirations, resentment of the tax-gatherer and the burgeoning desire to assert individuality in the wage-earner, who senses the new power that opulence has given him to free himself from redundant government.

CHAPTER 36

1969

Roll Back the State

> A new approach and a new battle-cry to resist the encroachment of the State into individual, family lives and voluntary organisations for communal activities: the State would have to be "rolled back." * The phrase became familiar fifteen years later under the Thatcher Conservatives. By the early 1990s the battle of ideas for rolling back the State had been won, but the politicians had not done much to resist the obstructors—the bureaucratic, occupational and academic vested interests in State structures.
> (*The Daily Telegraph*, July 1969.)

Mankind is plagued by a pestilence even more perplexing than poverty, ill-health, or tension between classes and races. It has yet to learn how to disperse, domesticate, discipline power.

The tyrannical power of a Hitler, a Mussolini or a Brezhnev is easy to identify and difficult to eradicate, except by revolution. The benign, benevolent power of democratic government is easier to discipline but its danger more difficult to dramatise. Its intentions are good, its methods humane, but it could choke its charges with cotton-wool and solicitude.

The power of the government of Britain, France, Germany, Sweden or Norway is measured by the two-fifths or more of the national product it controls through taxation. Even America, Canada and Australia are dangerously near a third. Only Switzerland, in Europe, keeps below a quarter. Alexis de Tocqueville in 1841 phrased the danger of benign government in a passage that present-day politicians in Britain, Conservative, Labour and Liberal, should repeat three times a day before meals and the Speaker should recite, slowly, before Question Time.

> Above this race of men stands an immense and tutelary power . . . absolute, minute, regular, provident, and mild. It would be like the authority of a parent, if . . . its object was to prepare men for manhood; but it seeks

> . . . to keep them in perpetual childhood . . . such a government . . . provides for their security, foresees and supplies their necessities, facilitates their pleasures, manages their principal concerns, directs their industry, regulates the descent of property, and subdivides their inheritances—what remains, but to spare them all the care of thinking and all the trouble of living?

Do democratic governments "prepare men for manhood"? I would say that, by and large, with some backsliding, Canada, Australia and America do; Britain does not. In Britain conventional party men rarely see this as their job; and the few who do rarely say so for fear of losing influence. It is two men who reject their party's unthinking, pretentious paternalism who most clearly sound this note: Desmond Donnelly and, on some issues, Enoch Powell. And it is a reflection of contemporary political attitudes that they are depicted not as independent-minded men of integrity and vision but as cranks out on a limb. Yet it is they who reflect underlying private preferences undiscovered by the ballot box, and the party hierarchies that are out of touch with the public.

In Britain the perverse, hilarious, hysterical doctrine still rules that the larger the wealth of the nation, the higher incomes rise, the more men can do for themselves, the more the State must do for them—and tax them so that it can so do it. That is the implication of the unrelenting expansion in comprehensive State education, the National Health Service, council housing, State graduated pensions. Instead of "preparing men for manhood," British governments have been keeping them in "perpetual childhood," destroying the hope held out by the English classical economist Nassau Senior in 1861:

> We may look forward to the time when the labouring population may be safely entrusted with the education of their children; . . . the assistance and superintendence . . . of the government for that purpose [is] . . . only a means of preparing the labouring classes for . . . the latter part of the 20th century . . . when that assistance and superintendence shall no longer be necessary.

We are now in "the latter part of the twentieth century." Yet that "assistance and superintendence" is clamped down more tightly not only on "the labouring classes" but also on everyone in sight. Somehow or other there must be a way of loosening it, of rolling back the State, of reducing the province of government.

What should we permit the State to do? Why does it do what it now does? What must the State do?

National income is about £37,500 million. This year the government will take £16,000 million, or 45 per cent. It need take no more than half of that. The general principle is clear enough: it was laid down by Adam Smith, Abraham Lincoln and Maynard Keynes: that government should do only what individuals cannot do for themselves.

Necessary State functions are of two main types, communal services or public goods and redistribution of income. The first comprises external defence, internal law and order, public health, environmental and preventive services, drainage, street lighting, water, parks, etc. (although some of these services could be paid for by charges), and tax collection. That's about the lot. A total of perhaps £4,000 million for services in kind, or 12 per cent of national income.

Second, though nothing in the Smith–Lincoln–Keynes principle requires *State* education, a *National* Health Service, *council* housing, *State* pensions, basic or graduated, it may require *cash* for people with low incomes to enable them to pay fees for education, rents for homes, and to insure for medical care and pensions; and cash for hospitals and other places that care for the physically or mentally incapacitated. All this may take another £3,000 million, or 8 per cent (falling off as incomes continue to rise). The total, so far, 20 per cent of national income.

About 5 per cent (£2,000 million) is required for interest on the National (government) Debt. The remaining 20 per cent, paid as subsidies to persons who do not need them or to industries—mostly manufacturing, farming, fishing, transport—which would in time be better without them, could be returned to, or left with, taxpayers.

This is the policy required to prepare men for manhood. Government welfare services in kind that people could pay for, out of incomes or government grants, could be taken over largely by private suppliers.

Nationalised industries in transport, fuel, telecommunications, etc. would be self-supporting, perhaps by letting them be run by private organisations, as Austria has been doing in rail transport. People would be helped, and industries would be expected, to stand on their own feet, not on the taxpayer's corns.

There is no technical or political reason for supposing that the State cannot be rolled back to half its monstrous weight in Britain, but there is a decision to make between two methods. The first is the slow, gradual, hopefully painless way—the soporific—spread over ten or twenty or thirty years.

The danger is that the soporific may become a comfortable habit; the patient will not willingly drop the crutch. The second is short, sharp, but not necessarily painful surgery, spread over a few years. People with accumulated expectations—prospective pensioners, railwaymen, miners, farmers—should be bought out. National Insurance, largely a fraud, should be wound up. There should be a year of education at the government's expense in the reasons for rolling back, and three years' preparation.

Not least, if the next government wishes to reduce the power of the State and reduce the taxation that finances it, the private organisations in education, medical care, housing, pensions that are to replace it must be nourished and encouraged. Otherwise it will be even more difficult to roll back the State in 1971 or 1973 than today.

People fending for themselves will be further depressed by Mr. Roy Jenkins's withdrawal of tax refunds on insurance loans, Mr. Richard Crossman's pensions and medical care intentions, Mr. Edward Short's noises on independent schools, Mr. Anthony Greenwood's restriction on the sale of council houses. Yet their opposite numbers, Mr. Iain Macleod, Lord Balniel, Sir Edward Boyle and Mr. Peter Walker, remain strangely reticent.

The independent-minded in British society must be encouraged to keep going until a government in office that does not fear or decry independence can remove their disabilities and encourage them to grow as bridgeheads for further advance. They need to be told, now, that the next government intends to replace State by private endeavour wherever people prefer it. An affirmation of principle would undo the harm done by recent and prospective expansion in the power of government.

Big Government means Little Men, with sparse hope of manhood. The next government may find comfort from another morsel of nineteenth-century wisdom; in 1821, Talleyrand said: "In our time it is not easy to deceive the public for long."

The 1970s will require a long jump rather than a slow shuffle to manhood. A short step out of a quagmire lands a man flat on his face; only a leap can land him in safety.

PART V

Wither the Welfare State

C: First Steps in Reforms, 1970–1992

CHAPTER 37

1970

The Great Pensions Swindle

> Conservative and Labour ministers have accused each other of misleading the public. Both claimed their State schemes were essential because private pensions would never cover all employees. The historical trends on what was likely belied their predictions. * That is the pretence the political process tempts able politicians to use for party advantage. It may continue as long as government dominates the economy.
>
> (*The Daily Telegraph*, February 1970.)

This is the title of a short book to appear in the next few weeks. But "swindle" is not my word.

On 27 January 1959 Mr. Crossman said in the House of Commons that if Mr. Boyd-Carpenter's scheme were described as a swindle it would not be exaggerating. On 6 March 1969 Mr. Boyd-Carpenter said that if his scheme were a swindle Mr. Crossman's was a bigger one.

What is the big idea both have urged? Instead of "flat-rate" contributions and pensions, the same for everybody, they should vary with earnings. People with higher earnings would pay higher contributions; and their pensions would also be higher, thus helping them to maintain their standard of living after retirement.

What could be simpler, "fairer," more reasonable, more productive of "social justice" than that? Of course, it is hilariously impertinent in a democracy for government to *order* a man who earns rather more than another to save more for his retirement. If he earns more he can save more how he pleases. And if he must be told to save more—which I contest—there is no case for forcing him to save through the State.

The whole scheme is suffused with a patrician anti-working-class flavour. It does nothing for present poverty among pensioners. It would prevent the wage-earner with a rising income from making decisions about saving for retirement. It would prevent or retard the further spread of occupational schemes down the income scale. It reflects none of the emancipating power of self-help through voluntary effort that inspired the early democratic socialists. But then this is a piece of social engineering initiated by the governors, not social democracy originating in the governed.

To inform public opinion of the economic, social, political and personal consequences behind the seductive statistics, a group of people with no financial interest in pensions has been formed. Its name is STOP: Save The Occupational Pension—for people who do not yet have one as well as for those who do.

Mr. Crossman's scheme is full of promises, hopes, estimates, guesses, assumptions, questions, and more promises. How can he dispense such attractive benefits all round? Does "the State" really contribute anything?—or is it a convenient disguise for the consumer/shopper/taxpayer? Does the employer really pay—or is his contribution partly passed on in higher prices? How much will the wage-earner pay in the end? Why is Mr. Crossman raising money by "national insurance" instead of by open taxation? For how long would occupational schemes be allowed to "contract out" and continue undamaged?

On all these grounds Mr. Crossman is weak. But let us take him on his strongest ground. When driven on the defensive he attacks manfully. He says it is "a wicked deception" to suppose that occupational schemes could ever cover everyone. And he gave six "hard facts" to substantiate his charge.

1. *Only 56,000 out of a million employers have occupational schemes.*

Only 5.6 per cent? that sounds shocking. But Mr. Crossman's mini-figure is misleading. At the end of 1967 employers with schemes were covering 12.2 million out of their 22.1 million employees, about 55 per cent. Only 1.5 million employees had employers with no schemes at all. As Dudley Moore might say: "Funny!"

Further, these figures are two years out of date. Since 1967 more employees have been covered; more employers have schemes. And even up-to-date figures would understate the coverage. Occupational schemes usually take in employees after they have been with a firm for a few years, so they may join at twenty-five or later.

The development of occupational schemes has been held back by the very expansion in State pensions, which has increasingly mortgaged employers' and employees' contributions. For fifteen years the incessant chatter by Mr. Crossman and his sociologists has created uncertainty about the finances of occupational schemes. The trade unions have shown little interest. The rules applied by the Inland Revenue have delayed new schemes, restricted benefits. And government has done little to help. In 1956 the Conservatives at least introduced tax rebates on individual pensions for people without access to occupational schemes. Since 1964 Mr. Crossman's Government has done nothing. Yet coverage since 1957 has spread from 8 to 12½ million. How many more wage-earners might now be covered if there had been less discouraging action?

2. *Only a minority of occupational schemes provide half or two-thirds of pay.*

As his case on inadequate cover becomes weaker year by year, Mr. Crossman likes to refer to the small benefits paid by some schemes—£3 a week is his favourite figure. Many schemes are young—some five to ten years. Their benefits—as in Mr. Crossman's twenty-years scheme—take time to build up. Even by 1977 Mr. Crossman's scheme would be paying only a quarter of its full benefits.

3. *In some important industries, like building and farming, there is virtually no pension provision and no prospect of it.*

How much is "virtually"? Schemes are run by some farmers and builders. Doesn't Mr. Crossman know? They are not yet numerous, but what has the government done to help workers in seasonal or declining trades—or to facilitate "federal" schemes for small firms in large industries?

4. *Only a quarter of working women are covered in occupational schemes. Married women cannot rely on their husbands' pensions because they may die.*

Occupational schemes increasingly give life assurance lump sums and widows' pensions. In a survey of 620 member firms of the British Institute of Management at the end of 1968, a year after Mr. Crossman's figures, Pilch and Wood, the pension pundits, found that 66 per cent of schemes provided a lump sum for a man's family if he died before retirement, 8 per cent a widow's pension, and 21 per cent a mixture of both. *Funny!*

5. *Only a third of male members of occupational pensions are "unconditionally" covered for widows' pensions.*

That figure was for 1967. In 1963 it was under 20 per cent. At that rate it would be over 40 per cent by 1972. Mr. Crossman says it is never likely to approach 100 per cent. If his Bill becomes law the figure might grind to a stop.

And why only "unconditional"? Seventy per cent of men in private-sector schemes have a choice of leaving a pension to a widow if they die after retirement. *Very funny!*

6. *By 2000 it is estimated that a third of pensioner households will be without an occupational pension.*

Another "estimate" that no one can check? Not everyone is in work that carries occupational pensions. Nearly 1⅓ million men and ⅓ million women are self-employed (and some—too few so far—have 1956 annuities). In some work frequent change is desirable or unavoidable, so pensioning is difficult. Some people may prefer higher pay to buy a personal pension. Others may like to save for retirement by life assurance, unit trusts, shares, antiques, buying a house (or two). There is no reason why everyone should have an occupational pension.

Continuing development has spread occupational pensions in coverage, size and variety of benefits. They could go on developing if public opinion prevails against the Boyd-Carpenter–Crossman tragi-comic pretence. Whatever their imperfections, occupational pensions are at least based on the security of profitably-invested funds that grow with time. What are Mr. Crossman's pensions based on? A "contract with future generations" who are not present to sign on the dotted line. Some contract!

CHAPTER **38**

1971

Top Up the Poor Man's Pay

> Concentrating aid where it was most needed might be attempted by a "reverse" income tax. There were difficulties, but the government did not enquire into possible solutions. The USA experiment seemed to find the optimum compromise between giving most help with the least disincentive to earn. * Twenty years later there has been no such experiment in Britain.
>
> (*The Daily Telegraph*, July 1971.)

Help for people with inadequate income should be designed to emancipate them from dependence. The secret of success in giving is to make it superfluous as quickly as possible. Giving is good when, as the economist Alfred Marshall said of State pensions, it contains within itself the seeds of its own disappearance.

By this crucial test of humanity for the poor and dignity for the citizen, the towering structures of social benefits in most Western countries are tragic failures. Some benefits are too small, too hard to obtain, or too late. Others, the vast bulk, are too large, too easy, too inflexible. And they all linger long after the conditions that called them into being have been forgotten. Most miss their mark: they do not help the needy at all. The United Kingdom is probably the worst offender: probably over £6,000 million out of £10,000 million raised in taxes and paid in social benefits does not help people in need. The USA is rather better. Even in Australia, better still, benefits remain for bizarre reasons (free milk because dairy farmers want high consumption, not to ensure good nutrition).

Little wonder that some countries are turning to a new device. It seems simple. People who earn little shall be given money; those who earn more shall be given less. This is selectivity par excellence: assistance matched more or less precisely with need.

This is the idea behind the American "negative" income tax advocated by the formidable Professor Milton Friedman; President Nixon's Family

Assistance Plan, stopped in the Senate but probably to be a major plank in 1971; the British "reverse" income tax; and Sir Keith Joseph's Family Income Supplement, which will add up to £3 a week to low earnings.

But nothing is new: in 1795 the Berkshire magistrates, meeting in the Pelican Inn (on the site of which now stands a doctor's surgery) in Speenhamland near Newbury, arranged for an "allowance" from the rates to make wages up to 3*s.* a week and 1*s.* 6*d.* for a wife and "every other of his family" when the gallon loaf of bread cost 1*s.*, rising by 3*d.* and 1*d.* for each penny increase in the price.

It is easy to see that "topping up" earnings seems a simple solution. It is less easy to see that it bristles with possible abuses and uncertainties.

It does not inquire into the reason for low earnings; whether personal—old age, ill health, incapacity, torpor, fecundity, parasitism; or institutional—industrial change, trade unions restrictions, government-induced market failure (which prevents housing from passing down the income scale), inflation, high taxation. So all are treated alike: the worthy and the unworthy.

Topping up makes help too easy. The less you earn the more you receive. Manna from Whitehall! Which low-earner would exert himself to earn more? Which man earning rather more would not be tempted to earn less? Income from government would become as reputable as income from work. But what of the hopes of encouraging people to stand on their own feet by fertilising self help?—the most heartening refrain in British politics since Churchill's call to the British to resist Fascism.

Breaking the link between work and earnings could make for suspicion, demoralisation, pauperisation.

The bonds of the family would be weakened if a man is not expected to keep his wife and children but can push them on to the State (that is, his neighbours). Large families might multiply.

The cost could then escalate out of control. When supplementary benefits are raised to keep pace with, or to outpace, inflation or living standards, more people are made "poor" by a stroke of a pen. But their standards have not declined; they are being raised. In the same way, topping up low earnings could feed on itself: its aim could change from alleviating poverty to creating equality.

People with middling earnings might press for higher pay to keep up their "differentials" and so inflate costs.

Employers and employees would be corrupted by collusion in paying low wages made up from taxes. Free collective bargaining could be frustrated.

Democratic politicians would be even further demoralised by bidding for votes through increasing "topping up."

These are possible dangers. They might never come to pass. But it would be foolish to brush them aside. The Speenhamland system spread, with varying scales of allowances throughout the parishes of England. It was sanctioned by Parliament in 1796. There seemed no practicable alternative; hardship from the war-time high prices and low wages was spreading.

And it lasted for nearly forty years. But after the war against Napoleon in 1815 increasing criticism of its demoralising and pauperising and "over-populating" effects led in 1832 to a Royal Commission and in 1834 to the Poor Law Amendment Act. It laid down that poor relief be given in workhouses to make the status of its recipients "less eligible" than that of self-supporting earners in field and factory.

Now, nearly two hundred years later, the poor are a small minority, not the general mass of wage-earners. And strong unions hitch wages up, sometimes too fast (and often at the expense of the lower-paid). Not least, topping up alleviates the *symptoms* of poverty; by itself it does nothing to remove its *causes.* The only "cure" is to move people out of low-paid jobs by retraining, education and *embourgeoisement,* and to mechanise the hewing of wood and the drawing of water.

And yet . . . Are all these possibilities decisive objections? Or risks we must run? The cure will take time, perhaps fifteen years. Until then it would be degrading, repugnant and wasteful for society to stand aside and see people suffer, even if poverty is their own fault.

Even if on a much smaller scale than two hundred years ago, the remaining poverty is a bar against the spread of freedom that the wage-earner could newly enjoy together with the well-off and the wealthy. As long as anyone cannot pay, the supporters of State welfare argue that everyone shall have it "free." This is equality run to seed in sour sulking. It is to make every recipient of State benefits "less eligible" than the customer who pays. But worse than that: people with low earnings can be given the same "eligibility" as those who earn enough.

The problems would be obvious. First: the optimum compromise between removing poverty and retaining incentive will have to be found by experience. Making a man lose £1 of topping up for every £1 of earnings (that is, a 100 per cent tax) would remove the incentive to earn, except through self-respect and reluctance to sponge. The British Family Income Supplement envisages a 50 per cent tax: only half will be lost. Perhaps 60 per cent or 40 per cent will be found even better.

Second: administration may be difficult. The sceptics are having a field day conjuring up chaos, confusion, corruption and catastrophe. They may be right. But their opinion is unsupported by evidence.

On the contrary the US experiment in a reverse income tax since August 1968, allotted $5 million by President Nixon, suggests that the conjectures are unsupported prejudgments.

Up until October 1969 effort at work *did not* decline. None quit their jobs to qualify for more "topping up." Except for the old and disabled they provided monthly records of income without help. Payments are varied monthly according to earnings and are posted fortnightly (so there is no lack of "take-up").

Third: topping up is not merely a palliative. I see it as a great experiment in emancipation from standardised, unresponsive, autocratic State services that have outlived their day. As topping up is developed, cash benefits unrelated to means can be withdrawn and services in kind can begin to pay their way.

Fourth: most fundamental of all, topping up must be seen as an interim programme while the long-term causes of poverty are removed. Study of the causes has been overshadowed by emphasis on short-term symptoms and palliatives by bodies like the Child Poverty Action Group. A Movement to Abolish Poverty (MAP) is being formed to study the causes and their cures as well as the palliatives. Will government now do its bit to test the treatment? Will Sir Keith Joseph allot £2 million from his vast budget of £5,000 million for an experiment in topping up? It would do more good for poverty than pouring £3,500 million of it every year into the pockets of the not-so-poor and the not poor at all.

CHAPTER 39

1971

Tory Advance: Reluctant Officials

The new government variation of assistance with need was an advance on universal benefits. The reforms might go further with lessons from other countries. The advice of interested civil servants anxious about their jobs could be checked by disinterested outside advisers. * In the 1990s Ministers continue to be over-influenced by their officials.

(*The Daily Telegraph*, October 1971.)

The post-war "consensus" Labour–Conservative Welfare State lasted a quarter of a century, 1945 to 1970. This morning Mr. Edward Heath's Conservatives discuss further steps in the new Tory Self-Help Welfare State.

The old Welfare State was designed to give the same benefits to all, in need or not. It may have been egalitarianism, dogmatism, even Socialism. It was certainly not common humanity, common sense, or respect for individuality. It was the universalist creed run riot. The new Welfare State is based on human circumstances: benefits go to people who cannot help themselves; the happily increasing number who can, pay for the dignity of choice.

So far most of the measures are in the right direction. What more could be done?

Mrs. Margaret Thatcher was quick off the mark with the re-assertion of variety in secondary education. The increased emphasis on primary schooling, the work of experts and officials, is more difficult to judge in the absence of an effective voice for parents. Even then, it would mean little in the absence of fees to show the costs of alternative forms of education.

The argument for the additional year to sixteen would be more convincing if Mrs. Thatcher showed the cost in services sacrificed elsewhere—in education, or hospitals, or more money for people unable to work.

"Direct grants" should go to parents, not to schools: to consumers, not to producers. And not only where Labour local authorities decline to take places in independent schools. Much more generally government could make a start at withdrawing from the business of building, owning and running schools, at which it is not very good because politics should not get mixed up with education, and providing finance to low-income parents and loans to students.

It would begin with nominal fees for State schools, a principle approved for nursery schools by Lady Plowden and several members of her committee. It could encourage self-help by tax rebates on school fees, fares, etc. (up to £140 for each child in Australia). And it could, as in the United States, experiment with vouchers and "performance contracting." Private companies are employed (in Arkansas and Indiana) to teach backward children and are paid by results. The results are very good.

Sir Keith Joseph's increased use of pricing in the National Health Service is his most hopeful step in the right direction. But to make his emphasis on better management in the NHS a reality he too will have to use payment by results. Good management, as in private industry, requires competitive incentives for efficiency and penalties for inefficiency. Sir Keith and Mr. Michael Alison know all this: they have yet to apply it.

The introduction of better methods or businessmen, a little more centralisation here or more decentralisation there, will not suffice. What the NHS requires is more competition both within its vast bureaucracies and from outside. More internal competition requires a massive move to a more federal structure, with much more regional or local autonomy. And this requires power to raise money locally. The straitjacket of attempted equality must be loosened for the sake of higher standards all round, for psychiatric and geriatric patients as well as for normal acute and emergency medical care.

And competition from outside requires heroic decisions to encourage private capital to build hospitals and private insurance to cover more than the meagre 5 per cent of the people. There are millions of pounds that could be channelled into medical care. British health should come before the National Health Service. Mr. Enoch Powell has said "Britain is stuck with the NHS . . . for my lifetime and beyond it." He must be proved wrong. The NHS receives too little—barely 5 per cent of the national product because it limits us to taxation. With the whole battery of taxation, social insurance, private insurance, fees, charges and reimbursements, France and Germany, Belgium and Norway, Canada and the United States raise 6 to 8 per cent and more. And in periodic refinement of their methods they never dream of copying the NHS. Not even Senator Edward Kennedy, who praised the NHS the other day, is advocating it in his country. Why then should British Conservatives see the 1946 creation of Bevan as untouchable?

Mr. Peter Walker and Mr. Julian Amery have taken the longest step in the right direction. Their housing allowances in cash will put low-income private tenants on the same financial footing as low-income council tenants with rent rebates.

They should now be persuaded to take an even longer stride nearer their goal. Rent rebates retain non-market rents; housing allowances promote market rents. Rebates frustrate the rationing function of rents and necessitate rationing by officials; allowances strengthen rationing by rents and choice by tenants. Not least, the dual rebate-cum-allowance system segregates council from private tenants.

Messrs. Walker and Amery could put this right by introducing cash housing allowances for *all* tenants. They have been used in Europe for many years. Or, if the change is too sudden, *all* tenants, council and private, could be given housing vouchers. The perspective must be long run. The United States Department of Housing and Urban Development under Mr. George Romney is sponsoring research by the private Urban Institute in Washington to discover the possible effects of housing allowances of varying kinds—cash or vouchers—in raising rent in the short run and increasing the supply of housing in the long run. They would, moreover, cost much less than local government building.

The new pensions scheme will shift the emphasis from State to occupational and private pensions generally: another step in the right direction.

But the introduction of graduated National Insurance contributions to pay for the uniform State pension will create pressure for graduating the pension. Sir Keith Joseph and Mr. Paul Dean may have solved the immediate problem of finding more money without raising taxes, but they will be making severe difficulties for Conservatives in the 1980s.

Far better to make a start with winding up the whole National Insurance system. Australia has managed very well without it. Her pensioners are better off than ours; and less money has to be raised in taxes. The Prime Minister, Mr. William McMahon, is resisting Australian academic Labour-like talk of "national superannuation" that Mr. Heath's Tories have rightly rejected.

The Reserve Pension Scheme must not become a backstairs to State control of industry, as envisaged under Mr. Hugh Gaitskell and as is happening in Sweden. The board of management must be strong enough to segregate its funds from general revenue. There are worrying doubts here.

The solution is to expedite the expansion of occupational and private pensions—not least by removing their control from the Inland Revenue—so that only a small and diminishing number have to resort to the State's Reserve Scheme.

The Family Income Supplement is yet another move on the right lines. But if 60 per cent do not ask for it, the Cabinet should recognise its weakness—that claimants have to initiate a claim—and go the whole way to reverse income tax. In time it could replace family allowances and other wasteful benefits. (Canada has been discussing means-testing its family allowances.) And it would take over from the half-way measure of vouchers.

The main doubt is the effect on incentives. A recurrence of Speenhamland demoralisation is not inevitable. The New Jersey experiment so far indicates no marked disincentive. Abuses are probable, but controllable. They should not distract Conservative attention from the central aim of mastering poverty so that *all* can pay for welfare. The abuses are tiny compared with the thousands of millions raised in taxes and paid back to taxpayers in universal benefits.

But is a government changing the direction of social policy affecting half of public expenditure effectively serviced by a civil service working in a twenty-five-year-old groove? British civil servants are incorruptible, but they are not chameleons. They are able, experienced specialists with opinions, value judgements, feelings of their own. Ministers out of office evolve new thoughts: civil servants continuously "in office" generate inertia.

If the American system of bringing in senior officials with each President has defects, though in Washington recently I saw its advantages, new solutions may have to be evolved. Perhaps more systematic reference by Ministers to unofficial outsiders acting as a second string to provide a constant flow of second opinions. Like the NHS, bureaucracies should have competition both within and from outside. The Tory Welfare State may stand or fall by it.

CHAPTER **40**

1972

Timid Tories and State Welfare

> The strategy and tactics of Conservative governments. None of the supposed obstacles was insurmountable. Political prudence could be combined with principle. Crossman knew how to resist his obstructors; Conservatives could hardly be less "bloody and blunt." The paternalist thinking of Crossman had been echoed by paternalist Conservatives. * So far the 1992 Conservative government speaks with two voices—for smaller government and for bigger government.
>
> (*Crossbow*, August–September 1972.)

If the 1970s Conservatives are to remedy the errors of the post-war years and build a society in which men stand on their own feet instead of on one another's corns, they must allow the citizen to spend more of his money. Much of the domain of government must be conducted by government. Much of it need not be. Some welfare services must be run by government, central or local. Most need not be. This is the scope for Conservative reform of the Welfare State.

The immense opportunity should inspirit, comfort and fortify Conservatives when the going is rough. Half of the £40,000 million GNP is disposed of by government. Half of government disbursement goes on State welfare. But most State welfare in cash goes to people who are not poor. Most State welfare in kind goes to people who could pay. Perhaps £7,000 million could be left with taxpayers, ratepayers and social insurance contributors to spend on private insurance or direct payment to competing suppliers, State or private, of education, medical care, housing, retirement income.

This opportunity to strengthen self-help and independence has been created by the 1945–70 Conservative/Labour consensus. Six obstacles stand in the way, none insurmountable.

The most immediate is the 1970 Manifesto. It said the 1970 Conservatives would redirect housing subsidies from all and sundry to the poor. They are keeping their word. It did not say, *specifically,* that they would replace universal by selective benefits in education, medical care or pensions. Ergo, they must not be expected to do anything, or much, about elephantiasis, standardisation or denial of parental choice in education, about the deficiency of resources, waste and unresponsiveness of the NHS, about the vast disbursement of pensions to people who have not paid for them in National Insurance and are not poor. But if, as Mr. Richard Crossman implies, both parties are coming to rule by manifesto, and if, as it seems, the morally more austere Heath Ministers rule by the whole manifesto and nothing but the manifesto, Conservatives who wish to see the hopes of 1970 fulfilled must work for specific undertakings in the manifesto of 1974 or 1975.

The second obstacle is the consensus. Conservatives, say some Conservatives, must rule by the centre: they must not drive through Parliament anything that vexes, incenses or envenoms Labour. There may have been occasions in British history when party or class bitterness would have disrupted economy and society as well as policy. But Conservatives who believe it applies to welfare policy in the 1970s have lost before they have tried.

After a quarter of a century of State medicine, almost half a century of State pensions, more than half a century of State/local government housing, and a century of State education, the beneficiaries will not release their gains without protest, anger, or resistance. The 1970 Conservatives have to devise not a new strategy but new tactics. They are right to want to remove social benefits from people who are not poor or who can pay; they are wrong to attempt to do so without easing the pain, the anguish, the frustration of the withdrawal symptoms. Millions of families accustomed to pay 5 to 10 per cent of income in rent instead of the 20 to 30 per cent they use in real resources have been habituated to arrange the rest of their household budgeting on the 90–95 per cent remaining instead of the 70–80 per cent they will have left after rising to market rents. Little wonder that Conservatives face condemnations of hard-faced ideologuery from politicians who think the Welfare State the final state of mankind or who believe the poor and the deserving will suffer in the quiet Conservative revolution.

Not least, the Theory of the Middle-Ground Consensus does not withstand examination. It does not encourage a tendency to middling moderation that strengthens political cohesion, but an asymmetrical gravitation towards growing government. Opposition to bigger government (and less power for the people) is described as social divisiveness that must be resisted. Opposition to less government (and more power for the people) is described as social cohesiveness that must be respected. Whatever it is in theory, the consensus in practice is a one-way street to socialisation. Political criticism of the 1970 government, derived from a philosophic anxiety to strike a working-class chord, expresses itself in opposition *à outrance.*

The third obstacle is the continuing delusion among politicians (of all parties) that journalists, in the written or the spoken word, materially reflect or influence public opinion. British journalists are often brilliant "wordsmiths" with strong opinions and humane instincts whose access to a large readership makes them advocates of causes; and reporting is often entangled with advocacy. For example, Mr. Joe Rogaly of the *Financial Times,* a journalist of incisive mind and persuasive pen, ended a recent article (28 March 1972) that found fault with the reverse (negative) income tax in Mr. Anthony Barber's "tax credit" scheme:

> . . . at this stage it must be said that there is only a 50:50 chance that his scheme will emerge with that general degree of acceptance that is necessary if any change so radical is to work in this country.

A year earlier (2 March 1971) he had been even more emphatic and prophetic. The Minister was going to do absolutely nothing about enabling the private sector to serve more people. The few trifling NHS charges would be mostly not worth collecting.

> . . . the NHS will be developed and expanded in a manner only marginally different from that to which Ministers have become accustomed over the past 20 years.

All this not in a spirit of neutral reporting but with unconcealed satisfaction at the discomfiture of those who had been urging reform (dismissed as "Right-wing pamphleteers," an odd description for a BMA committee of ten doctors and two laymen, the present Solicitor-General and me).

The fourth obstacle to welfare reform is the monstrous regiment of *apparatchiki*—from the cool, collected Whitehall bureaucracy to the calm, kindly social worker. (There is now even a "fair" rent officers' association!) Mr. Crossman's penetrating analysis of the relationship between ministers and bureaucrats (*Inside View*) would suggest that some 1970 Ministers cannot have found willing hands and minds to apply their new thinking. This is not only a clash between professional permanent civil servants and amateur transient ministers *per se.*

> There must be a fight and a triumph. It's like a man and a woman in a Victorian novel . . . They are females. They aren't prepared to give way without a good fight.

There is also a clash between civil servants whose philosophic approach may coincide with their occupational interest in big government and Ministers elected to inaugurate less government. Professor Maurice Kogan brilliantly illuminates the interrelationship between unchanging civil servants and changing Ministers. He was Private Secretary to Sir Edward Boyle and Mr. Anthony Crosland. His book, *The Politics of Education,* suggests at least one reason why their policies differed so little. It also indicates that Mrs. Margaret Thatcher must have encountered subtle or sullen resistance. And there is a widespread view, *pace* Lord Blake in the January 1972 *Crossbow,* that Sir Keith Joseph's attitude to the NHS is not "a model of the proper way to equate principle and practice" but another example of a high-principled Minister with a kindly disposition not being ready, in Mr. Crossman's terms, to

> Select a few, a very few issues, and in those issues be bloody and blunt because . . . you get no change except by fighting.

Sir Keith has done more to apply 1970 principles to pensions, but even there the application is a half measure: graduated contributions are to pay for uniform pensions. This is national "insurance" half true, half false. It is an unstable structure that may not outlive the realisation that it is an abuse of national "insurance" goodwill to bolster a disintegrating financing mechanism without the political obloquy of bolstering it by taxation. Instead of winding up a system that unnecessarily socialises income, the Minister is enabling the next Labour government to extend and perpetuate it by raising graduated contributions to pay for graduated pensions.

The Whitehall bureaucrats, able men of integrity as they are, cannot escape the general judgment of American bureaucracy reached by the American economist-turned-bureaucrat Dr. William Niskanen who is returning to academic life because he found that government could not be reformed from within:

> . . . There is nothing inherent in the nature of bureaus and our political (representative) institutions that leads public officials to know, seek out, or act in the public interest.

"Know, seek out or act . . . " Do British bureaucrats know the public interest in welfare? General elections and local government elections do not provide the information on personal preferences in education, medical care, housing or pensions. Elections are suitable for discovering *generalised* public opinion on communal services or policies—from defence and overseas aid to Rhodesia or Northern Ireland. They are not suitable for discovering *personal* preferences. And most education, medical care, housing and pensions are personal services.

"All governments tend to be over-awed by the Treasury Knights . . . This government has been no exception" said Lord Blake. And the Treasury is not the only over-awing Department. The power of the bureaucracy has increased, is increasing, and, for the good of the bureaucrats, should be diminished. It could be by adaptation of the Franco-Belgian *Chefs de Cabinet,* the German minister-official, the American presidential appointments of the top two layers of officials, by the Australian use of a private office, or by developing unofficial advice as a "second opinion" that strengthens Ministers by disciplining officials.

The fifth obstacle is philosophic. Mr. Crossman, one of the outstanding thinkers in Mr. Wilson's Cabinet, has evolved a new theory of Social Damage. Individual preference and choice does social damage in education and medical care, though not in housing or pensions. This is a remarkable development of Socialist theory that would be recognised by none of the theorists from Marx or Engels through Tawney or Cole to, say, Harold Laski or John Strachey. More surprising is a formulation that approaches it from the Conservative camp. Although more liberal (in the classical sense) in temper, Mr. Timothy Raison has said "there can be plenty of room for private provision" in education and health services and

> normal provision for retirement and housing should shift gradually from the social (governmental) to the economic (private) sphere

but

> basically health, education . . . will continue to be essentially State-provided social services . . .

Mr. Crossman sounds the authentic note of intellectual Socialist paternalism that has little root in working-class aspirations. Mr. Raison here speaks like a Tory paternalist rather than a Whig individualist, streams which, as Lord Coleraine has reminded Conservatives, were conjoined by Edmund Burke to form modern Conservatism. I hope that before he achieves high office in the coming twenty-five years, Mr. Raison will change his mind. As a non-Conservative of working-class origin and upbringing I find their well-intended paternalism offensive. I would suggest to Mr. Crossman (Winchester) and Mr. Raison (Eton) that they are misguided on three counts. First, the emerging working man will want to do better than the State can provide, or than his neighbour may choose to provide for himself, in education and medical care no less than in housing and pensions. At Putney in 1647, Colonel Rainboro said for the Levellers:

> Really I think the poorest he that is in England hath a life to live as the richest he.

Second, differentiation through private provision in housing and pensions will spill over into education and health. A well-housed child will do better at school than a child from a slum; a pensioner with a good occupational pension will make better use of the NHS than one with a smaller one. The welfare services cannot be segregated: half differentiated, half uniform. Third, the *attempt* to segregate them will make for the very social divisiveness that is condemned: private provision in education and medical care—which will spread the tighter the State controls education and the NHS—will create two classes: the (growing) minority who pay and the majority who take the State service "free." The only equality the State can create is in the status of common State *beneficiary* by outlawing private education and medical care. The only equality that can be created in an open society is the common status of *consumer* who pays in the market: by returning taxes to the middle- and lower-paid, by topping up low incomes, and by vouchers to all.

And this discussion conveniently introduces the sixth obstacle to welfare reform. If public desire for a thawing out of the Welfare State is resisted from within, it can be expressed only by seeking welfare outside the Welfare State from private suppliers—schools, doctors and hospitals as well as by home ownership and private pensions. But here there are two constrictions. One is that citizens who would want, in Mr. Crossman's words, "to buy themselves something better" in education and medicine have to go on paying for the State school or hospital they do not use; that is a difficulty other countries have removed. The other constriction is that the private suppliers are mostly non-profit organisations with a sense of mission, rather than commercial businesses with a sense of urgency to sell more on the best terms. Both are desirable. The non-profit organisations mobilise voluntary work and charitable capital. They have mostly kept pace with personal incomes and some have grown faster. But not fast enough to enable any but a politically insignificant 5 to 10 per cent to buy the welfare of their choice. They should be supplemented by providing more scope for commercial enterprise to respond to the latent demand for more choice in welfare from the middle- and lower-paid as well as from the higher-paid.

These are tasks the 1970 Conservatives will have to tackle in their second term. They will require a lot of thinking and research in the next two years. In the meantime some hope must be held out that private suppliers will be allowed to serve parents, patients, or pensioners who want to pay for something better than the State can supply, and that they in turn will be welcomed and encouraged for their independence and integrity, and for adding funds and resources not accessible to the tax-levying State. The 1970 Conservatives must see that the more they encourage personal provision of welfare the easier will be the political task of thawing out the Welfare State in the face of the occupational resistance of its *apparatchiks.* They must begin to prepare now for tax refunds and vouchers, about which some Tories are sceptical, as political stop-gap fortifiers until taxes can be reduced as more cash benefits are withdrawn from the non-poor and more benefits in kind are charged for.

If the 1970 Conservatives are to continue the long overdue reform of the Welfare State in their second term, they must resolve the Crossman/Raison dichotomy and heed the Tory paternalists, the collectivists on the Opposition benches, the bureaucrats, and the journalists less than the common people whose aspirations they misconceive or misrepresent and who want what was set out in 1970. This course is political prudence as well as adherence to principle. For it could make the second term itself more certain.

CHAPTER **41**

1978

The State Is Usurping Parents

The rediscovery of the family by Prime Minister Callaghan in the approach to the 1979 General Election, with the predictable promise of increased State support, was countered by the precisely contrary view that the Welfare State had undermined the family. * The Welfare State and its rising taxes are still preventing parents from resuming the family provision originated in the late nineteenth century.

(*The Daily Telegraph*, October 1978.)

As a father and grandfather like James Callaghan, I applaud his moving words on the family as "the place where we care for each other, where we feel our responsibilities for each other, where we practise consideration for each other." Yet it is his political thinking and his party—copied by some Liberals and Conservatives—that have undermined the family he now champions.

In the election campaign we shall hear a lot about child benefits, the taxation of married couples and single people, working mothers, single-parent families, juvenile crime and vandalism, etc.; but not about the real culprit: the State itself.

The trouble started more than a century ago, when the State began to interpose itself between parents and children. Since 1870 it has gnawed at the bonds of family by *preventing* parents from "caring for" children, *discouraging* children from "feeling responsible" for one another or for parents, *hindering* members of families from "practising consideration" for one another.

The family is the unit of British private and social life. It is the home of the next generation. There is no substitute for the natural love that parents and children feel for each other and would express if they were not prevented, discouraged or hindered. The natural tendency would be for parents to feel responsible for their children until they were able to care for themselves; for children to look to parents for guidance in learning how to take their place in adult life.

From the way Mr. Callaghan has spoken since he became Prime Minister about the necessity for vast "public" expenditure on welfare, you might suppose the British family would have disintegrated if it had not been for the State. The truth is the very opposite. When families needed help the State helped them in the wrong way. The British family today would be much stronger if the State had not replaced the natural paternalism of parents by the political paternalism of government.

This truth runs counter to the myth of the Fabians, the welfare Liberals and the paternalist Tories that the Welfare State marked a vast social advance. While 1978 is an improvement on 1948, or 1925, or 1911, comparison is futile. The improvement is the result of higher productivity *despite* the centralisation, bureaucracy, inefficiency, jobbery and taxation brought by the Welfare State. The real question is: did State welfare bring better education, health care, housing, saving for retirement—the four foundations of the family—than would otherwise have developed?

Long before 1870, when the origins of State education were introduced, parents were increasingly paying small school fees out of low incomes. School attendance and literacy in 1850 in England exceed that in the world as a whole in 1950. Two-thirds of working-class children were receiving daily schooling.

This development would have continued since then if parents had not been taxed more heavily to provide "free" State education. By now the British would be paying more for education *voluntarily* than they are having extracted from them by taxation. The reason is obvious to any father or grandfather (and mother or grandmother). They would have been able to see the family benefit.

They would certainly not have tolerated the falling standards of recent years. State education has damaged the family, especially the poorer.

By the 1890s most adult men were *voluntarily* insured with friendly societies against sickness (and to that degree against old age) and death. As the membership of friendly societies grew faster than the population, the uninsured were a shrinking minority. The implication of Mr. Callaghan's argument, that British heads of families would have callously neglected their wives and children, is a myth.

What is not a myth is that from 1911, when State insurance for sickness was made compulsory, from 1925, when pension insurance was made compulsory, and from 1948, when payment for health services was made compulsory through taxation, families could not spend as much as they would have done and would now be doing voluntarily. They would by now be spending more on sickness and health services and pensions by voluntary insurance than they are being made to do by taxation. The reason, again, is that they would be seeing the family benefit, which they now cannot.

Although incomes were much lower sixty years ago than now, more and more families were buying their homes and becoming owner-occupiers. By 1915, 11 per cent of British families were buying their homes. By now the percentage would be not 55 but nearer the 65 of America or the 75 of Australia. And it would have included many council tenants.

Ordinary British families eighty years ago were also saving for rainy days and retirement through building societies, friendly and collecting societies and co-operative societies, trade unions, other workers' societies, life assurance, industrial insurance, railway banks, trustee banks, Post Office savings banks. Mr. Callaghan's insinuation that, if it were not for compulsion through the State, British families would have neglected their health, their education, their homes or themselves in old age is a bald assertion and a slander on Labour voters. His implication that, if it were not for the State, the British family would long have broken up, is historical hysteria.

The truth is again the opposite. From 1870 State education has spread to the point at which 95 per cent of families are discouraged from giving education as much thought as entertainment. From 1915, when rent control began and led to local authority building in 1919, council tenancy has spread to 6½ million families who are prevented from giving housing and homes as much thought as holidays. From 1911 and 1948, compulsory tax payment for health services has spread to the point at which 98 per cent of families are hindered from giving choice of doctor or the timing of medical treatment as much thought as they give their choice of decorator or the timing of Christmas parties.

What has Mr. Callaghan's State Welfare done for the family? Since education is provided by the State, parents cannot feel they have much to do with it: they cannot satisfy their sense of responsibility to educate their children for life. And children sense their parents' incapacity: they do not look for their parents to provide their education, for they see it provided by teachers, officials and politicians.

Since the state provides medical care in sickness and accident, parents feel they cannot do much for their children in these crises. And children sense it: they do not look to their parents to have much influence in restoring them to good health.

And they tend to leave aged parents or subnormal brothers, sisters, uncles, aunts, children in hospitals that are increasingly misused as hostels. (Half the beds are occupied by what the trade calls "geriatrics" and "psychiatrics").

Since government supplies housing for one family in three, parents cannot feel they are doing much about providing a home for the family. And children sense their parents' impotence and lack of influence or authority.

Since the State provides income in retirement, children increasingly leave their aged parents to government.

Is it any wonder family bonds have been loosened? Since children look not to their parents, but to "public" authorities, social workers and officials outside the family for education, health care and homes, is it any wonder that children in trouble do not seek comfort, advice or guidance from parents? Is it any wonder that parents leave children in trouble to outsiders?

The politicians' solution is more government power, more officials, higher taxes to pay for more State services to interpose themselves between parents and children. Their cure for the failure of paternalism and coercion is more paternalism and more coercion.

The family is a unit that must be allowed *self-government* if it is to thrive. There are some elemental requirements the State must leave to the family to learn by practice and experience. It must be left a large measure of autonomy, self-rule and family judgment in four elementals: education, health care, homes and saving for rainy days and retirement. If some families are short-sighted, less provident, or incapable, they can be helped by information, advice, example: if poor, by money, perhaps with a requirement of minimum health insurance. But they must take decisions themselves.

The tragic error of the past century was to help poor or other needy families by State benefits in kind which teach nothing but passive acceptance, instead of benefits in cash, which families could have learned to spend more wisely and responsibly than even the best-intentioned official. (And not all officials are selfless saints.)

The family is an oasis of subsidisation, a bulwark of privilege. Even Beveridge saw this truth. No wonder the egalitarians have undermined it by teaching children to scorn their parents' values. The sociologists are seeing their error, but too late. To force families is to paralyse them. Only one right policy is open to British politicians: to help families develop in their own ways.

There is no alternative. As incomes rise, families will want better education, health services, homes, retirement income, than the State can provide equally for all out of taxation, which, moreover, is paid so reluctantly that the distinction between (legal) avoidance and (illegal) evasion is increasingly blurred morally and ignored.

Family aspirations can be suppressed only by coercion. The dream of

Fabian egalitarians, Liberal welfarists or Tory paternalists that the British family could be coaxed or coerced is empty. The taxpayers' revolt shows the British will not take more useless and nasty medicine.

The Californian Proposition 13, against taxation, would have an even larger vote in Britain. The parents' protest in Kent against zoning is a warning to politicians. Mr. Callaghan's election bait of yet more government, bureaucracy and taxation will turn out to be a boomerang, especially if the alternative of more freedom for the family is presented imaginatively and dramatically.

CHAPTER 42

1980

Move Universities to the Market

An invitation from an "establishment" journal provided the opportunity to reinforce the earlier argument of 1962. The best hope of strengthening independence from political influence lay in market-cost fees with scholarships for promising students and supporting loans or vouchers. * An additional purpose in the 1990s is to supplement pure scholarship by teaching the preferences of students and the requirements of industry.
(*New Universities Quarterly*, September 1980.)

Higher education has moved too far from the market. Its dilemmas and heart-searchings arise mainly from that divorce. And they will remain after the cuts are absorbed, until it moves nearer and is more responsible to self-financing consumers of its teaching and research.

The divorce from the market is reflected in the air of unreality in the exchange of the editor with Sir Alec Merrison and Professor Maurice Peston. At one point I thought it was approaching reality when it asked whether "the country" wanted engineers more than sociologists, but it then lost sight of "money" and turned to "vision," that is, from reality to conjecture.

None of the participants pursued this fruitful line of thought. None asked if the *country* necessarily wanted to cut down on higher education even if there was agreement that the *government* had overspent, over-borrowed and over-printed currency. But the replacement of country by government is an unavoidable risk so long as the financing of education is channelled through government. The decision on where to cut down on expenditure is then political, even party political. And, whatever the party in power, the short-period decisions of government are not necessarily likely to reflect the long-term interests of the country or of academia.

It is hardly necessary to resist the argument that the UGC protects higher education from political influence. It would be improper and undemocratic if it did. As a taxpayer I expect my MP to account to me for the money he takes from me and passes to Oxbridge or Redbrick. And that is party politics.

In supporting and consolidating the system of financing from taxation through government (national or local) and party politics, higher education has made the same mistake as the doctors. The doctors have bought financial security at the high price of political influence and subjection to government resources as decided by economic conditions and fluctuations and the reactions to them, not least in "incomes policies" and other irrelevances for scholarship. The doctors, too, dreamed of a Health Corporation stocked with tax funds that doctors would spend without accounting for it.

If a sizeable part of higher education were financed by students paying fees and by industry placing research contracts and investing in faculties of business administration, financing and marketing and scientific technology, more money would now be going into the universities, despite the slowing down in industrial activity, or because of the falling rate of economic growth.

Universities might then be nearer the industrial base from which their incomes—taxes on profits and production and earnings—ultimately come. They might be under more pressure to produce graduates equipped for industry: the requirements of vocation might loom larger and the potential of pure scholarship loom less. That would redress the imbalance that has persisted too long in the era of indirect political financing and university unreality. But it would do the universities little, if any, harm and industry much good. In any event, better relatively weak pressure from several industrial sources, from which it is possible to escape, than strong pressure from one ubiquitous political source to which higher education is now harnessed.

The universities may think they can hope for a sympathetic rather than a sceptical minister—a Shirley Williams than (say, but I do not know) a Mark Carlisle. But that is playing politics. It is to put scholarship, learning and research at the mercy of political chance. In any event, for some years a succession of Carlisles is more likely than the dream of a succession of Williamses—until Labour regains its capacity as a governing party, if ever. And if the Carlisles are replaced, it may be by the nightmare of Kinnocks rather than of Williamses. And the Kinnocks will not meekly hand over large sums without asking the universities to serve "the national interest"—as defined by autocratic Kinnocks, benign but blinkered Heffers, and romantic technocratic Benns. Their definition would be very different from the judgment of the universities as well as the wishes of the students or their parents, or the requirements of industry responding to consumers in the market place.

The *rationale* of financing from a predominantly single source has never been persuasive. It implies a wholly unfounded confidence in what Professor Albert Hirschman called "voice" to the neglect of the power of "exit." Universities arguing, however persuasively, with government for more money—or fewer cuts—have poor bargaining power if both sides know there are few other sources of money in the event of disagreement. Even if only as a reserve power, the universities will have to develop other sources—student fees, research fees, grants from industry, foundations and private benefactors—as a means of strengthening their "voice." Why has higher education sold itself to a monopsonist—and a political monopsonist to boot?

The case for government financing from compulsory taxes voluntarily agreed by democratic majority is that higher education is a public good from which all taxpayers gain but the financing of which some would shirk to obtain a "free ride." This valid theoretical concept lends itself to massive, grotesque, unlimited and even hilarious inflation. In his incisive little book on the nature of public goods, Professor Peston reproduced a celebrated passage from Lord Robbins on the ubiquity and universality of public benefit. Almost every activity unintentionally generates benefit to third parties: our house has a thatched roof and passers-by stop to admire it. They smile and talk to companions about it—or to us if we are nearby. That is not a case for subsidising me. On that ground we should all be taking in one another's externalities. External benefits may be a necessary but they are not a sufficient reason for State subsidy or financing, not least because "market failure" (caused by poverty, inequality of income, short-sightedness among consumers, monopoly among suppliers, etc.) is often exceeded by "governmental failure" (caused by party politics, inequality of power to influence government, over-centralisation, bureaucracy, resistance to change, waste, corruption, etc.).

If all the arguments that university education confers benefits on all in Britain by producing home-born and overseas-born graduates were true and the cuts will do damage, the universities have neglected to justify much larger sums from the taxpayer–government–UGC. Yet there must be a point at which the marginal advantage of higher education is exceeded by its opportunity cost—the marginal advantage of hospitals, kidney machines, nursery schools, home helps, meals on wheels, roads, child benefits, retirement pensions (for most, not wealthy pensioners), art galleries and museums, opera and ballet, and so on, almost ad infinitum. "External benefits" is a claim we can all make. The universities are not unique.

Some universities (or departments) can properly claim that generalised measures for overseas students may damage the more productive institutions with a high complement of overseas students rather than the less productive, or at least less attractive. The damage they may now suffer is a consequence of macro-cuts, which are scythes that lop off the heads of flowers as well as weeds.

But the solution is not smaller cuts *all round* that would save some flowers but also some weeds. The much more sensitive solution is the micro-measure of charging by each university (or department) according to marginal or long-run average costs—and also according to income if it wishes to select students with more potential but little money rather than those with less potential and more money. The ultimate safeguard of scholarship is to make higher education more self-supporting in the market. That would strengthen the good teachers, researchers and scholars, though some of the rest would not survive. But "higher education" is not a homogeneous product. The present system finances the less good or relatively pedestrian as well as the better and superlative.

The Government spokesman, Dr. Rhodes Boyson, has said it has no plans to close down any British university within the next five years. I do not see why not. British higher education is overgrown, undisciplined, wasteful. It would improve by pruning. The weeds are stunting the flowers. I have little doubt that remoteness from the market breeds indifference to costs not only in schools but also in colleges, polytechnics and universities. The lights would be turned out sooner—literally—if income were derived from selling to the market rather than from bargaining with bureaucrats. Professor David Friedman suggests that the costs of private production are characteristically half those of "public" production. No doubt there are many exceptions. Yet if John Pardoe's private colleges can train office staff at a third or a half of the cost of government colleges of further education, I should expect State universities to have higher costs than private universities.

In the absence of market tests—the willingness of students to pay fees, assisted by loans (or vouchers, as argued by Professor Michael Crew and Dr. Alastair Young in an IEA Hobart Paper, *Paying by Degrees* in 1977), the willingness of consumers to pay for research, the willingness of private industry to endow scholarships it judges will be fruitful—how does higher education justify the large funds it asks taxpayers to provide? Why must we assume that *every* university, *every* faculty, *every* department, *every* professor, reader, lecturer or demonstrator has earned its/his keep by using resources more productively than they would have been used elsewhere—from hospitals to ballet and thousands of other alternatives? Why should higher education be sheltered, more than competitive industry, from the verdict of the consumer? How, to put the point starkly, can university vice-chancellors ask for more money from taxes when children are allowed to die from spina bifida in the tax-financed NHS?

I do not say this case cannot be made. But the universities have not made it. And they will never be able to make it in a form that convinces the public as long as they depend on tax-funds. That is why they must move nearer the market.

I would go further. One less Redbrick—or half-a-dozen—would be no loss if replaced by one—or half-a-dozen—new Buckinghams (and all different from one another). We should then be experimenting with more intensive cost-saving innovation such as two-year degrees, which the first Buckingham has pioneered in peacetime. And I think the academic establishment, well represented by Sir Alec Merrison and Professor Peston, must expect it to happen. The revulsion from the State, now increasingly evident in medical care and school education, will spread to higher education. So will the case for pruning as the effect of the lower birth-rate passes upward from the schools. The State-funded universities should welcome competition from private universities. In the absence of private competition it is never possible to say that State-funded higher education is efficient. Private competition would enable it to make that claim—as State universities in the USA can now make it more plausibly than Essex or Sussex or Salford or Warwick.

The British Council brings students to Britain and others to learn about British thought. A senior Polish economist, head of a key organisation, recently wanted to visit the IEA to learn about our work on market and pricing systems, especially shadow or transfer pricing inside large firms. After an hour I found I had more in common with him than with politicians, planners and bureaucrats in Britain who think resources can be allocated from the centre by all-knowing benevolence. He even scouted Oskar Lange's notion that the centre could be instantaneously informed of events or demands at the periphery by speed-of-light computers. He wanted to come to Britain to see what he could learn, and I was glad to see him. Splendid. But, especially as a market-minded economist, would he not have paid his costs without subsidy?

The finances of the universities would be most secure if individual consumers or clients or benefactors received (or saw) better value the more they paid. But no taxpayer—student or parent, client or benefactor—receives (or sees) better value by paying higher taxes. And as long as the universities are financed out of general taxation apportioned in the Cabinet Room, no taxpayer can be asked to support higher education by paying higher taxes, since there is no way for him to ensure that *his* taxes will go to the universities. This divorce between taxpayer and recipient of taxes, as Professor Peston knows, has exercised the new "public choice" economists. Here representative democracy is unrepresentative and produces government failure. The only solutions seem to lie in the constitutional reforms of referenda and earmarked taxes.

Until that day, which seems distant, the universities' best bet for all three objectives—maximising revenue, increasing efficiency, and strengthening independence from political influence—lies in charging fees, with rebates or scholarships for promising students, and supporting loans and/or vouchers. New evidence on the response of parents and students and the general public to loans *vis-à-vis* grants is analysed by Professor Cedric Sandford of Bath University and two colleagues in a forthcoming IEA Research Monograph. The conventional importuning of politicians and the defensive responses discussed by Sir Alec and Professor Peston will no longer suffice. Higher education must not confine its financing largely to taxation; it must tap all possible sources. It must redress the imbalance of political funding by selling itself in the market.

CHAPTER **43**

1988

Political Bar to Economic Progress

A series of four articles on the reconstruction and transfer of welfare from the State to the market as economic conditions change, concluding with a six-point outline of reforms. * Reform awaits the emergence of younger Conservatives untied by the past of their elders and of Left-inclined politicians and academics who finally accept the market.

(*The Sunday Telegraph*, August–September 1988.)

Economic advance since 1979 has in many ways been unprecedented in British history. But a stubborn obstacle remains—the dominance of the economy by politics.

We can run our lives in two ways. One is political, by voting for spokesmen to represent us in legislative assemblies making decisions collectively on the use of our resources. The other is the commercial way, by making decisions individually for ourselves in the market.

We in Britain are still using politics far too much, commerce far too little. Government runs or regulates most economic activity. We could cut its tax "take" of the national cake from a half to a quarter, probably less. The income tax rate could be cut from 25 to 15 per cent.

But we must be ready for a cultural shock. Since the war we have said, when anything has gone wrong, "The government must do something about it." Many still say it, in all political parties. We still do not think instinctively "Keep the politicians out!"

The City pages present responsible commercial activity. In production and distribution, buying and selling, saving and investing, good decisions bring personal reward, bad decisions can bring ruin. This is generally not true in politics. Its rewards are only loosely connected with good decisions in doing public good. And the penalties for bad decisions in doing public harm are rare. Contrasted with commerce, politics is irresponsible.

The reasons are clear but ignored. The nineteenth-century hope that representative government would benevolently serve the whole people once they all had the vote remains a hope. Conventional political observers still see parliamentary democracy as the ready instrument of the popular will. The economist asks about the costs and benefits of government to individuals and families, which can be measured.

In the commercial market we "represent" ourselves directly. We spend our money on food, clothing, furnishing, motoring. We use our money—"votes" to buy what we want as individuals, families. If we don't like one supplier we can change to another.

The political "market" is very different. Politicians spend other people's money. We the people are "represented" indirectly in a tortuous chain of public meetings, conferences, motions, references back, elections, private conclaves, lobbies, compromises, hard bargains.

We submit to majority decisions on intimate personal services like education, medical care, housing and transport. And if we, as individuals or minorities, don't like what this Tower of Babel produces, we cannot escape.

In spending our own money, we make every penny count. In the political "market" our cross on the ballot-paper makes not a scrap of difference. The cost of voting, in time, earnings lost, inconvenience, can be high; the benefit is doubtful, immeasurable or absent.

So it is rational to "vote" in the commercial market for what you want, but "irrational" to vote in the political market because you have no precise idea what you are likely to get. No wonder one in four of us does not bother at all in general elections and more than two in four at local elections. Yet our political representatives are spending as much of our money as we are ourselves!

Dig deeper. In the commercial market we compare prices and qualities, select the best colours and accessories, expect guarantees and after-sales service, and our money back if dissatisfied. And we are getting better about choosing investments now that there are more alternatives.

Contrast politics. We select people and policies by slogans about "needs," promises about "priorities," rhetoric, the arts of the demagogue. What a way to run the railroads, the schools, the hospitals, the day nurseries, the libraries or airports. And can you imagine the reply from your "public servants" if you asked for your money back when dissatisfied, as you often are? Investment in politics is a dangerous gamble.

Commercial prices are sometimes imperfect in registering values. But political prices are often non-existent. If Sir Roy Griffiths had run Sainsbury without prices, as politicians now expect him to run the NHS, the Sainsbury family, shareholders and employees would be paupers.

To influence commercial suppliers we withdraw our purchasing power. To influence political decisions on our daily lives we have to become politicians, join committees, boards, councils. But not all of us are good at the life political. And most of us prefer the life domestic with our family and friends. But that is the logic of the political process. The politicians love it. Ninety per cent of us would hate it.

The political classes have a new name for it—"community." Be not deceived. It is another word for collectivism, socialism, statism—the politicians' happy hunting ground.

It is urgent to cut government down to size. Professor David Marquand, a former Socialist who is trying to see the light, said last week that the aim of the "democratic left" (itself a contradiction) is "to make market forces the servants instead of the masters of democratic politics." But the lesson of the post-war years is that the people can exert themselves better in the market than in politics.

The purpose now is to confine politics to its essential roles, which are minor, to get it out of the way of the market.

Government and politics loom too large in our lives because once they get in, for good or bad reasons, they can't (or won't) get out. The supreme example is school education and all it means for the happiness of children, the family, industry, the economy and national finances.

Parents were increasingly paying school fees in the nineteenth century, despite low incomes, and more would undoubtedly have joined them. In 1870 the politicians thought the gaps should be filled by tax-financed "free" schools.

That was the error that has ended in the unresponsive, inefficient, politicised State education for more than nine out of ten children that the government is trying to reform.

The Britain of the 1980s is worlds apart from the Britain of the 1870s. Incomes are much higher. Parents understand even better than did their great-grandparents and grandparents the value to their children of basic schooling.

They have much higher standards in their private and family lives—their food and clothing, their furnishing and housing, motoring and holidaying.

Here most have a choice in spending their higher incomes, and here they have learned to become demanding in what they buy.

But not for the nine in ten in State schools. Politicians and educationists have not understood the vast economic and social advance of the last 118 years.

The State schools are still mostly run by the political process. We still elect "representatives" in Whitehall and town hall to decide for us. Yet we could all decide for ourselves. And nearly one in ten does decide in 2,500 schools with about three quarters of a million children.

Each year more of the nine could decide the schooling of their children. More will decide, and more are deciding. As real incomes rise annually by some 3 per cent, they will have increased by almost 50 per cent by the year 2000.

Moreover, increasing numbers will share in sizeable sums, perhaps £50,000 to £100,000 or more, inherited from their home-owning parents.

So, as more down the income scale come to experience higher standards everywhere else, they will demand better schooling than government, under any party, can provide out of taxation. And more and more will be able to pay for it for the first time. The one in ten will grow year by year to two and three and more.

The luckier parents in the better jobs and expanding industries and regions will reach this stage before A.D. 2000, others not until 2010 or even 2020. But the less fortunate do not have to wait.

The difference between State and private schools is precisely that fee-paying parents can exercise more influence than tax-supported parents. The evidence is now accepted by the critics of private education.

That is why they talk incessantly of "parent power." But they do not see that it rests on the method of payment.

The old hope on the Left for social cohesion when all parents had to accept State schools has passed; no party will abolish the private schools. The prospect of One Nation now lies only in the nine joining the one.

But there is no reason to wait twenty or thirty years. It could be done in the next two or three.

Mr. Kenneth Baker's Act will not do it. Opting out by schools sounds a revolutionary idea, but it will not produce much improvement as long as the money for schooling goes straight from government to the schools, which will therefore continue to be controlled by the political process. No school can be independent if it is financed by the State.

The Baker reform obscures the human nature and *Realpolitik* of school government.

That the schools' income will come from central rather than local government will not change its political flavour. The decision to opt out will be subject to the familiar paraphernalia of politics, with its majorities on boards of governors and among parents—and all *that* means in lobbying and hard bargaining.

Governors and heads will control on average untold wealth of £1 million (roughly £1,000 for each of 1,000 pupils). They will band together to hold what they have. And only the usual breed of activists will become parent-governors. Boards of governors cannot represent non-political parents.

The reality of school "politics" is that government will impose restrictions on the powers of parents to move children (especially to new schools, which will therefore be discouraged), on the hiring and firing of teachers and on the powers of parent-governors.

It was not true that in the nineteenth century most of our low-income great-grandparents would not pay for education. But it is now true that it is dog-in-the-manger government that is stopping most parents from spending more than it can find from taxation.

If we now wish to increase the "investment" in our children, the secret is to change education from a "public service," which is a smoke-screen for a political battle between party activists, into a parental decision.

That requires not government cash funds direct to schools but the return of taxes to parent-taxpayers and topping up lower incomes so that all parents can pay.

Any other solution will waste ten more years in which it will be said that the Baker reform should be given time to see what it can do. It will do nothing fundamental unless it moves from financing schools to financing parents. But the Thatcher Conservatives will have to prevail over the statists.

Medical care is, after education, the largest refuge for superfluous political power that has taken control but cannot change with social advance and technical progress.

As with State education, the National Health Service is fighting a rearguard action it cannot win. Current official re-thinking on health policy will not produce the best results unless it unmasks repeated myths about the NHS.

It was created in the 1940s in the light of the social conditions of the 1920s and 1930s, though it irresponsibly almost destroyed the voluntary health organisations built up by ordinary working people over fifty years. To survive, it must urgently prepare for the twenty-first century.

Like State education, it applied the wrong solution—political supply of "free" services instead of purchasing power to enable all to pay. But this is precisely the fatal error that the vested interests of doctors, managers, officials and employees wish to perpetuate. "Free" is the camouflage for tax-paid. But customers control a service only if they pay directly by prices (charges), not indirectly by taxes.

The elephantine structure originated in 1948 now obstructs vital reform in 1988. Tax financing, centralised price-less rationing of resources, monopoly organisation, professionals and trade unionists who prefer payment by the impersonal State to payment by satisfied customers—these are the obstructions that must be countered. The required reforms will not come from inside the NHS.

The NHS persists in presenting itself as a "welfare" service when it is increasingly a consumer service. The nearest it has moved to new thinking is "*internal* markets" to make better use of its *existing* resources in beds, equipment and staffing in neighbouring areas.

But the urgent revolutionary reconstruction is "*external* markets" to generate *more* resources by competing with the vast range of other services on which the British spend their rising incomes.

The NHS must therefore jettison methods and practices, ideas and attitudes in which the withdrawal symptoms will be painful. It will have to change from a "public service" that "gives" medical care to grateful patients to a competitive service that sells to its customers.

Its ideological supporters, who defend State services on principle, however outdated, still claim it is the envy of the world. But in the forty years since 1948 the world has ignored it.

The systems nearest to the NHS are in the Communist countries, where State-controlled, bureaucratic, insensitive, corrupt medical systems are made tolerable only by privileges for the powerful and black markets for the populace.

But in the Western world only Italy tried it (in the early 1980s). It collapsed after a couple of years, not least because the Italians are even better at tax evasion than we are.

The confident defence of the NHS that other systems would produce "double standards" according to purchasing power conveniently obscures the *multi*-standards of the NHS according to cultural, occupational and political power.

The dedication of doctors and devotion of nurses are components of elemental human compassion; they have nothing to do with State medicine. They dignified medical care in my childhood when doctors in the East End of London, whose charge for a visit was 2*s.* 6*d.*, asked my mother for 9*d.*, and she was proud to pay it. State medicine is politicised medicine: its entanglement with taxation, national finances and general elections has seduced doctors and nurses into replacing human compassion with financial calculation.

Strikes against the patient were unheard of before the NHS. Now it misleads doctors and nurses into striking against the patient under the guise of striking against the State.

The NHS cannot provide the higher standards expected in the coming decades as long as tax financing limits its revenue, now around 6 per cent of national income, far below the 8 per cent in Europe and Australasia or the 10 per cent in North America with their mixed systems of State and private, compulsory and voluntary insurance.

Is it seriously argued that the British care less about their health and would pay less to preserve it than the French or the Germans, the Americans or the Canadians? The tragic difference is not of national character or of incomes but of method of payment. It is the NHS that is discouraging us from spending more on our health.

Then there is the myth that the NHS is cheap. In *quality* the NHS is very expensive: in time, peace of mind, waiting with painful hips, varicose veins, haemorrhoids, inability to choose your surgeon or hospital, to ensure contact with your family in emergency and your workplace in convalescence, lack of privacy at all times. The personal and national loss is incalculable, but ignored in the NHS.

The claim that the NHS is run cheaply, taking only 6 per cent in administrative costs, is thus bogus. Any system can be run cheaply if it throws costs on to its customers in a take-it-or-leave-it service that ignores their preferences.

The final myth is that the NHS is popular. It is based on naive opinion polling that asks a national sample if it "approves" of the NHS without stating the tax cost. How can you "approve" of anything if you are not told its price, the missing link? You may "approve" of apples and buy them at 40p a pound, but not at 70p.

British health services will not be safe with doctors, managers or politicians, but only with the people who value it sufficiently to pay for it voluntarily.

We can now think of replacing the Liberty, Equality, Fraternity of the 1789 French Revolution by the Liberty, Prosperity, Fraternity of the 1979 British Revolution.

That is the right order. Liberty comes first to liberate the merchant venturing long repressed by the State. The result is the prosperity that flagged in

Britain in the 1960s and 1970s, so that living standards fell to among the lowest in Europe. And prosperity will enable the British to express their innate fraternal compassion for others.

The moral critics of commercial society claim fraternity as exclusively their "value." That is bad history. The British displayed spontaneous fraternal feeling for one another long before the State almost destroyed it and then tried to enforce it by socialised welfare.

The "free enterprise" Americans are much more generous in their local community United Funds for good causes than the "welfare" British. The Welfare State put the cart of charity before the horse of prosperity; no wonder it ended with neither.

The economic reforms since 1979 in transferring power from State to citizen must now proceed from industry to the "welfare" services.

Education and medical care are the two that are *thought* to be the politically most difficult. That view is also denied by history. A government that transferred education and medicine from politics to the family would soon have public opinion on its side as standards rose. (A parent from Stoke-on-Trent writes that his complaints are ignored: "we have got nowhere because we have no financial hold over the teacher to do better.")

Radical reform in housing and pensions would, politically, be even easier. Less than one in ten parents and patients has opted out of the State but, in housing and pensions, six or seven are owner-occupiers or accumulating private pensions. Opting out could be extended even further to insurance for sickness, possibly unemployment.

People were building schools and hospitals and buying homes (by mortgages in Leeds and elsewhere) long before shallow Fabians, like the Webbs and G. B. Shaw, urged politicians to usurp the parent. The State has no business owning a single home, hospital or school. In these intimate affairs of the family it is a stranded whale that has missed the tide of social progress.

Instead, it persists with the pretence that 90 per cent of us would neglect the education of our children, the health of our wives or husbands, the well-being of our ageing parents. If any are guilty of these crimes against themselves, it is the State that is guilty of crimes against the family.

The perverse logic of impertinent paternalism is becoming too apparent to deny. Brent is not the only council that provokes tears or laughter. Local government, Tory, Democrat, Labour, continues to supply its comic list of "essential services," from libraries with pop tapes to pools with wave-makers.

Public libraries were established in the 1850s to supply good reading for working men. Swimming pools are mostly used by the active young but partly financed by the inactive elderly. Perhaps the best reply to the statists is ridicule.

The failure of "public ownership" has brought a new understanding that it takes private ownership to make you care for personal and national assets. How can we "care" for "our" nationalised railway engine? Private ingenuity can be applied also in the very heart of government: in parts of law and order, police duties, defence; even on the seabed and in air space.

These vast potentialities for liberty, prosperity and fraternity will require radically new attitudes and policies.

1. The most fundamental is a moral, psychological, cultural change in attitudes to the notion of "public." This honourable word has been debased as a camouflage for political. "Public" expenditure is political expropriation of private earnings and savings. The "public" sector comprises the politically-manipulated industries in which the real public has little influence and no say, and so on.

2. People want to keep the money they earn and spend it themselves. Anyone who says he knows more than the people how to spend it is denying them the opportunity of learning from experience how to spend it better.

3. Many bureaucrats are still surplus to needs. They should be allowed to decide where and when they will move to the growing private industries that will require the best of them. Holding their pay relatively to inflation for three years would encourage movement to the market.

4. The growing private industries in welfare and former government functions will require a strong dose of buccaneering merchant venturing. Only one millionaire seems to have emerged in the private school industry. Professionalism and the non-profit motive are desirable, but not enough. Profit-making hospitals are the most efficient in the United States.

   Entrepreneurs, perhaps from Europe or America, are required to *anticipate* the growing numbers who will want to escape from the State. We must hope for more welfare millionaires.

5. Creating "voices" on committees is not enough. Only the tiny minority of assertive activists will "join" them. The common people

must be enabled to "beat" them by creating *exits* through which the dissatisfied can escape. Money-votes are more powerful than ballot-box votes, especially to the uninfluential.

6. Britain has no written constitution, but means must be found to require government to reduce its tax take from 50 to 25 per cent over seven years.

There is more. But all that would make a good start.

PART VI

The Excesses of Over-Government

CHAPTER 44

1969

Whose Obedient Servant?

> Bureaucrats cannot serve "the public interest" because they have no machinery to measure it. And it conflicts with their interest in maintaining big government. Able men and women are wasted in activities that are not the concern of government. The true "public servants" are the entrepreneurs made to serve the public by the sanction of loss if they fail to supply what consumers want. * In the past decade the bureaucracy has been pruned but its powers have been increased. The education officials now have the control of the school curricula they have sought for twenty-five years.
>
> (*The Telegraph Magazine,* June 1969.)

The air is thick with self-righteousness. Politicians, academics, civil servants protest their devotion to "the public good," "the national interest," "the community well-being" . . . The paragons wear their haloes immodestly.

Politicians, with honourable exceptions, have in recent years damaged "the public interest" by sending us all chasing "national economic planning," "incomes policies," "wage freezes," "guiding lights," and other wild geese. From Harold Macmillan and Selwyn Lloyd to George Brown and others, they owe the rest of us billions in pay, savings, and exports their nostrums have destroyed before birth.

Nor do they even know "the public interest." They are simply out of touch. When did they ask your opinion about comprehensive schools, council house subsidies, graduated pensions, the Betterment Levy? Many of them expected massive opposition to prescription charges; they were wrong. Many fear rejection of benefits related to means; they are wrong.

Even if they did ask, they lack the machinery for giving the public what it wants. The ballot box, which must be used for opinion on medical care, education, housing, pensions. Yet it is their pretext for doing what "majorities" as few as fifty-one out of a hundred (of the two-thirds or three-quarters who bother to vote) want. The rest of us have to lump it.

The growing horde of pseudo-scientists called sociologists, who have outsized social consciences and undersized common sense, declaim their compassion for the poor; they "care"; they have a "commitment" to welfare. Yet they preach that State aid must go equally to all, whether living on £500 or £5,000 a year. So people who need more receive no more; and people who need less receive as much. Compassion? The national interest?

They have a passion; they "care"; they are committed—to the false god of *equality,* the fetish that frustrates the "public good."

The most recent merchant in "the national interest" is the "public servant," traditionally beyond public criticism as a paid employee of a political master—Whitehall Minister or local councillor. But he has become a little more talkative. Sir William Armstrong, the distinguished head of the Home Civil Service, has spoken of the civil servant's work and "traditional satisfaction of service to the community."

State employees are often men of high ability and impeccable integrity. But are they entitled to the special label of "public servant"? They often work hard; they save inexperienced Ministers from precipitate decisions; they carry weak Ministers through crises. But they often have so much power left to them by over-stretched Ministers that they may rule without risk to themselves. They sometimes warn on what is "politically impossible," which is beyond their competence and not their business. Their claim to be "public servants" is questionable because they, too, do not know what the public wants.

When did a civil servant last resign because he felt he was helping to do public harm? How many have salved their conscience by telling themselves they could prevent harm by staying put?

The people who do most good are those who brag least—from village grocer and local builder to business executive and company chairman. Their job is to find out what the public—the customer—wants and set about supplying it. They work for a profit, a surplus over costs. If they judge well, they make money, a little or a lot. If they judge wrong, they lose money. Theirs is the difficult task; and many politicians, academics, and civil servants would make a hash of it.

But these are the authentic "public servants"—from thousands of unknown traders and small "capitalists" to Lord Stokes of British Leyland, "Norman Wates of Wates, Lord Cole of Unilever, D. H. Barran of Shell, Sir Edward Lewis of Decca, Lord Sieff of Marks and Spencer, Henry Lazell of

Beecham, Lord Sainsbury of Sainsbury. And many more, especially those who take risks, try new ideas, offer wide choices.

And businessmen work through machinery used by *everyone,* the market, that enables them to serve not only vocal, organised, strident majorities but also small, unorganised, inarticulate minorities.

If people in industry make a profit when they do not serve the public, that is the politicians' fault for neglecting the laws and institutions required to ensure that they do.

The moralists have a twisted sense of values. They execrate businessmen who use advertising jingles to sell relatively harmless things like soap, soup, cornflakes or instant mash. But they tolerate or laud politicians who tell not-so-white fibs in seducing us to entrust them with our very lives, our liberties, our standard of living. (Read the last six general election addresses.)

It is high time for more humility from the "public-interest"-mongers and more recognition for the people who *pretend* less but *perform* more.

CHAPTER 45

1972

Can Bureaucrats Be Neutral?

Two later essays pursued the pretensions of the "public servants" by the new sophisticated American analysis of the economics of bureaucracy, "public choice." The "public servants" should face the same tests as other people by internal and external competition. They should be disciplined by farming out, hiving off and denationalisation (later called "privatisation"). * There has been some progress but their power remains in substance.

(*The Daily Telegraph,* February 1972 and October 1979.)

Some of Britain's outstanding men, in ability and integrity, are "bureaucrats." For good or ill, they run the offices ("bureaux") of government. Although they may exercise more influence, and thus power, than the heads of businesses, trade unions, the churches, the newspapers, the universities, they have been much less known to the general public.

How many citizens—electors, taxpayers, ratepayers, social insurance contributors—have heard of Sir William Armstrong, Sir Douglas Allen, Sir Donald MacDougall, Sir Samuel Goldman? Sir William is head of the Home Civil Service and Secretary to the Civil Service Department; Sir Douglas head of the Treasury; Sir Donald head of the Government Economic Service and Chief Economic Adviser to the Treasury; Sir Samuel a Second Secretary, a very senior post, at the Treasury. And they are mostly paid more than their Ministers.

Then there are the "head" bureaucrats of each department, usually described, disarmingly, as Permanent Secretary or Under-Secretary.

In practice politicians and Ministers are partly in the hands of the bureaucrats. They must be, whatever party is in power. Until recently it was thought bad form to discuss the bureaucrats in public. They were hardworking, sea-green incorruptibles above the daily debates, the party squabbles, the sordid place-hunting of parliamentary democracy. They neither made government policy, nor executed it. They were neither to be blamed for failure, nor praised for success. They presented the pros and cons of alternative policies for Ministers in their wisdom or ineptitude to decide. And they went home and forgot all about it. The reality is different.

Ministers come and go; bureaucrats go on and on. Ministers are amateurs: they may have developed ideas while in Opposition (or in other departments), but they cannot know the practicability, the likely consequences of what they have thought up. That is for the professional bureaucrats to "advise" on. Ministers are concerned with principles, objectives, strategy. The bureaucrats know the details that can reduce lofty thinking to childish prattle.

So Ministers must be influenced—"managed"—by the bureaucrats. The power can be exercised on Ministers of all parties, but with a difference. Bureaucrats must want to maintain or enlarge their influence: their income, status, even family happiness is at stake. They will therefore work in more harmony with Ministers who maintain or enlarge the province of government than with ministers who reduce it.

The role of bureaucracy has now as never before been dissected by an American economist, Dr. William Niskanen. He is no ivory-tower spinner of theories. He was at the Rand Corporation, the massive research institution in California, when the methods of improving the management of government activities, "systems analysis" and "programme budgeting" were evolved.

When he moved to government on the staff of Secretary of Defence Robert McNamara under President John Kennedy, he found the Rand techniques were simply not being translated into action.

> I came to recognise there is nothing inherent in the nature of bureaus and our political institutions that leads public officials to *know, seek out,* or *act* in the public interest.

Further experience at the Institute for Defence Analysis in Washington crystallised Dr. Niskanen's thinking into a book that should once and for all reveal the Emperor's nakedness of a neutral, objective, efficient Civil Service. He is now a bureaucrat under President Nixon.

Bureaucrats' private interests may conflict with the public interest; if they do, it will come second. This must be true of every Western country. The conflict of interest is especially clear with a Government that wishes to reduce its powers and return them to the people.

For many decades there has been little difference in the philosophy of Conservatives and Labour on the extent of government. The dispiriting years of the consensus blurred the choices the people could have been offered, most notably in fuel, transport and welfare. Apart from the bonfire of controls after 1945, in which even some Socialists rejoiced, and a few sparks of "Tory freedom" (more correctly, economic liberalism) in the mid-1950s, both parties have remorselessly extended the province of government. This is the environment in which the top bureaucrats of the 1970s grew up. But in 1970 a new Government announced the opposite doctrine. Nationalisation, State control, bureaucracy is now on the defensive; at least, that was the promise.

Can the bureaucracy not merely *change* but *reverse* gear against the momentum of twenty-five years? Crashing gears, screeching brakes and roaring engines should be heard all over the land. There is some of each here and there; but elsewhere the silence is creating a sense of anti-climax. Is the bureaucracy slowing down the reversal of engines? Are the reverse gears rusty for lack of use? Can men who have risen to the top, who must have strong opinions, or loyalties, be expected to eat their words or remain silent if they think their country is harmed, if their consciences are offended, their values violated?

Many civil servants must go home at night feeling that their Ministers are, as was said of Byron, "mad, bad and dangerous to know." How can they serve them without intolerable strain?

And should Ministers be served by inherited, hostile, antipathetic advisers? The influence of top bureaucrats has been felt by ministers of both parties. Mr. Richard Crossman has hinted that important papers on pensions were kept from him. The *New Statesman* has reported that Mrs. Margaret Thatcher's chief bureaucrat, Sir William Pile, "is said to have stated—perhaps apocryphally—that although she arrived at the Department with five facts in her head (all wrong), within six months he had succeeded in teaching her eight others (all right)."

Ministers have been on the point of reversing the errors of consensus politics, yet very little seems to happen. Millions are still raised in taxes and returned. No widening of choice in education by vouchers for the working man. No student loans. No encouragement to choice in medical care. No hospital charges. Still too little competition in British industry. Ministerial decisions?—or bureaucratic obstruction?

The conclusion that must be pondered by people of all parties anxious about the future of parliamentary democracy is whether government can effectively reflect the wishes of its electors if it is served by bureaucrats out of sympathy with it. What can be done?

First, should a new Government renew not only Ministers but also the top layers of bureaucrats who work closely with them? It is done in America (and elsewhere) with, I would say, mixed but, on balance, good results.

Second, should the bureaucrats who stay be allowed to make their doubts known to the public and not work behind closed doors or their Ministers' skirts. That is now done in America and Australia.

Third, should unhappy bureaucrats with Conservative (Labour) sympathies "manage" or obstruct Labour (Conservative) Ministers with bees in bonnets and bats in belfries? Should they be tempted to emphasise cons rather than pros, deluge Ministers with piles of papers on dispensable detail to slow down decisions, omit reference to inconvenient documents?

Fourth, is it time for an even more fundamental reform in bringing bureaucrats to book? After a rarefied mathematical-economic analysis of bureaus as monopolies or competitors, Dr. Niskanen concludes they can be disciplined and made to approach nearer to the public interest by competition both from outside, and, perhaps most surprisingly, from within. The first seems simple enough: some local government services (water, refuse collection, fire-fighting, seaside amenities, art galleries, museums) could be "privatised," as well as national health services and State schools.

But internal "duplication" and other "wastes" may also be a price worth paying to change bureaucrats from monopolists into competitors.

Dr. Niskanen proposes competition, or more competition, even in defence: he condemns the "cartel" in American military missions. In Britain Lord Rothschild has made a good start by proposing customer-controlled research. But there is not nearly enough customer control in State education or medical care. There is a long way to go. Government action here amounts to peanuts.

The romantic reading of the British bureaucrat is that he is a mental automaton or philosophic eunuch. The realistic reading is that he is no less—and perhaps no more—human than the rest of us. That is the reason for a reappraisal of the functions and public accountability of the British bureaucrat.

CHAPTER 46

1979

Phase Out the Civil Servants

> The advent of a new Government intending to reduce over-government prompted a review of new ways to prune the excessive bureaucracy vulnerable to a 10-point indictment. Since post-war government has been doing twice as much as it should, there could be large reductions in superfluous staffing. * In 1994 the 10-point indictment stands. After fifteen years of pruning by Conservative Governments millions of superfluous bureaucratic "public employees" remain who could contribute more to the national well-being in private industry.
>
> (*The Daily Telegraph*, October 1979.)

The British bureaucracy is under systematic criticism as never before. Public opinion has become hostile as never before. The question is how to reduce the number of bureaucrats.

Some civil servants have been offended by the suggestion on this page recently that one way would be to use the price mechanism and reduce bureaucrats' pay. That is what happens in the real world. If pay in a firm, occupation, industry, region or country falls, people sooner or later move to where pay is higher. Why not British bureaucrats?

In defence, they claim their work is exceptionally important, demanding, or responsible; requires them to move unpredictably and disrupts their family life; denies or cramps the right to strike. In attack they reply that people in private industry have perks, not least cars, health insurance, expenses, and others not available to civil servants.

There is an immediate and obvious retort. Civil servants, local officials, public employees of any kind, are not tied to their jobs. Most can move. Some do, but only a trickle. If they remain, it must be because they like their jobs despite the drawbacks. They must prefer their regular employment, sheltered from market fluctuations at home or overseas, their security for life, their sense of power or importance, their OHMS briefcases, the prospect of honours, the pensions escalated in retirement, or other perks.

Those who cannot move knew before they joined, or ran the risk of being locked in.

But they are now having to face criticism more fundamental than pay—and it will grow in the next ten years—that, whether their pay is too high or too low, they are simply too numerous. Instead of being a relatively small elite supplying services that only government can supply, they are everywhere: in every railway coach or restaurant, pub or club. Walk into any public or private place and on average one in five is paid by taxes. That is a frightening figure.

For thirty-five years since the war, bureaucrats have lived in the balmy atmosphere of undiscriminating public approval. Where there was a social, economic, or political problem, government would find a solution. It would create a new department, authority or board; it would appoint a new commission, committee or panel. It would equip them with variously trained administrators, professionals, clerks, doormen and tea-ladies. And the solution would follow.

The reality is much less romantic. Abuses, scandals, corruption and other sordid episodes have taught us better. Or perhaps it was foolish to have expected otherwise. Bureaucrats are much like the rest of us ordinary mortals. They vary from the exceptionally talented to the timid who want shelter from competitive industry where services have to be sold and costs covered, from the most dedicated to the work-evader twiddling his thumbs and trying hard not to be noticed, from men and women worth more than their pay to passengers and scroungers.

But in all "public" services there is a buck-passing, responsibility-avoiding mentality which makes "public" servants tend to do as little as necessary to satisfy the letter of their duties, in sharp contrast to the initiative-taking mentality in private industry which makes people do as much as they can if the incentives are provided. Perhaps "public" servants could be enterprising expenditure-cutters if they were awarded 10 per cent of the economies they devised. But there would also have to be penalties for incurring costs higher than necessary. And it is more difficult to build such incentives into the "public" services than into private industry.

I would go further and maintain that a half or more of what government is doing it should not be doing at all. Two-thirds of government expenditure, financed mostly by taxes, is returned in cash or in services that could be better supplied by private industry. Half or more of all taxes traced to individuals is returned to the very same households from which it came. This is the vast bureaucratic engine, carrying coal to Newcastle.

But there would be more jobs in the private than in the "public" sector because privately-produced services would sell better. They would be more efficient, more tailored to customer requirements, as experience in the USA, Denmark and elsewhere indicates; cheaper, often probably half or less, as in training office staff, refuse collection, fire-fighting, ambulance services, not least house building. But we shall never know if government provides services without discovering costs outside. I therefore propose that where practicable, no services should be supplied by government unless it has discovered that outside costs are higher. And I predict that in five years many bureaucrats would be engaged more efficiently in private enterprise, be better off, and benefit the country, not least by lower taxes.

As a taxpayer who, like others, has a large slice of his income taken and spent by strangers, I ask the bureaucrats to consider a ten-part indictment of bureaucracy that goes to the roots of our open society and the free institutions that used to sustain it. And if they think of themselves as taxpayers, heads of families, husbands or wives, mothers or fathers, sons or daughters, they must agree with much of it.

- Every bureaucrat swells the nation's tax bill.
- Most bureaucrats restrict the taxpayer's choice by providing a monopoly service.
- Most bureaucrats service politicians with powers beyond their capabilities.
- Most bureaucrats work without direct consumer tests of their value.
- Every bureaucrat works for himself as well as, or rather than, the public whose taxes pay him.
- Every bureaucrat provides services without knowing what the consumer/taxpayer wants.
- Many bureaucrats remove a worker from productive industry.
- Every bureaucrat spends someone else's money.
- Every bureaucrat has an interest in expanding government whatever the interests of the public.
- Every bureaucrat has a vote he can use to further his interest at the expense of the public.

We are now confronted by the task of changing from bolstered old industries to hopeful new ones. There is now a chance for the British genius for improvisation, technical skill and personal service. We could replace an annual growth rate hovering around nil to something like the long-term British rate of 2½ per cent to 3 per cent. We might even aspire to the 5 per cent or more of Germany, Japan and smaller industrial countries.

The bureaucrats will slow down the process. Some Chief Education Officers are concentrating expenditure cuts on transport or books to inconvenience parents, rather than on teachers no longer required. We can imagine what other manoeuvres there are in the National Health Service, in council housing, and in the numerous other national, regional and local services.

If bureaucrats advise Ministers on where cuts can best be made, or themselves are left to make them, we must expect them to cut where it suits them, not the public.

What can be done? Buying out the bureaucrats is expensive. Transferring the younger and more mobile leaves the older and less adaptable. Waiting for the older to retire is too slow.

The only solution is large-scale and not too gradual farming out, contracting out, hiving off, and denationalisation.

CHAPTER **47**

1980

Government of the Busy, by the Bossy, for the Bully

A more realistic form of the conventional description of democracy by Abraham Lincoln, "of, by, for the people," discredited by the history of the political process: used as the title of this article after the new Government's first year.

(*The Daily Telegraph*, February 1980.)

The Conservatives were elected because Mrs. Thatcher said they would undo post-war Socialism by freeing the people of the yoke of government. They may pacify Northern Ireland, democratise Rhodesia, morally quarantine the USSR—but the Conservatives will not have done their job if they leave ordinary people as much dominated by government in 1984 as in 1979.

The Conservatives were not elected to improve the management of Socialism. They were not elected to run the schools or the hospitals better than Labour. They were elected to remove the power of the system over the people. Their task is to put the school parent over the councillor, the official and the teacher; the patient over the administrator, union official, even the doctor and nurse; the tenant over the political landlord. These three intensely personal services must not remain dominated by monopoly producers and their *apparatchiks* in 1984.

The ordinary voter in 1984 will not judge the government by the achievements of Lord Carrington and Sir Ian Gilmour at the Foreign Office. Nor are the key ministers to be found in the Treasury, since they are not in the front line of the battle to assert the sovereignty of the people over government. The three key ministers by whose works the Government will be judged are Mark Carlisle for education, Patrick Jenkin for health and Michael Heseltine for housing.

There is least doubt about Mr. Heseltine. He showed prompt understanding and early determination to turn millions of council tenants into home property-owners.

Mr. Jenkin, after a wobbly start, has stoutly asserted that the system of financing health services almost wholly by taxation should be replaced. We must hope the press report that his officials have (predictably) advised that a move to insurance is impracticable is only a pause on the road to the long overdue radical revision of the financing of medical care in Britain. The proposals for requiring motorists to insure themselves as well as third parties for medical costs, and for the victims of hazardous sports to pay medical bills, are a minor distraction from the central purpose of allowing people to pay for all medical attention—in emergency or not—in the ways they prefer. That is the objective; everything else is secondary.

But it is Mr. Carlisle who has been slowest off the mark. The only idea he is pursuing for asserting authority of parents in the schooling of their children is to give them a stronger voice in running State schools. But individual parent power requires much more than a stronger collective voice. Parent-governors, like other "representatives," simply strengthen the articulate—because of accent, connections or "bully power"—at the expense of the inarticulate. If Mrs. Thatcher is to win the hearts and minds of the millions who feel powerless in the vast, impersonal, political machine of State education, she must equip *each parent* with equal power to *escape* from officials or teachers who fail to educate their children.

That means the power to withdraw their money if they are dissatisfied. And there is no sign that her Education Minister has yet thought as far as that. This is the acid test of the government's determination to liberate the people from officialdom.

For some years I have studied various methods of escape, not preferences. A few days before Christmas a deputation of six, organised by FEVER, the voucher "lobby," presented a petition signed by parents urging the minister to empower local authorities to allow parents to withdraw their children experimentally, by voucher, from State to private schools. The Minister said he would look into the law.

One of the six, Mr. Paul Marland, the new MP who has taken over the mantle of parents' champion in Parliament since Dr. Rhodes Boyson was shunted to higher education, asked him to assign £1 million out of the £55 million earmarked for the Assisted Places Scheme to help local authorities try out the idea of escape from State to private school. The bureaucrats who accompanied the Minister had evidently not informed him of the possibility.

State education now takes £8,000 million in taxes. Much of it is spent on officials and teachers who think the system is run for their benefit. They are virtually unaccountable to parents. Nothing the Government is doing will make them more accountable. All the ferment on standards is stewed by the elites: teachers, educationists, sociologists, journalists, inspectors, officials, politicians. There are no parents in sight. Nothing will enable them to assert their authority over unacceptable teachers or schools except the power to *escape.* Even the current cuts are planned and executed by officials and teachers without reference to parents.

The Kent County Council study in 1978 calculated that vouchers for pupils in private schools, less the savings on teachers in the State schools, might amount to £1 million. But this figure overlooked two effects that would ultimately reduce school costs. First, schools dependent on income from parents would take more care with their costs—they would turn their lights off earlier; we shall never discipline the profligacy of the State schools until we introduce the cost-consciousness of the private schools by increasing competition. Second, parents would add millions for the chance to choose the school they prefer. Ultimately, therefore, parent power would provide more funds for schools and improved education at lower costs.

Mr. Carlisle said he expected local authorities to find the initial money. By the remarkable ingenuity of the Kent Council majority leader, Sir John Grugeon, private money has been found to finance experiments in moving old people and juvenile delinquents from "institutions" to real homes. He now hopes to find at least some of the money privately to establish the experiment in parent power. But why should Kent parents, who have waited for years for the experiment, wait more years until private money can be found?

Whose money is it? Parents are taxpayers. A reputable private firm says: "Satisfaction or your money back." Why should not State schools (and hospitals and everything else) give the same guarantee?

Politicians dispense patronage—or largesse—too freely. The Government is spending millions of taxpayers' money where they have little or no say. Mr. Carlisle is providing money for fashionable language laboratories that teach no better than chalk and talk. Sir Keith Joseph has given £300 million with a possible further £133 million to British Leyland where it will probably all be lost before long. Mr. Jenkin is giving £6,000 million to hospitals where some of the old are neglected and some of the mentally ill are maltreated. Mr. Heseltine is providing £12,000 million to local government that is riddled with waste and worse. Mr. St. John-Stevas is giving £60 million to the Arts Council partly for quixotic activities that few taxpayers use and even fewer approve.

After thirty years of State economy, British society has become a mad hatter's tea party in which the pipers spit on those who pay them. The 21,000 members of the National Association of Head Teachers are told by its secretary to oppose efforts by parents to provide funds for books and equipment. How many head teachers have disavowed their official for such pernicious advice? If equality means that no one may show example to the rest, the Welfare State is condemned to stagnation.

Millions are dissatisfied with State education. Ultimately it is immoral for government to misuse their money by locking them and their children into State schools to prevent them taking it to schools they prefer. And it is an arrogant invasion of family life to usurp the role of parents. Mr. Carlisle should give parents—all parents, not only the lucky ones with able children—more influence in the schooling of their children. It could be the tocsin of Mrs. Thatcher in 1980.

CHAPTER 48

1980

Price-less Opinion Polling

> In its two senses: polling without prices is worthless; opinion polling has asked unanswerable questions. Since the 1950s it has misled politicians, like the Labour leader who suffered by losing the 1992 General Election, the press, opinion-formers and the public itself by finding 80 per cent satisfaction with State welfare and a vague readiness to pay unknown taxes for unstated benefits. The confusion was intensified in the 1980s by sociological researchers. * In the 1990s the public policy pollsters should now use priced research. Or government should conduct its own scientific researches.
>
> (*British Public Opinion*,
> Spring 1980.)

How satisfied are you with the care you get at present from the NHS?" When NOP asked that question in November 1978, 45 per cent of its sample replied "Very satisfied," 39 per cent "Fairly satisfied." Total "satisfaction": 84 per cent. Favourable responses of such magnitude for the State health and other welfare services have been common since the Welfare State was established after the war.

In 1957 Political and Economic Planning (PEP) found general satisfaction with the NHS.

In 1962 Research Services, for the Institute of Community Studies, asked, "Would you say you were for or against the Welfare State?" and 94 per cent were "For."

In 1964 Research Services, this time for the Association of the British Pharmaceutical Industry, asked, "Do you think . . . the NHS is . . . working reasonably well or not?" and 88 per cent replied "Yes."

But of what value are such measures of opinion? "Approval" cannot be absolute; it must be related to alternatives.

Are the recipients supposed to compare the NHS with:

(a) other State services;
(b) medical services in Germany, Sweden or Greenland; or
(c) with what they would have been in Britain if run by other methods?

Such results have nevertheless built up an impression of general public approval of welfare services supplied by the State. And they have influenced politicians in all parties on public policy. It was, indeed, the conclusion that reform was "politically impossible" which explains practical men's response to the early Institute of Economic Affairs economic studies on pensions, housing, health, education. These found defects in State financing and made proposals for reform.

If economic analysis of the shortcomings of State welfare was to be ignored on such grounds, scholars would hardly bother to engage in fruitless investigations. But these measures of massive public approval were not being assembled in a manner that economists would regard as significant.

We use costs to reflect the alternatives in relation to which "approval" is measured. It is thus meaningless to talk about the demand for a product without reference to its price. At a low price demand may generally be high. At a high price it is relatively low. A service that is approved if thought to be free might be disapproved if known to be expensive.

To test the view that reform of State welfare was "politically impossible" and thereby to encourage economists to continue their studies, we had to go over the heads of the politicians and ask the public its preferences between State services and alternatives *marked with their prices.*

Together with Leonard England and Wendy Grosse in 1962 at Mass Observation—later as England, Grosse & Associates—we worked out methods of asking priced preferences between State and private education and medicine as the two largest State services in kind. (Pensions and housing were studied in different ways.)

Preferences were measured by the readiness to top up a voucher worth two-thirds of State education and a voucher worth two-thirds of the cost of insuring private health services in 1965, 1970 and 1978.

The results (referred to in the first issue of *British Public Opinion*) were very different from 80 per cent or 90 per cent approval. Instead of massive approval of State welfare indicated by the price-less polls, the priced surveys showed in contrast that, when the public knows the price, they declare increasing approval for the private alternatives: from 30 per cent for education in 1965 to 52 per cent in 1978, and from 30 per cent in health to 57 per cent.

There were tasks to solve in sampling, calculation of State and private costs, phrasing the questions to be intelligible without over-simplification. But at least they were faced. And insofar as imperfections were constant over the years, or gradually removed, the trend over time is broadly significant. The results were also internally consistent: for a lower-value voucher (one-third of school costs, half of health insurance costs) the take-up—"demand"—was lower.

It was soon evident that these priced researches were more significant than the price-less polls. Professor Mark Blaug wrote in 1967, "economists will recognise immediately that the [IEA] enquiry in effect elicited information about the slope of the demand [curve]." Timothy Raison in 1970 conceded that the price-less surveys in *New Society* in 1967 had been defective:

> This [*New Society*] survey was not wholly valuable as a policy-making aid . . . it only tells us what people think about what is—not about what might be . . . the crucial question of what research can or cannot do is to help us in the evaluation of alternatives . . . with which the IEA has experimented. One must talk about costs as well as [approval of] services.

There was no overwhelming preference for State over private welfare. The polls had misled the politicians.

The priced researches also cleared up an apparent mystery. Mr. Joel Barnett, then Chief Secretary to the Treasury, said in 1978 that, if you asked people, they wanted both lower taxes and more welfare. So, evidently, they were all confused. They offer politicians no guidance on public policy. And it is no use asking them.

Not so. Contradictory answers are given because of the absence of price. Everyone will want lower taxes if State services continue unchanged. Everyone will want more welfare if taxes are not raised to pay for them. It is not the recipients who are confused. Their answers are contradictory because the questions cannot elicit realistic replies. Measuring preference without reference to price is meaningless.

People are not stupid. Politicians may be condemned for expecting them to give rational replies to irrational questions and for misleading them for thirty years by talking of "free" services which are paid for either by others in subsidies or by themselves in taxes.

If the result of priced research is doubted then the Government—if it wishes to base policy on public approval—can check it in three ways. It can ask Jonathan Boreham to run surveys through the Office of Population Censuses and Surveys. It can conduct referenda. Best of all, it can provide choice in real markets and see what the people approve in practice when they know prices and are spending their own money.

As long as present policy continues (as the bureaucracy would wish), the Government will be perpetuating the suppression of public preferences.

CHAPTER **49**

1983

"New Right" and New Government

> Post-war New Mercantilism put producer before consumer interests and was strangling society. The first Thatcher government was reflecting the classical liberal teaching. The new approach was being retarded by Tory constitutionalists who advised "incremental" change. * If politics continues to suppress social and technological advance it will be ignored and evaded. The final adjustments will be more convulsive.
>
> (*The Daily Telegraph*, April 1983.)

The secret of the "New Right" in British politics—why it has emerged to dominate economic debate and has won instinctive public support in all parties—is that it has divined the key to the human dilemma, the conflict between mankind as producer and as consumer. And it has provided government with the method of undoing the self-inflicted damage of the post-war decades.

The guilds of mediaeval England were the characteristic device by which men put their interests as producers first. If producers had been allowed to coagulate into guilds, combines, combinations, cartels, trade associations, professional faculties, trade unions to protect their jobs and incomes, they would have excluded newcomers, retarded technical change, established monopolies, and exacted high prices from their consumers. Society would have stagnated, or strangled itself.

The only way to save mankind from itself is to put its long-run interest as consumer first, and its short-run producer interest in security of a job second. And the only institution that mankind has evolved for asserting his essential long-run interests and aspirations is the market, in which men work, whether commercially, co-operatively, or mutually, to serve one another as consumers.

For forty years in the nineteenth century the market predominated. But for nearly a century, as the Conservative party yielded too often to the importunities of employers and Labour was created by the trade unions, the open market has been pushed off the centre of the economic scene, and all British governments, certainly since 1945 and earlier to 1932, have yielded to the promptings and importunities of producers.

That is the essential teaching that the "New" Right in Britain, the United States and elsewhere, had absorbed from the "new" economists who for twenty years have rejected much of the old producer-inspired economics of Keynes (high employment), Beveridge (full employment), and the Fabians (public sector employment). This producer, employment-at-any-price nostrum was accepted uncritically by all political parties in all Western countries. The new economists, mainly in the United States but drawing their inspiration from two hundred years of economic thinking by English and Scottish economists and philosophers and from the nineteenth-century Austrian, German, Italian and Swedish economists, have created the "new" economics.

The dominance of "macro"-economics (employment policies based on national totals of output, income, expenditure, etc.) is being qualified and replaced by the restoration of "micro"-economics (attention to individuals, small groups, localities, single industries, plants, pits). Professor Lawrence Klein, who won the Nobel Prize in 1980 for macro-economics, has declared in a book only three years later (to be published by Blackwell this June) that macro-economics, like patriotism, is not enough.

Economists, led by United States' Professor J. M. Buchanan and Professor Gordon Tullock, have been subjecting government, fondly regarded as managed by benevolent saints or despots, to the close critical dissection that economists have long applied to the faults of private industry.

The key to productivity for over a thousand years is being analysed as typified by the enclosure of common ("socialised") land into private plots, which each owner has an interest in preserving, improving and developing. What is owned by everyone is owned (cared for) by no one.

The notion that government could "regulate" industry to the public advantage has been virtually destroyed by Professor George Stigler (the 1982 Nobel Laureate) and Professor Gary Becker, both of Chicago University. Professor Becker has opened a new world of economic enlightenment by analysing investment in human capital by education and training, and its effect on the family.

The new economists have retaliated against the conventional argument that government was necessary to prevent harmful effects of industrial activity on third parties by demonstrating that the "externalities" of government are usually worse, and less capable of repair, because government is less responsible and accountable than private industry.

The essence of the new economics has been applied for only the past two years of Mrs. Thatcher's "New" Right government. Even then the principle has been applied only very tepidly in many sectors—"natural wastage" is the euphemism for carrying unnecessary public workers at private taxpayers' expense. And the failure to close pits yielding coal-dust as though it were gold-dust could reduce Britain to ridicule. The principle has hardly begun in education, and has apparently been ruled out in medicine. It is, therefore, comically premature for a new book to entitle itself *After the New Right*. The author makes some graceful acknowledgements to the new economists, although he has fault to find with some, yet his is the first attempt from the Left to analyse the new economics behind the New Right. The Left and the Old Right have had a century. Perhaps the New Right should be allowed at least twenty years before it is judged.

But at least the debate on the intellectual foundations of the New Right in Britain has now begun. The Left is gradually coming to see that it has lost its intellectual dominance.

Mrs. Thatcher's main achievement so far is to have begun to educate the nation out of its producer obsession. She has a second (perhaps a third) term to change producer-dominance into consumer-dominance. But she has instinctively sensed that the new economics behind the New Right is not only superior to the Old Wrong (of Left and Right); it reflects suppressed popular aspirations, not least in family life.

It is not true, as Lord Beloff of Oxford and Buckingham renown, vice-chairman of the advisory board to the Conservative Research Department, seems to think, that the English want only "incremental" change. Intense field studies at the Institute of Economic Affairs have discovered a widespread desire in all classes for family influence in education and medicine.

That reform could not be "incremental." It would require government to create wide-ranging new powers to strengthen the family. All British parties are in a state of flux as underlying social opportunities open out. If the patrician Old Right will not allow Mrs. Thatcher to respond to popular desire, it may not be only the Labour Party that splits and disintegrates.

Incrementalism is a comforting constitutional doctrine if it takes place continuously by degrees, at the pace of social and economic change. But if incremental change is suppressed, as it has been by thirty-five years of the

Welfare State, it accumulates to large-scale reform: at 2 per cent a year, 70 per cent by now! And the longer the suppression is tolerated, the more convulsive the ultimate reforms will be. By 1993 it will be 80 per cent. If political institutions do not change with human experience and family aspirations, they will be ignored, defied and evaded, as unacceptable laws and taxes have been for decades. And that should worry the constitutionalists.

CHAPTER **50**

1988

New Left: Beware Politics

> Discussion of a proposed Left-inclined academic "think-tank" provoked a warning that politicians were occupationally unable to apply the best solutions. The academics should adopt the IEA formula of presenting all scientific conclusions for policy, not only those the politicians judge "politically possible." * The lessons of the 1980s confirm that influencing sympathetic politicians requires the long-range intellectual "artillery" of reasoned research before bombarding them with the "infantry" of "practicable proposals."
>
> (*The Guardian*, June 1988.)

There is much talk at present about the creation of a new, left-of-centre academic "think-tank" modelled on, among others, the Institute of Economic Affairs. Since I am about to retire after thirty-two years' work with the IEA, perhaps my thoughts may be of interest to those embarking on this venture.

Think-tanks have emerged in response to the felt frustrations of both academics and politicians. Thus it was with the IEA, and thus it is also with the new proposal. But this does not mean that the interests of academics, politicians or, indeed, of the think-tank itself are identical with one another.

Traditionally, many academics were exclusively concerned with research and teaching. There were always those seized with the mission of advising and persuading the political party they thought most likely to adopt their thinking. In the post-war period their insights were often either lying fallow or were diluted or tailored to the expediencies of party politics.

Some of the most eminent were sceptical of the prevailing Fabian–Beveridge–Keynesian dominance in economic thinking; and some of the younger were too awed to speak their minds. The eminent required coaxing out of their ivory towers and the not-yet-eminent needed fortifying by the discovery that many others thought like them.

The missing intellectual midwife was a centre that would focus their work on neglected solutions to pressing problems, present it intelligibly and graphically, yet induce them to canvass *all* solutions suggested by their analysis, not only those considered "politically possible" by politicians.

This, I would say, is the formula that produced whatever effectiveness the Institute of Economic Affairs has been said, by friends and critics, to have had, for good or ill, in recent years. And it is the formula that the mooted Labour-sponsored think-tank will have to adopt if it is to make the most effective use of the able economists and other academics on the Left.

But the enterprise may be more difficult for the New (market-socialist) Left than it was for what the Old (statist, corporatist) Left calls the New Right (a misnomer for classical liberalism in modern dress and context).

Some who have called for an IEA-like think-tank to serve Labour know that IEA authors have been asked to analyse awkward issues rigorously and to conclude with the emerging proposals whether they would be adopted by a political party or not. That was the process of making the desirable possible.

The purpose was not to tailor proposals that *politicians* thought politically possible, but to present the most desirable measures and make them politically possible by public education in their advantages over current policy.

The IEA was not the academic arm of the Conservative Party. Ralph Harris, now a cross-bench peer, had been a Conservative candidate (a rare experience for the son of a bus conductor); I had been an active Liberal (not so rare for the son of a cobbler); and our early associates, Graham Hutton, Colin Clark and others had been Fabians. About one in five IEA authors have had sympathies left of centre. IEA papers examined flaws in the case for markets as well as strengths. Professor David Collard said in a Fabian Tract in 1968: "I concede a consistent and honourable attempt to remove a major blemish of the free market system."

This was the long-range intellectual "artillery" necessary to re-educate public understanding to accept the "infantry" of practical proposals for reform. It was not service for party politics, but re-education for a climate of opinion in which party politics could better serve the public.

A think-tank to "service" Labour would not produce its best scholarly work. Its politically-tailored proposals would not perform the preparatory task of public education.

It would not command the academic respect of intellectual sceptics. And it would lose the intellectual initiative to party tacticians.

The subject of debate between liberal and socialist economists, between the New Right and the New Left, is now not whether the market should be used, but how. A think-tank on the Left will have to confront awkward truths. Its recruitment would be easier than for the IEA, because academics on the Left are generally more inclined to work for their "cause" than are academics on the Right.

But they more often allow their ideologies to obscure their scholarship (as in the new *Palgrave Dictionary of Economics*). And their emotions more often confuse their reasoning. (Economic liberals are no less "caring" or "compassionate" than socialists. And the market-based policies emerging from their analyses are potentially more effective in the treatment of avoidable inequality and poverty than are the politicised solutions of State welfare created by government of the busy, by the bossy, for the bully.) But these are differences that scholars can resolve better than politicians.

The more difficult task will be to keep the work of the new think-tank distant from party politics, which the IEA has done by being equally accessible to politicians of all parties. The new think-tank would have to show comparable catholicity, which would be less likely if it were working for "the next Labour Government."

If the profession of the scholar is to make his highest contribution to the national life by providing his best thinking, individual economists, political scientists and philosophers should exchange their best ideas, not only those that *politicians* think "politically possible."

Here academics on the Left may not share my view of the economics of politics, which has coloured the work of the IEA. Politicians suffer from an incurable occupational disease. It is not a criticism of them, but it limits their powers to do good. They are prevented by the political process as it now operates from choosing the best policies.

They prefer politically easier second-best to politically more difficult first-best solutions. They yield to the loud-voiced who organise because they have much booty to gain at the expense of the meek who do not organise because individually they have little to lose from each dose of largesse but much in total. Party politics distorts the economy by favouring the citizen as producer over his/her more fundamental interest as consumer.

No political party, given the state of public understanding, can implement the best thinking available to it from social science. Intellectuals of the "New Right" cannot regard Mrs. Thatcher's Conservative governments as representing the best of the economic liberalism they propound. Many applaud her for doing much more than previous Conservative prime ministers in liberalising the economy, often by measures thought "politically impossible" before 1979. But her governments have implemented half-measures (in education opting out by schools rather than by parents) that will delay the best solution by a decade. And Conservative ministers, including the most able and upright like Lord Joseph, have not only not implemented liberal solutions but have discredited them by seeming to claim they had been examined and found impracticable.

A Labour government would also frustrate the best academic socialist thinking, not least its politicised efforts to incorporate the market mechanisms that Alec Nove, Raymond Plant and other socialists have shown are essential for "feasible socialism."

Academics of all philosophies, liberal and socialist, in think-tanks of the "New Right" and the "New Left," have the task of resisting the short-termism of well-intentioned but politically constrained party politicians, and devising ways of enabling or requiring them to put the unorganised before the organised, the consumer before the producer interest, the ultimate public advantages before the immediacies of pressure groups. Economic liberals maintain all this can best be done in market-based capitalism. Socialists have to show how it would be better done under socialism.

Not the least task of socialist-inclined economists like Julian le Grand or Ray Robinson will be to devise ways of correcting for the differences in *cultural* power that influence (or decide) access to services supplied by the State, especially education, medical care and housing.

The corresponding problem for liberal academics, which some have tackled at the IEA, is to even up the differences in *financial* power (income or assets) that influence (or determine) access to services in the market. Their solutions are to work on the demand side rather than on the supply side—to top up incomes by tax refunds, reverse taxes, cash grants or earmarked purchasing power (vouchers). A joint research effort might produce the solution that has eluded both so far.

Intellectuals must not become the servants of politicians. Their task is to reveal the truth even if not politically timely or rewarding. It is to help party politicians to surmount the horizons of party and make the desirable, and nothing but the desirable, politically possible.

CHAPTER 51

1986

Capitalism Is More Corrigible Than Socialism

Political tremors in East Europe indicated that capitalism would replace socialism. The fundamental contrast was not only in their alleged strengths; it was even more in their weaknesses and the ease of correction. * Capitalism has now been accepted as the best hope of raising living standards. The advantages of free markets are appearing despite the dislocation following their suppression by forty to seventy years of State economy. The end of socialism is forecast for the Soviet Union and China.

(*The Daily Telegraph*, March 1986.)

When I was asked by the New Zealand Employers' Federation to write a credo for private enterprise it was not difficult to see why they wanted a restatement of the case for what they were doing. The paradox of the century, not yet examined by the psychiatrists, is that the economic system that has created the wealth of the world—private enterprise, the *most* successful known to mankind—has been condemned by the mass of activist intellectuals and its practitioners given a guilty conscience. In its place the intellectuals have advocated the *least* successful system known to mankind—the varying forms of (unnecessary) State control from social democracy to Communism.

The system that allows men the *most* freedom to exchange their wares in a market has thus been condemned as "capitalism" by accusers who would replace it by a system that gave men *least* scope to come together as buyers and sellers to enrich one another.

I had been wondering about this paradox in preparation for a lecture on capitalism and socialism at the University of Edinburgh. Instead of contrasting the *strengths* of each system, I found myself doing the opposite: listing their *defects* and asking how easily they could be removed. I concluded that private enterprise in a market economy—the "capitalism" of the socialists—came out even more strongly superior to any form of State economy, from the "mixed economy" through the welfare bureaucracies of social democracy to the fully articulated apparatus of socialism or Communism.

As an economist who passed through a phase of socialist faith in early years, I later reacted against the confident but empty claims for a socialism which was unsupported by example by thinking it was much more fruitful to see where the capitalist system was working badly and removing the causes.

Capitalism has serious faults. At least, in the way in which it has been allowed to work by government, it throws up objectionable features. It yields wide differences in income, so that people with the lowest incomes still have too little access to the minimum services that the community thinks all should have for civilised living. It exhibits sometimes long-lived and deep-lying monopolies. It separates the ordinary man and his wife from ownership of the assets that would ensure independence and dignity. And it seems to neglect the "social" effects of private exchange in the market, and the damage sometimes caused to innocent third parties and the environment by noise, smell, congestion and other forms of "pollution."

This is the valid indictment of capitalism. It does not include unemployment or inflation, both of which are even worse, but concealed, in socialism.

Now to say that private enterprise has had these defects is not to prove that it cannot deal with them. It has tried to deal with some of them, though not always successfully. It has made a bit of a hash of dealing with poverty and "inequality." This is its most difficult task, and it remains the most damaging criticism.

But the market economy will not cure poverty or "inequality" until it uses the market here as elsewhere. Instead of providing the relatively poor with the required purchasing power and so enabling them, along with everyone else, to use the market, we have destroyed the market by providing most of these services "free."

We have been more successful in combating private monopoly, and we are still refining the anti-monopoly laws, but we have more than undone this good work by creating new government monopolies which we have only begun to think about dismantling.

We could also have done more to encourage the ownership of assets to give everyone a stake and a direct interest in ensuring it is used efficiently. So far the only large asset ordinary people own is their home, and the capital market has not done much about turning it into income when they retire.

We have a long way to go widening the direct personal ownership of industry through stocks and shares. Indirect ownership through life assurance, pension funds and unit trusts is better than nothing, but is too remote. Workers' participation through "industrial democracy" is no substitute for ownership, and nominal ownership through nationalisation is no use at all: no one can do anything about ensuring that his fifty-five-millionth "share" of a railway engine, a school or a hospital is used efficiently.

We are only now beginning to deal with the "social" effects on the environment and individuals. The law could give individuals the right to compensation, some industrial processes could be rendered harmless, and others could be discouraged by charging those who cause the damage.

These defects remain for "capitalism" to remedy, but to claim that they can be remedied only by replacing capitalism by socialism is no argument at all.

It is wishful thinking, fairy-tale spinning, romancing. Poverty is worse under socialism because the system is less productive. "Inequality," the question-begging word for differences in income, is usually worse because there is no market in which people can move freely from lower-paid to higher-paid work. Monopoly is clearly worse because it is controlled by the State, which no one can discipline, while the regime is less inclined to do anything about social damage because, in the absence of a free Press, the political bosses and the bureaucrats are not under public pressure.

Moreover, socialism without markets has defects of its own that are more irremovable than the defects of capitalism, even if there was a will to remove them, which there is not. They are irremovable because they are essential to the economic system and its political control from the centre.

Socialism is ignorant of the people's wants because they have no market in which to express them. Controlled elections are useless for this purpose.

Socialism is therefore inefficient. It produces goods and services in the wrong quantities or (more often) the wrong qualities. It produces shortages that create queues and surpluses sold off at low prices to disguise the blunders.

Socialism creates dissatisfaction that threatens conflict because it rides roughshod over regional, cultural and racial, sexual or other minorities.

Socialism enthrones monopoly.

Socialism must use coercion to reconcile individuals to decisions made by tiny coteries of bosses or bureaucrats.

Socialism creates corruption because there are no uncontrolled open markets in which people can trade freely with one another.

Socialism lives on secrecy. Information is falsified or suppressed.

These are the results that common sense indicates and knowledge of every socialist country confirms. They are found, to a greater or lesser degree in the varying forms of socialism in Britain; from nationalisation through the Welfare State to local government. Yet socialism goes on being advocated—in its latest British version by Messrs. Benn and Heffer—as though common sense could be ignored and socialist countries did not exist.

It is possible the British will opt for more socialism on the grounds that the only reason why it has failed so far is that there was not enough of it. Yet socialism abroad is increasingly seen to be failing. My understanding that it is relatively easy to remove the defects of private enterprise because it goes with the grain of human nature, while socialism requires increasing coercion, leads me to three resulting "predictions."

China will become increasingly capitalist. Soviet Russia will not survive the century because it can keep its people subdued only by increasing coercion as they learn of the rising living standards of the West. Messrs. Benn and Heffer are depending on a mounting tide of British ignorance and gullibility, and Labour as we have known it will not govern Britain again.

This last "prediction" may comfort the semi-socialist Conservative "wets" but it should embolden the non-socialist Conservative "dries." There is a lot of socialism in British society. Other politicians could respond to public rejection by replacing it with individual freedom.

CHAPTER **52**

1988

Policies: The Difficult and the "Impossible"

> Politicians may think desirable policies "politically impossible." They have an interest in avoiding policies that require exceptional effort in "selling" to the electorate. Economists reply that the more "impossible" policies are thought the more good they may do. * The best policies of the 1980s' governments were thought "impossible" by earlier governments. If the British economy is to be rid of its weaknesses it will require many "impossibles."
>
> (*Managerial and Decision Economics,* South Africa, 1988.)

I choose this variation of W. H. Hutt's *Economists and the Public* (1936) as the title of this essay to emphasise his prescient anticipation of the economics of politics, developed two decades later in the study of public choice. The short book in which he formalised his thinking on the political frustration of economic policy came much later in his *Politically Impossible . . . ?* (1971), which I asked him to write for the (London) Institute of Economic Affairs (IEA). His critique of economists for subservience to politics was reflected in his middle period and his later writings, not the least of which was the extended 1977 version of *Theory of Collective Bargaining* (1930), suggested to him at the 1976 meeting of the Mont Perin Society at St. Andrews University in Scotland.

Hutt's most important work is usually considered to be *The Theory of Idle Resources* (1939). It was in part a reaction to Keynes' *General Theory* (1936), but his other works on Keynesianism have been underrated and shabbily neglected, even by economists who shared his general outlook. His insights into the economics of the labour market in his books on trade union power have also yet to be fully acknowledged. Yet, in view of the burgeoning of public choice, and its explosive effect on political science (which few political scientists so far have had the wit to recognise), what seemed a small work of secondary importance on the economics of politics deserves more attention than it has received even from public choice economists and certainly from political scientists.

Why are some of the inferences of economic analysis adopted with alacrity and others rejected with contumely? Since economists are fallible humans who hope for recognition, approbation, perhaps applause, even influence on the times in which they live, it is predictable that they will work on subjects that yield conclusions for policy that will commend themselves to politicians in a world dominated or regulated by government. The corruption of academia in State-dominated economies, in which government provides funds for economists to work on ways to improve or extend the domain of political control, on the plausible grounds that the State must be concerned about the efficiency of the services it supplies has yet to receive exhaustive examination. The more apparent obstacle to scientific inquiry is the invincible political judgment it confronts that, however beneficent for the general public weal, a proposal for reform may be judged by the politicians to be commendable, ingenious, praiseworthy, desirable but, alas, *politically impossible.*

In its lamentable corporatist phase in the early 1960s British industry was apt to ape its political masters. At a conference of the (then) Federation (now Confederation) of British Industry the assembly murmured its approval of the argument of the economic adviser to a world-renowned British company that industry had to accept the view of the (then Conservative) government about the course of economic policy and that "politics was the art of the possible." Some years later, at a small gathering of liberal market-oriented economists who were urging a course of action on the then Prime Minister, an academic of some repute contributed the conventional wisdom: "I agree, but, really, only the PM can say what will be acceptable." The State-dominated economy is productive of trimmers: able, honest, earnest scholars who can truthfully say, hand on heart, "At least, if I am there, I can prevent *some* harm . . ."

To these sophistries Hutt brought his clear mind, disdainful of the seductions of influence or office. *Politically Impossible . . . ?* was the first, and keynote, paper in a new IEA series of studies devised to examine "the circumstances influencing or deciding the translation of analysis into action"; its avowed editorial aim was "to extend economic analysis into political economy." The Preface said the series would look into "the possibly wide range of influences that bear on the formation of policy: from ideas to financial interest . . . the authors will be concerned, strictly as economists, with the interplay between ideas and policies." Hutt was asked, in short, to judge between Keynes' emphasis on ideas as the influence that, he had said, "ruled the world," and Marx's obsession with vested interests, with John Stuart Mill's judgment of Solomon that "conspiring circumstance" was the ultimate determinant.

The book was subtitled "Why Politicians do not take Economic Advice." In a note on "Readings for the Student of Political Economy," Hutt listed James Mill's *Essay on Government,* which, he said, discussed "the dangers lurking in representative government," Morley's *On Compromise,* two books by T. W. Hutchison, Schumpeter's *Capitalism, Socialism and Democracy,* Bassett's *The Essentials of Parliamentary Democracy,* Buchanan and Tullock's *Calculus of Consent,* Tullock's *Towards a Mathematics of Politics* and *Entrepreneurial Politics,* Arrow's *Social Choice and Industrial Values* and Downs' *An Economic Theory of Democracy.* Clearly we could have expected a characteristically Huttian analysis of public choice in the 1970s and 1980s if his attention had not returned to trade unions, Say's Law and again, Keynes. He might also have taken further his idea, outlined in the war-time *Plan for Reconstruction* (1943), for buying out the vested interests that lose from, and therefore obstruct, change. But, we must remain content with *Politically Impossible . . . ?*

In its ninety-nine pages of classical scholarship Hutt illustrated his analysis of the roots of supposed "political impossibility" from monetary policy, income redistribution, Keynesianism and the trade union use of the strike-threat. His approach was to investigate the conditions in which politicians rejected beneficial policies on the grounds that the people could not, as voters, be helped to see their true interest. Public choice economists, increasingly since the 1950s, had been discussing the effect of voting systems and constitutional rules on the voters' choices. Hutt in 1971 was questioning whether, whatever the electoral system, a proposal for the benefit of the voter could ever be held to be "impossible." Economists who limited their advice to government to proposals that politicians considered popular with, or at least acceptable to, voters were betraying their trust as scholars. Hutt could see why they did so: because even a second-best policy that was enacted was judged better than the first-best policy that was abandoned. Not least, it enabled economists to give practicable advice and so enabled them to be seen as solving problems. But, in "solving" an immediate problem they did longer-term harm. To end the 1929–33 depression the classical prescription was reductions in wage costs to make goods saleable and increase the demand for labour to contain and reduce unemployment. Keynes thought that the classical medicine was politically impossible: government would not act on it because the trade unions would not accept wage reductions. The solution was to leave money wages untouched but reduce real wages by raising prices through monetary expansion and budget deficits: *QED.* The day would be saved by duplicity, as well as by providing politicians with an academically reputable excuse for unbalancing budgets.

Hutt's conclusion, from this and his other three illustrations, was that economists should give their advice in two versions: the second-best if it were impossible to explain the alternatives to the electorate; and the first-best if it were. In the dispute between Keynes' and the classical remedies, price inflation was the second-best policy, reductions in real wages the first-best. But, the failure lay with politicians, not with economists.

Why is the public assumed to be incapable of understanding the first-best? Keynes' prescription has been shown to be not only defective in economic analysis. The public choice analysis of Professors J. M. Buchanan and Richard Wagner has also shown it to be politically unrealistic. Politicians have to deal with the public not only in the market process, as buyers or sellers of products or services, but also in the political process, as voters and electors. If it was politically naive to assume that workers would accept reductions in real wages in the short term it was no less politically unrealistic to assume that politicians would faithfully operate budget surpluses in the long term to remove inflation once budget deficits had created them. So the price of avoiding reductions in real wages to end a depression was a long vista of unbalanced budgets, with repercussions over half a century into the 1980s to President Reagan and the financial "crisis" of October 1987. The price of Keynesianism has been very much higher than he—or, after his death, his followers—admitted. A policy may be acceptable if its costs are low; the same policy may be rejected if its price is revealed as very high.

Would it have been politically impossible to explain the alternatives to the public in the early 1930s? We shall never know. What is clear is that budget deficits were more acceptable to *politicians* than confrontation with the unions. That is why economists too often make assumptions, for which they are not equipped, about proposals that are, or are not, likely to be politically acceptable, and that is why they too often offer second-best policies.

The list of policies that politicians have proclaimed "politically impossible" is very long in Britain: measures to encourage movement of labour from declining to growing industries, with the risk of unemployment; the resistance to strike-threats; the repeal of trade union legal immunities; the abolition of exchange control; de-socialisation of industry; thawing out the local government control of education; ending a State pension scheme; introducing competition into the National Health Service; returning housing from local government to private ownership . . . the list grows longer every year.

There must have been many British economists or other academics who, down the decades, gave "politically possible" advice—Hutt emphasises Marshall, Sidney Webb (who lauded unions in public and denounced them in private), Keynes . . . We do not know who else there were among famous men who made political pre-judgments, nor who rejected the prospect of influence in order to safeguard their academic integrity.

A recent instance is that of a bright young economist at the University of York, Professor A. J. Culyer, in debate with my colleague at the IEA, Dr. David Green. Culyer has argued that deregulation of State medicine (which would stimulate medicine in the market) is *politically* unlikely, and that proposals for it therefore distract attention from research that would yield *politically* more acceptable remedies for the inefficiencies of the National Health Service:

> Academics have an inglorious record at assessing political feasibilities. [A profound truth that could be framed on every academic's desk . . .] but, given the international omnipresence of the [State] institutions and the considerable power of the [medical] professions they protect, I think it highly unlikely that I am wrong [in thinking that deregulation and competition between medical services are politically improbable].
>
> . . . those who suggest . . . that relaxations of professional restrictions are necessary for economic efficiency in health care . . . distract our gaze from important research into questions we *can* answer . . . [such as] clinical budgeting to lead to improved efficiency in the NHS or the more imaginative use of rigorous procedures for appraising investment or for reducing "frivolous" demand.

In short, since alternatives to the NHS are politically unlikely, it is improper for academics to pursue them to discover whether they might have advantages for the sick that would have emerged in Britain if the NHS had not suppressed them.

This is precisely what the "distracter" Dr. Green, a sociologist and political scientist who knows the case for the NHS especially well as a former sympathetic socialist active in local government, had done. He has performed the indispensable service of the academic in "distracting" the gaze of other academics from established institutions, that are not working well because they have the fatal flaw of pricelessness, to others that might or would have developed if the existing institutions had not been endowed with virtual monopoly power by the State. He has distracted their attention, and undermined their confidence by two forms of research: into the history of the voluntary medical services that had emerged in the market before the NHS and into the medical services that have emerged in countries that allowed the most freedom for them to develop unsuppressed—the USA and Australia. He has concluded that present-day medical policy in Britain would achieve better results if deregulation allowed both known and so far unknown medical services to emerge than if the NHS continues to be patched up after nearly forty years of inefficiency protected by the State.

That the alternative medical services have been lost to Britain is for politicians to explain, or explain away. Of more direct relevance to Hutt's diagnosis is the conclusion that they would not have been studied by academics who conceived their task to confine their study to the politically possible. And the likelihood that they will study only the politically possible is heightened the more the institutions and academia itself are financed by the State.

The false notion of political impossibility has bemused thinking on, and obstructed reform in, the British Welfare State, not only in the NHS but also as a whole, including education, housing, pensions and insurance against unemployment and ill-health. Until recent years there was what politicians refer to as "all-party support" for the maintenance and expansion of the Welfare State. *A priori* reasoning and common sense might have made some of the more reflective politicians, certainly Conservative, possibly even Labour, doubt this "consensus," but if any of them wondered, they did nothing, or very little. It might have occurred to some of them that, in a period of gradually growing affluence with rising personal and family incomes and general living standards, it was strange, even foolish, for the State to supply education, medical care, housing, pensions and much else for all and sundry, young and old, in bad or good health, rich and poor. Yet there was paralysis of thought in politics, almost a conspiracy of silence, an implicit but uncritical supposition that it was politically impossible to question the Emperor's clothes, to see the nakedness of the idea that when more people could provide for themselves the State should, almost every year, continually provide more for them—at their expense, of course.

The paralysis of party politics should have been evident to British economists not long after the post-war Welfare State was institutionalised in 1946. Yet, if any of them sensed it, few spoke up. To us at the IEA the paralysis was especially evident because doubts about the efficiency, relevance or equity of the Welfare State were stilled by the plaintive phrase, "It is still young; give it time"; or by the supposed public anxiety that removal of some State welfare services would leave a frightening void—who would supply schools, doctors, nurses, hospitals, homes, pensions?; or by the evidence of opinion polls that periodically found large percentages in favour of the Welfare State in general and the NHS in particular. Since reform of the Welfare State was therefore "politically impossible," said the politicians, research and proposals for reform to allow the market in welfare to re-emerge after decades of repression were fruitless. There were also some academics who said that, since the NHS served the mass of the people, intellectual effort was better directed to improving it than to encouraging alternatives that were in any event "politically impossible."

Yet, the growing incomes since the 1940s were enabling more people down the income range to want better education, medical care, housing or pensions than the State could provide out of taxes that were, moreover, being increasingly avoided or evaded. More people knew of other people who had shifted out of the State to the market. The opinion polls were flawed: they contained no prices, no information on opportunity costs. When pricing was introduced at the IEA the true state of public preferences, or aspirations, emerged. Increasing proportions, it transpired, would shift from the State to the market, the more their abortive taxes were returned. The first of these priced surveys was attempted in 1963, the fifth in 1987. After nearly twenty-five years, some politicians in the Conservative and Social Democratic Parties (but not Liberal or Labour) were abandoning the paralysis of "political impossibility." In 1987 real reform of the Welfare State may have begun—"may" because the measures proposed may be false starts. At least the spell of political impossibility has been broken—not by politicians but by market forces.

At the IEA, where this propensity among economists was detected in its early years, a firm injunction was issued enjoining authors to pursue their analysis wherever it led them, even to unpopular, seemingly "politically impossible," solutions. Hutt has said that even the renowned Alfred Marshall tended "to write in a manner which would not upset the politicians of his day." If so, he would not have been admitted to the IEA in my day. When Morgan Reynolds asked Hutt (for the *Journal of Labor Research*) about his argument in *Politically Impossible . . . ?* on how far "economists should compromise the truth for political purposes" he replied: "Never . . . if we feel we can influence policy in the right sort of way we can go into politics, [but] our authority as economists is relinquished." What of economic advisers to US presidents (or British prime ministers?)? Hutt replied: "If you are a paid mouthpiece, you can always resign. If you accept the position with that understanding . . . you could do good work there . . . " Would he act as adviser to a head of government? Not if it required silence "on issues which concern the public." The danger remained that economists in such positions may be thought to "be trying to . . . improve the electability of their [political] masters."

There's the rub, as Shakespeare put it. Hutt here, as so often elsewhere, put into stark terms the dilemma of the economist who prizes his intellectual integrity but who yearns to "do good." When, many moons ago, I asked a distinguished American economist if he would accept the chairmanship of the USA Council of Economic Advisers he replied that he would decline the invitation because he could do more good by offering unofficial advice outside it. How many economists have similarly escaped the dilemma? Several in the USA have resigned more recently after two or three years' service with President Reagan. The stronger the yearning to do good, the more the danger that association with politicians will induce sentiments of loyalty, admiration, even affection, that may blunt the edge of intellectual judgment even where they stop short of transforming the academic into an acolyte trying to "improve the electability of [his] master." Yet not to take this risk is to see politicians advised by ambitious academics ready to tell the part of the truth that is palatable and "politically possible" rather than the truth, the whole truth and nothing but the truth that the public weal demands but politicians fail to teach.

The error of the economist tempted to advise politically possible expedients is to assume that their client is the best judge. Yet politicians are not independent, objective, dispassionate or neutral judges of the "politically possible." Their conception of it is subjective, myopic and, not surprisingly, self-serving. By "politically impossible" they characteristically mean politically *difficult*—requiring skill, patience and the capacity to persuade Cabinet colleagues, party officials or financial supporters to confront vested interests, reject the importunities of rent-seekers, resist hostile press or television interrogators and to placate irate spouses who object to disruption of their private or family lives by repeated absences of the Minister at emergency meetings. With rare exceptions—a Churchill in war, a stubborn Mrs. Thatcher confronting a primitive Marxist like Arthur Scargill in a coal-strike, a Reagan reducing the US budget deficit by unpopular reductions in welfare expenditure rather than break his word on resisting tax increases—politicians are less interested in politically *possible* than in politically *easy* policies. No less than the rest of us they want a comfortable, agreeable, quiet life based on a congenial job. They want easily saleable policies. The notion that politicians yearn to put the public interest before their private interest is a fiction that the public-choice economists have finally destroyed. They may—sometimes do—serve the public interest, but as a by-product of self-preservation, which they plausibly cite as the condition precedent.

But, politics entails the arts of salesmanship. The doctrine of political impossibility is largely an illusion based on circular reasoning explained by the economics of collective decision-making in the political process. The dilemma of representative government is that it makes short-term expedients politically more profitable than long-term interests, and satisfying producers electorally more rewarding than satisfying consumer interests. Representative government is tempted to yield to organised pressure at the expense of the unorganised, because the direct concentrated benefit to coalitions of pressure groups is more visible than the indirect dispersed loss to the multitude. In an ideal world politicians would put long-term before short-term interests, yield to consumer before producer interests and go over the heads of the articulate organised to serve the inarticulate unorganised. They would resist policies that inhibited the production of wealth in the long run, reject privileges demanded by vocal professional or trade union pressure groups, spurn the short-term stimulants to production exerted by inflation. The record is that they have not, because politicians are not saintly seers but operators of a political process that prevents them serving the public interest.

How to escape from the impasse? Hutt's solution was communication and consultation: public education in the consequences of alternative policies. The best politicians are part-time public educators in this sense. Yet it may not always be clear where strenuous explanation of disagreeable but desirable policies, such as the termination of social benefits or charging for hitherto free services (which the libertarian Conservatives under Mrs. Thatcher have slowly attempted), ends and the rationalisation of blatantly partisan measures, such as subsidies to affluent landowners or small farmers in Europe, begins. What is certain is that "representative" government is under ceaseless pressure from the activists, who may be relatively affluent, for measures that are yielded at the expense of the inarticulate, who are often the relatively unaffluent. The solution of the Oxford philosopher, John Gray, derived from public choice, is to replace piecemeal reforms (such as the removal of trade union privileges) by widespread reforms affecting many vested interests:

> . . . reforms should be so large, so comparatively sweeping, that it is hard for anyone to identify the winners and the losers. If . . . the results of these large-scale changes in the direction of freer markets will benefit most, if not all, over some period of time, then the . . . thwarting of liberal policy by small-scale groups can be avoided.

Piecemeal liberal policy has not worked because it has provoked the opposition of producer groups whose loss is concentrated, identifiable and damaging, without mobilising the support of consumer interests whose gain is dispersed, indirect and potential.

In short, liberal reform seems politically impossible because it is cautious and designed to minimise political opposition rather than radical and designed to maximise political support. (A clear example is the British proposal to decentralise the control of schools from local government to school boards of governors: it provoked opposition from all the vested interests of local politicians, bureaucrats and teachers without mustering support from parents.) This escape from the rent-seekers offers hope. It requires politicians who will risk the loss of support from producer interests but who see the prospect of large gain by building a public philosophy that rejects concessions to pressure groups as offensive in a liberal society. The difficulties are two. First, producer losses are immediate, consumer gains are gradual. Second, the representative political process imposes a short horizon of five years (the UK), four (the USA) or three (Australia) between elections that discourage longer vision. The market is the only economic institution that enables the interests of man as consumer to prevail over his interests as producer, but it requires a high rate of technical innovation to dissolve coagulations of industrial power and fairly rapid social advance to breed rejection of established producers. Again there is a virtuous circle to evolve: free markets to encourage technological innovation and social advance; technical and social change to strengthen markets. Again we have to look to a new ethic that welcomes initiative and enterprise as moral imperatives.

There is a difference between the neoclassical and the modern public-choice attitude to politicians. The neoclassicists censured them for lack of vision, conviction or courage in pursuing the public weal by "politically impossible" but desirable policies. Public choice has shifted the criticism from the politician to the political process in which he has to operate. Politicians vary in the personal efforts they exert to make the politically desirable politically possible, but all operate in a minefield. Politics in representative democracy often means a hard life. Yet politicians choose it in preference to the law, journalism or housework, and must be expected to take the consequences.

Economists who help to make life easy by providing "politically possible" solutions are supporting a privileged elite at the expense of the people. They have no cause for satisfaction from a sense of serving the public interest. Perhaps, like the Americans, they should avoid direct political service and wait for politicians to ask their advice as scholars. There is no clear positive correlation between the number of economists in British government ministries and the gross national product or the public wealth.

In 1987 public choice is a fully developed branch of economics, recognised in the world academic community by a Nobel Prize. Sixteen years ago, when Hutt wrote *Politically Impossible . . . ?*, public choice was barely halfway through its thirty years of unprecedented development. Professor Buchanan has said that its truths can be traced to the instincts of John Stuart Mill and the early classical economists. Hutt has remained an economist in the classical mould. He was never seduced into offering politically easy solutions nor been tempted to make politicians popular. His writings instinctively sensed the insights of public choice. He shed light on the economics of politics and the relationship between economists and the politician, as he did on every other subject to which he turned his evergreen, liberal mind.

CHAPTER 53

1990

Too Little Government Is Better Than Too Much

> Optimum government is unattainable. Government is not an exact science: it usually misses its target, aiming too high rather than too low and staying too long: it is not good at correcting error. The most crucial decision by the electorate is to choose between too much and too little government. The safer choice for a free society is too little. * That is the superiority of the market, which corrects mistakes sooner than the State.
>
> (*The Financial Times,* September 1990.)

The European economic revolution of 1988–9 ranks with the English Revolution of 1688 and the American and French Revolutions of the eighteenth century as a political climacteric. The world will never be the same again. Whether old falsehoods have been discarded with open relief or bitter heart-searching, the best minds in economics, political science and philosophy are re-examining long-held propositions in the replacement of socialism by capitalism.

The collapse of communism as a creed and socialism as an economic mechanism has persuaded socialists that capitalism which maximises the market and minimises government has finally won the argument. Liberals who have upheld the market and Socialists who have accepted it can now join in devising a less imperfect market capitalism.

The contrasting experience of the politicised and market-based societies of Europe, North America and the Far East suggests points from which to start the debate.

Freedom for the common people is better ensured by the economic democracy of the market on the formula of one man, one vote every day, than by the unpredictable political democracy of the ballot box franchise of one man, one vote every thousandth day (more or less). On the other 999 days, political democracy serves politicians, bureaucrats and their clients in the organised interests of industry, the professions, the trade unions, the arts, the Church.

Money-votes in the market are unequal; but so are influence-votes in the 999 days between political elections. Markets are superior because it is easier to even up money-votes than influence-votes; this is the experience of capitalist America, social democratic Europe and Australasia, the communist East, and the socialist Third World alike. "Democracy"—the "social" democracy of Sweden and probably of Poland, the "liberal" democracy of Holland or Belgium, or the "Christian" democracy of Germany and possibly of Hungary—is not enough.

Political "democracy" that takes half of personal incomes to spend on welfare or industrial services which give voters as taxpayers little say and less escape can be as oppressive as communist socialism that takes even more than half but is tempered by underground markets it cannot suppress.

After 140 years, Abraham Lincoln's "government of the people, by the people, for the people" is still an unrealised dream. In the real world, political democracy is of the activist, by the politico, for the organised: of the Busy, by the Bossy, for the Bully.

Government cannot be depended on to redress market failure. Its electoral short-termism, its ignorance of or indifference to individual preference, its vulnerability to pressure groups and its corruption create government failure that is worse than market failure because it is less corrigible.

The market incorporates more effective self-correctives than the State: it is easier to escape from commercial than from political monopoly or coercion.

Government cannot be "accountable" to "participating" citizens by transforming every man and woman into a politician. The effort to validate, justify or camouflage big government by "active citizenship" is an escape from reality, since only a small minority, perhaps no more than 5 per cent, are political people. It is a prescription for consolidating inequity since it aggrandises the political people over the mass of domestic people. It prescribes a waste of human talents.

Politics is a profession; it requires specialised character, temperament, talent. Generalists unschooled in the political activity of organising, agitating, lobbying and putting pressure on politicians are induced to engage in public or backstairs politics to ensure a hearing. Government heeds "demos" more than *demos.* Democracy is degraded and downgraded.

"Active citizenship" is an invasion of personal life. To make the political life the test of "citizenship" is to jettison the classical advantages of the division of labour. Most citizens excel in buying and selling. Large numbers are better in artistic, sporting or other non-political creation. And most want to enjoy domestic life with family or friends, to care for neighbours, to serve good causes. For them "politics" is oppressive, unproductive, obtrusive or boring. It is not the source of justice but of injustice.

The power of the voter over government is indirect, remote, unsure. The power of the consumer in the market is direct, immediate and powerful.

And it can be made more so. The common people would be better empowered by the market. Government should therefore concentrate on the irreducible minimum of goods and services that cannot be supplied in the market. This is the necessary realm of the State, the essential socialism in a capitalist society.

A basic ethical requirement is a public philosophy that proclaims that man as consumer shall prevail over himself as producer; that as producer every individual shall be free to better the product of any other by competitive access to free markets; and that it is immoral for group interest to bypass the people by blackmailing government.

The poor are served better by maximising production than by equalising distribution. To maximise productivity and provide resources for people who cannot earn sufficient for independence, the market should be given its head despite short-lived abuses or excesses.

The market is the most powerful equaliser of incomes. Equity is better secured by reducing barriers to movement from low-income to higher-income occupations than by political redistribution.

Optimal size of government is unattainable. In the democratic political process the choice is between too little or too much: too little government ownership or too much; too little regulation or too much; too low taxation or too high; too high inflation or too low. The better choice is the risks of too little than of too much government.

CHAPTER 54

1992

Laissez-faire in the Twenty-first Century

> The experience of over-government in the last century compels a fundamental reconsideration of the functions of government in the twenty-first century. * The decision that faces humanity now is whether government can keep pace with the potentialities of economic progress in a twenty-first-century version of "laissez-faire." If not, it will lose prestige and authority and fail in its capacity to ensure the law and order of civilised society.
>
> (*Laissez-faire*, 1992.)

The eternal debate between classical liberals and pragmatic socialists (in all Western political parties, left, right and centre) on the role of politics in human life has to be reasserted and refined. Politics plays too large a part in the daily life of the common people. Its manifestation in "representative democracy" has not vested authority in the supposed sovereign franchise. The most responsible politicians have not found ways to make themselves accountable when they are unavoidable and retired when they are superfluous.

The liberal instinct is scepticism of the political process and the apparatus of coercion it erects in government. The liberal concludes that the safest course for mankind is to minimise government. The socialist instinct is faith in politicians deploying government coercion to correct the (real or alleged) defects of spontaneous human activity in production and exchange. The socialist concludes that politicians are a race apart that uses government to save human beings from themselves.

The persistent faith of scholars in the beneficence of politicians in government is unhistorical. There has never been incontrovertible evidence to suppose that government has benefited the human race. There is evidence that good has sometimes followed government action, but no evidence that government produced it.

The fallacy of *post hoc, ergo propter hoc,* against which students of economics are warned in their first year, continues to mislead historians into following a sequence of events in time rather than analysing a process of cause and effect. In judging the power of government for good or evil, its effect on human beings, interest lies in tracing the consequences of different forms of government, or of less government, or even of no government.

Over the last century the dominant act of supposedly benevolent government in Europe and other continents of the West has been the creation of the "Welfare" State. This jewel in the politicians' crown is their most tragic failure, the largest blot in their copybook. The truth, rarely revealed by government, or by politicians contending for power at general elections, is that the "Welfare" State has transferred dominant economic power from the people to the politicians. In Britain, the politicians now control more resources than the people, even after a decade of Conservative government that set out to roll back the State.

The conclusion of most political scientists, sociologists, philosophers and even economists has been that the political process in the democracy of the West produced better educated children, healthier adults, better housed families and the abolition of poverty in old age than in earlier times. That is hardly surprising; improvement would have been expected under any conceivable politico-economic order. The task is to judge how the condition of education, medical care, housing and pensions would have developed under different government measures, or with less government, or in the absence of government and with the spontaneous methods of developing welfare that would have emerged.

The implied assumption of conventional history is that individuals, in isolation or with others, could not in the past and still cannot today in the approach to the twenty-first century provide these elemental personal services without delegating power to politicians to create them in the legislative assemblies of representative democracy.

The classical liberals—Adam Smith, John Stuart Mill, Nassau Senior to Alfred Marshall, Lionel Robbins, Friedrich von Hayek—sensed the destructive power of government that would destroy the spontaneous urge of individuals to improve their condition. But it is only in recent years that the evidence of early spontaneous individual initiative has been assembled. Professor E. G. West has revealed the extent of spontaneous education, Dr. David Green of spontaneous insurance for medical care and other historians the spontaneous development of housing and methods of accumulating income after working life in the nineteenth century long before government created them by law. Professor Bruce Benson has demonstrated the early spontaneous origins in past centuries of the apparatus of law and order.

Professor West described the clumsy reaction of government as jumping onto galloping horses. Its effect was worse; it slowed them down.

Even when nineteenth-century incomes were very low, individuals were not the short-sighted improvidents of conventional history. The plausible conclusion, amply attested by the growing discrimination of the common people of Europe, North America and Australasia in spending the rising incomes of the twentieth century, is that by now they would have demanded higher quality education, more responsive medical care, more suitable housing and more flexible pension systems than politicians in unaccountable government have provided. And competing suppliers would have emerged in the market to satisfy them.

There can be little doubt, especially after the ignominious collapse of government economies in Eastern Europe, that the further advances in personal incomes in the twenty-first century will induce and enable the large numbers who have hitherto tolerated government services to demand higher quality, more varied and more responsive education, medical care, housing and pension systems. It is now clear that government will not be able to meet the demands unless they change the politicised, bureaucratised and producer-dominated structures of State welfare and that they cannot do this unless they expose it to the rigorous discipline of escape.

If the politicians, who have voluntarily made government their life-time profession, had been able to produce welfare without politicised procedures, with less bureaucratic administrations but with consumer-primacy, their instinct for self-preservation by winning electoral approval would have led them to do so. So far in Britain their minor concessions in permitting controlled "opting out" of schools and hospitals, selling one in five government homes to their occupiers and tolerating private pension schemes have left the substance of the Welfare State undisturbed—its political control, its bureaucratic administration, its producer-dominance. The latest nostrum of "charters" that promise higher performance on paper without permitting exits in practice if it is not forthcoming will bring little change because there is no open market to which the dissatisfied can escape. Even describing "patients" as "customers" is a transparent attempt to create the image of the market by aping its language.

The latest effort to justify a continuing Welfare State by claiming the readiness of the people to pay higher taxes for it is based on shallow statistical techniques in priceless opinion polling.

So much for the loud claim of politicians to "care" for the people by the Welfare State. The failure of politicians to demonstrate the benevolence of government by putting individual consumers, taxpayers or voters first before themselves, the bureaucracies and the vested interests organised as producers is demonstrated no less in all the other services they provide. In a wide range of industries dignified by mislabelling as "nationalised" or, even more transparently, "public," from transport through steel to fuel, political benevolence has succumbed to political self-interest. Ageing equipment and obsolescent technologies have been maintained for decades up to a quarter of a century or more to avoid damaging disapproval from the organised producer interests.

Even in functions that, it is argued, are performed by government because they cannot be financed by voluntary payment in the market, the so-called "public goods" of defence and a few others, better described as unavoidably collective functions, which are not as extensive as the etatists conveniently suppose, political benevolence is more difficult to detect than political self-interest. The brave attempt of a liberal scholar, the Oxford philosopher Dr. John Gray, to define the boundaries of government as decided by "weighty externalities"—the third-party effects of private bargains in the market—fails because it depends on the unrealistic assumption that the criterion of "weighty" would be decided by the people. It would require more than a present-day reproduction of Athenian "direct" democracy in ancient Greece to assert "people power." The familiar processes of voting in the "indirect" democracy of representative government have long replaced Abraham Lincoln's vision of government by and for the people by a very different reality: government of the political activists, by the political managers, for the politically organised—government of the busy, by the bossy, for the bully. Dr. Gray described his proposal as "limited government." The end result of validating government in providing services with "weighty" externalities would be unlimited government.

The main lesson of the twentieth century on the performance of government in providing services to correct the imperfections of spontaneous production and exchange is that it has not hit the target. Its self-interest leads it to over-correction: it takes into "public" ownership ("nationalises") too much. It regulates too much. To finance its over-corrections it taxes too much, borrows too much, debases the currency (inflates prices) too much.

Government is like a prehistoric monster that cannot adapt itself to a changing environment. It nationalises and regulates and taxes and borrows and inflates not only too much but also too long. It continues its over-corrections for years and decades after they have been outdated because it is reluctant to yield the political power for which politicians have entered politics. Over-correction creates barnacles of vested interests that obstruct the withdrawal of government from controls which sustain them.

The people would fare better with too little than with too much government because they would learn from their early mistakes more than from the mistakes of government. Early mistakes in spontaneous education, medical care, housing and pension schemes would have been corrected more easily and sooner than the many and repeated mistakes of the Welfare State, not least because government hides its mistakes more easily than can suppliers surrounded by competitors or disciplined by potential competitors ready to take their place. Government as supplier has proved to be the enemy of the people; in the market competing suppliers are its friends against the rogue-elephants.

Government replaces the signals of pricing by the decisions of committees or of individuals acting on outdated information, faulty forecasts, estimates, guesses and hunches dignified as political "judgment" born of rare talent, flair and experience. The horrendous mistakes made by government in all the services it supplies—not least in defence, where it wins wars not because it is competent but because other governments are even more incompetent—are derived from the ignorance of individuals sitting in committees without the guidance of prices.

In defence, and other "public goods" and unavoidably collective functions, pricing may be impracticable and the committee system is the alternative. But in most of the services supplied by government—from welfare, transport and fuel to libraries and car-parking—market pricing has been abolished as a political tactic to win votes by presenting them as free gifts, or as indispensable in curing poverty, one of the most damaging errors of government in ignoring the solution of providing purchasing power.

Politicians have wilfully blinded themselves to the only way of discovering the personal preferences of individuals they claim they wish to serve.

The inefficiency of priceless government in failing to base its services on knowledge of individual preferences is now compounded by an even more inefficient substitute that claims to provide government with the information it lacks. In recent years in Britain the techniques of social research have been dressed with a veneer of sociological science to provide government with evidence it lacks on the readiness of the people to pay higher taxes for more or better government services. They are offered periodic opinion-polling. The irony is that, like the government, it is also price-less.

The deficiencies of representative democracy have become increasingly evident. A single-issue pressure group in Britain, Charter 88, claims to offer the solution, a written constitution to enshrine a Bill of Rights and the rule of law in open government (which suppresses its mistakes), freedom of information (selected by bureaucrats), proportional representation in elections (no voting procedure discovered so far can reproduce individual preferences), replacement of the House of Lords by a non-hereditary second chamber (with occupants nominated by politicians), the control of the executive arm of the government by a "democratically renewed parliament" (which makes the rules governing renewal), remedies for the abuse of power by the government (easily evaded by politicians) and other desperate measures.

"Once every few years [says Charter 88] politicians listen to the people." The diagnosis is partly true, but the remedy of the paper—constitutional reforms—misunderstands the solution. Democracy may listen to the people every few years; but it soon forgets what it has said because it runs an economic machine that requires detailed daily adjustments in which the electorate cannot be "heard."

Democracy offers one man, one vote, few choices (political parties), every thousand days but its offence is that democratic government suppresses the mechanism—the market—that could offer *one* man, *many* votes, *many* choices (suppliers) *every* day. Representative democracy has so far no device for eliciting daily changes in preferences (such as could be extended for electronic consumer shopping or banking). Even if such a continuous political referendum by electronic voting could be created, the decisions of individuals would be based on ignorance of individual costs and benefits and the centralised structures of government could not rapidly adjust economic performance to changes in voting. Constitutional reform would not remove the remedial disease of democracy unless it reduced the power of government to its minimal functions. The cause of the fundamental disease is not lack of control of democratic government but the over-government of democracy.

Price-less opinion polling offers no solution for the ignorance of government that causes its massive misdirection of resources. If it did, governments would have used it often, in more detail and on a larger scale than the opinion pollsters. If warring political parties that respected the voters wanted to know their preferences in order to give them what individuals wanted they would have stolen a march over their opponents and invested in political "market research" based on knowledge of prices rather than television advertising appealing to sentiment, prejudice and fear.

In contrast to the vapourings lavished on the process of voting, the process of shopping is the locale of reasoned reflection on comparative prices and qualities, responsible care for family, concern for the sensitivities of friends and neighbours. The political process induces even honourable men and women to defend their interests, dignified as "affairs of State," by suppression of evidence, temporising, nepotism, ultimately *in extremis* by lying, bribery and corruption.

The opinion pollsters who purvey unpriced polling have been misleading British politicians of all parties. For several years they have been asking national samples questions of the general order "Would you pay higher taxes for more/better schooling/health services?" The replies have, not surprisingly, been approval by some 80 per cent. The sample has not been told how much more each individual would pay (nor how much more or better services each could expect). The question is an appeal to sentiment—"caring compassion"—rather than to informed calculation of costs and benefits. Few people are likely to reply a brusque "No" to a question that invites them to show their compassion in return for a conveniently unstated cost. The opinion polls trade cheap sentiment for political influence.

Not surprisingly the political parties have accepted the findings uncritically as validating their predilection to tax for "free" benefits. They would have reached different conclusions if they had considered what the people *do* rather than what they *say.* The millions confronting honest information in the shops every day "do" very differently from the few thousands caught in national samples who briefly or brashly say what they would do in unimagined circumstances. Their actions in the real world show they dislike both taxes and government welfare. The difference is that they can escape from the taxes but not from the services. Millions increasingly escape from the taxes by avoidance, evasion and barter: the official statistics from Scandinavia to Italy are gross under-estimates. Relatively few—not only with high incomes; some with low incomes but with concerns for their children and families—escape from government services for which they have to pay whether they use them or not.

The twentieth century was the age of growing politicisation of life through the increasing power of politicians in government. Its source was the influence of politico-economic thinking that saw the State as the benevolent remedy for the myopia of individuals. The last years of the century saw the final destruction of the etatist illusion.

The people do not require politicians to run their daily lives. Rising incomes—growing not because of but in spite of the activity of government in productive industry—will enable the people to dispense with the political process in most of government activity and replace it with the market process. The twenty-first century could be the Golden Age of *laissez-faire.* The Liberal Winston Churchill saw the truth revealed by Adam Smith: set the people free—*laissez-faire*—to produce, to exchange their surpluses, to enrich themselves and one another.

INDEX

The text for this book is set in Minion; the display type is Meta Plus Book. Both are relatively new faces, chosen to reflect Seldon's influence on and activity in contemporary social and economic thought. Minion was designed by Robert Slimbach for Adobe in 1990. In spirit and intent it derives from the Garamond tradition. Meta, designed by Erik Spiekermann in 1993, with open spacing for legibility at small sizes, has grown into an extended family and is now widely used.

Printed on paper that is acid-free and meets the requirements of the American National Standard for Permanence of Paper for Printed Library Materials, z39.48-1992. ♾

Book design by Barbara Williams, BW&A Books, Inc., Durham, North Carolina
Typography by Graphic Composition, Inc., Athens, Georgia
Printed and bound by Edwards Brothers, Inc., Ann Arbor, Michigan